MORMONISM:
A GOLD PLATED RELIGION

MORMONISM:
A GOLD PLATED RELIGION

Michael and Ann Thomas

Aylesbury, Bucks HP22 5BL
England

First published by SP/Valley Trust Ltd 1997.

ISBN 1 898938 32 6

British Library Cataloguing in Publication Data.
A catalogue record for this book is available from the
British Library.

Published in cooperation with
REACHOUT TRUST
24 Ormond Road, Richmond, Surrey TW10 6TH.

Designed, Edited and Produced in England for
ALPHA an imprint of
SP/Valley Trust Ltd, Wendover Road,
Stoke Mandeville, Aylesbury, Bucks. HP22 5BL by
Gazelle Creative Productions Ltd.,
Station Road, Harpenden, Herts AL5 4SE.

To Doug Harris and Reachout Trust
without whom this book would not have been written.

And to John Tancock and Linden Christian Fellowship
without whom the best chapters of our lives
would not have been written.

CONTENTS

Preface

Mormonism is a remarkable religion. From humble, even heroic, beginnings it has grown to become the most successful of all the traditional cults, boasting a worldwide membership of over 9 million members with organised congregations in 156 countries. Its full-time missionary force numbers over 47,000, operating in over 300 missions.[1] Its resources are enormous, its influence impressive, and its authority absolute in the lives of its members.

The last time the Mormon church disclosed its expenditure was in 1959 when, in a general conference, it was reported that 72,794,306 dollars had been spent the previous year on church programmes. The church no longer publishes such details, regarding them as 'undesirable'. In 1976, however, it was estimated that church holdings of over 2 billion dollars placed them among the top fifty corporations in America. The church's income in contributions and in sales by church-controlled corporations was estimated, at that time, to be in excess of 3 million dollars a day.[2] Arguably the most acceptable of cults, the church enjoys a respectability that must be the envy of many religious groups. It is a hard-won respectability, the product of careful public-relations work and intelligent exploitation of every opportunity that has presented itself.

In 1885, at the age of seventy-six, John Taylor, then third president of the church, was said to have gone into 'retirement'. From February of that year, until his death in July 1887, he was actually in hiding. 500 dollars was offered for information leading to his capture on charges of polygamy. 300 dollars was the price on the head of his counsellor, George Cannon.[3] In January 1953 Ezra Taft Benson, later to become thirteenth president of the church, took the oath of office as Secretary of Agriculture in President Eisenhower's administration. At the time he was already a member of the Quorum of the Twelve Apostles.⁴ In less than seventy years Mormon leaders had progressed from being outlaws to being key administrators in national government: from being law-breakers to being lawmakers. This is an achievement that easily provokes both envy and admiration.

At the head of the church is a man who is regarded as no less than the prophet of God, and whose words must be accepted without question as God's words. When the Prophet speaks all debate is ended. His authority is indeed absolute.

Of course the church has questionable episodes in its history, but few organisations, religious or secular, can escape the attention of the dirt-diggers. It has risen above all these things to become what it is today: a clean-living, image-conscious and socially integrated religion. So what's wrong with the Mormon church?

For us the issue has always been that of basic principles. We have no axe to grind with Mormons, no personal grievances. We have nothing to blame the church for, and much for which to offer it our thanks. We left simply because we found that the way of salvation was not to be found among the Latter-day Saints. That is the first and by far the most important thing wrong with the church.

The Mormon apologist Hugh Nibley has said: 'Of all the churches in the world only this one has not found it necessary to readjust any part of its doctrine in the last hundred years.'⁵ This is demonstrably not true. The self-delusion necessary for someone like Hugh Nibley to make such an assertion must be enormous. The deception necessary to keep over 9 million people loyal to such a delusion has to be colossal. Our second concern, then, is that people should be freed from such deception.

Here we go again

A common objection raised against this kind of book is that it tends to quote other authors with no recourse to original documents for confirmation of facts lifted from these other authors' works. Thus, the argument goes, errors and misrepresentations are perpetuated. We wish to emphasise that we speak from personal experience of Mormon doctrine. We know what we were taught and what we believed as Mormons. We still have many well-thumbed church publications and vivid memories of a doctrine that was once of paramount importance to us. While we do quote others who have gone before us in this work, we still have plenty of personal experience to draw on and against which to test what is claimed. It has been our experience over the years that when Mormons have disagreed with our 'interpretation' of Mormon teachings, they have been found to be at odds with their own church and not with us.

Why pick on us?

It seems inevitable that when we talk to Mormons we get accused of intolerance. After all, the argument goes, isn't it healthier and more Christ-like to respect each other's religions? Shouldn't we be seeking common ground instead of finding fault? Those who say such things need to be aware that it was the Mormon church itself that opened hostilities in what many see as a war for truth. And it is they who have failed consistently to show respect for other faiths.

From the outset, Joseph Smith declared all churches corrupt and an abomination to God, and today Mormons still believe that:

> This is 'the only true and living church upon the face of the whole earth' (Doctrine and Covenants 1:30), the only organization authorized by the Almighty to preach his gospel and administer the ordinances of salvation, the only church which has power to save and exalt men in the hereafter... There is no salvation outside this one true church, the church of Jesus Christ.[6]

Throughout its history, the Mormon church has challenged and provoked honest Christians to stand in defence of their own faith. With almost 50,000 Mormon missionaries now in full-time service, bringing these attacks to our own doorsteps, the need for vigilance and clarity is greater than ever.

In challenging the Mormon church, we are acting in accordance with the wishes of its own leaders. Mormon apostle Orson Pratt said, 'If, after a rigid examination, [the Book of Mormon] be found to be an imposition, it should be extensively published to the world as such.'[7] More recently Joseph Fielding Smith, tenth president of the church said, 'If Joseph Smith was a deceiver, who wilfully attempted to mislead people, then he should be exposed; his claims should be refuted, and his doctrines shown to be false.'[8]

We also have the admonition of the apostle Paul to 'test everything. Hold onto the good' (1 Thess 5:21). We invite all then to test the Mormon church and, if it is found wanting, to 'investigate' the truth that has stood the test of time. The truth of the gospel of Jesus Christ as found in the Bible – the only book of Scripture inspired by God, written by prophets, preserved by his power, and testified to by the Holy Spirit of truth.

Notes

1. *Ensign* magazine, April 1995 conference issue, p 22.
2. *Utah Holiday* magazine, 22 March 1976, pp 4-6, quoted in Jerald and Sandra Tanner (eds), *The Changing World of Mormonism*, 1981.
3. Chapter 8, *My Kingdom Shall Roll Forth: Readings in Church History*, 1979.
4. *Ensign* magazine, July 1994, pp 8-20.
5. Hugh Nibley, *No Ma'aam, That's Not History*, p 46, quoted in Jerald and Sandra Tanner (eds), *The Changing World of Mormonism*, 1981.
6. Bruce R. McConkie, *Mormon Doctrine*, 1979, pp 136-38.
7. Orson Pratt, *Divine Authority of the Book of Mormon*, (our brackets), quoted in Floyd C. McElveen, *The Mormon Illusion*, 1979, p 7.
8. *Doctrines of Salvation*, 1954, p 188.

Introduction

The faith of Mormonism can be described as a counterfeit, just like counterfeit money: designed to look so much like the real thing that only an expert can tell the difference. When you compare Mormon beliefs with those of the Bible, they often look the same at first glance, but deeper investigation shows that they are very different.

For example, here is a passage of scripture which may, initially, look familiar:

> Therefore, in the beginning the Word was, for he was the Word, even the messenger of salvation –
>
> The light and the Redeemer of the world; the Spirit of truth who came into the world, because the world was made by him, and in him was the life of men, and the light of men.
>
> The worlds were made by him; men were made by him; all things were made by him, and through him, and of him.
>
> And I, John, bear record that I beheld this glory, as the glory of the Only Begotten of the Father, full of grace and truth, even the Spirit of truth which came and dwelt in the flesh and dwelt among us.
>
> And I, John, saw that he received not of the fulness at first, but received grace for grace;
>
> And he received not of the fulness at first, but continued from grace to grace, until he received a fulness.
>
> And thus he was called the Son of God, because he received not of the fulness at first.

The reason this passage looks familiar is because it is written in biblical-sounding language, and contains parts lifted from John chapter 1. However, it is actually a passage from the Mormon scriptures Doctrine and Covenants, section 93, verses 8–14, and contains false doctrine. In this passage, Jesus is demoted to second place as the Son of God because he did not receive of the fullness at first. This is contrary to Jesus' claim to be equal with God.

An example of the confusion that this counterfeit faith can cause is shown in this extract from a letter written by a lady who left the Mormon Church, became a Christian, and then was drawn back in again:

> I do not think it really matters where you worship God so long as you worship him in spirit and in truth. I know many of the Mormon concepts of God are in error, as are many of the doctrines. However that does not make Mormons evil or dishonest, it just makes them wrong in some of their concepts, they still worship the same God and Jesus and their commitment to serving God is just as sincere as it is for those in the free churches.

Christians who share their faith with Mormons often come away confused, as the Mormons agreed with everything they said. So how can Mormonism be so close and not right? Let us examine the characteristics of counterfeit Christianity.

Characteristics of a counterfeit

The most obvious characteristic is that Mormonism sounds like Christianity. It uses the same terms to talk about God, Jesus and salvation, but the definition of those terms is not the same as in Christianity. For example, the Mormon God has a physical body, the Mormon Jesus is the brother of Satan, and was conceived by physical union between God and Mary, and in Mormon salvation some sins are not covered by Jesus' atonement.

Secondly, the counterfeit always offers greater blessings than the orthodox religion. Mormonism offers hidden knowledge through its extra scriptures and temple ceremonies which brings special privileges in heaven. This encourages arrogance, not only towards Christians who 'just' have the Bible and not all the further knowledge that God has revealed, but also within the church between those who have been to the temple and those who have not.

Thirdly, it is important to remember that members are always sincere and zealous. Following a counterfeit faith is not easy, and they work very hard. They love God and try to follow him in the best way they know how – they have simply been deceived into the wrong path. We should not mock or attempt to tear their faith to pieces.

How to recognise a counterfeit

1. Origin

Most counterfeits originate with someone appointed by God as a special saint, guru or messiah who represents divine authority. In the case of the Mormons, this is Joseph Smith.

2. Claim of special discoveries: mysterious, otherwise unavailable information

The Mormon church has three extra books of scripture, revealing many beliefs additional to traditional Christian beliefs in the Bible, and sometimes contradicting them. In addition, as mentioned above, there are secret ceremonies which reveal signs and passwords for entrance to heaven.

3. Bible

Most counterfeits have additions to the Bible. The three extra books mentioned above: the Book of Mormon, the Doctrine and Covenants, and the Pearl of Great Price, are regarded on an equal footing with the Bible, and where there is a contradiction they are preferred above the Bible.

Counterfeits prove many of their beliefs from the Bible, which can be very confusing for the unwary Christian. However, reading in context will often show misinterpretation. They use segmented Bible attention – focusing on one verse or passage of the Bible to the exclusion of others. For example, Mormons believe that their priesthood can only be passed on by the laying on of hands by those in authority, and base this on Hebrews 5:4 – 'No one takes this honour upon himself; he must be called by God, just as Aaron was.' This precludes

the priesthood of all believers. However, reading on: 'So Christ
also did not take upon himself the glory of becoming a high
priest. But God said to him, "You are the Son; today I have
become your Father."' (Heb 5:5). The reference is to Jesus'
authority, not ours.

4. Essential doctrines

Even among Christians there are differences of opinion about
some tenets and practices. Counterfeits, however, cannot be
accepted into Christian circles because they are wrong on certain fundamental doctrines of the faith such as the nature of
God, the person and the work of Jesus, the Holy Spirit, creation and the fall, and salvation and atonement. All counterfeits believe in salvation by works, and do not have a certain
hope of salvation. Mormons are no exception.

Dr Martyn Lloyd-Jones wrote:

> Any teaching or movement which says that you can have this
> or that blessing without first believing in the Lord Jesus Christ
> as the Son of God, as the saviour of your soul, and as your Lord,
> without whom you have nothing, is a denial of Christianity. Any
> blessing you may get apart from the Gospel of Christ is a denial
> of Christianity.

In Galatians 1:6–8 Paul warned about those who teach
'another gospel':

> I am astonished that you are so quickly deserting the one who
> called you by the grace of Christ and are turning to a different
> gospel – which is really no gospel at all. Evidently some people
> are throwing you into confusion and are trying to pervert the
> gospel of Christ. But even if we or an angel from heaven should
> preach a gospel other than the one we preached to you, let him
> be eternally condemned!

Other faiths are clearly seen to be different from
Christianity, but the counterfeit sets out to bring 'another
gospel' and so lead many astray.

Part One

BEGINNINGS

Chapter 1
First Contact

It's a Thursday evening and after a long day at work, you both settle down to discuss something that has become an increasing concern. Alongside all the responsibilities of a growing family, your thoughts have turned lately to spiritual matters. As you go over the same old ground, 'worrying' your concerns into shape, the doorbell rings.

At the door you find, to your surprise, a friend from work and another couple. After brief introductions and an apology for turning up unannounced, they state their purpose for calling. They have come to talk about God. You look at your friend and see that he is awkward but determined. This seems a remarkable coincidence and you joke with yourself that it must be God-sent, feeling uncomfortable at the same time to find yourself half believing it. You invite them in and, after another round of introductions and a scramble to provide appropriate refreshments (you know your friend doesn't drink alcohol), you settle down to listen.

'Well, we've worked together for some time now,' your friend begins, 'so you know, of course, that I go to church...'

'That's right,' you interrupt him. 'In fact, incredible as it may seem, we were discussing this very thing before you arrived.'

He sits forward in his chair. 'That's wonderful!' he replies, warming to his subject. 'You see, I've brought my friends along to help me explain something I'm very excited about and want to share with you. It seems our timing couldn't have been better.' He slowly sits back and looks self-consciously at his friends.

Before they can say anything one of you chips in, 'We've been over this a dozen times and, frankly, I can't see how we can resolve it. There are so many ways and such a variety of truths. It's all so confusing.'

'That sounds familiar,' the couple say, giving your friend a knowing look. 'You know you're not the first to be confused by such a variety of different churches all preaching different things.'

Soon your guests have launched into the most incredible story you have ever heard. It's about a young American farm boy, Joseph Smith, who at the age of fourteen found himself as confused as you are. His search for truth had taken him, it seems to you, over familiar ground. The questions he raised are old friends to you:

> In the midst of this war of words and tumult of opinions, I often said to myself: what is to be done? Who of all these parties are right; or, are they all wrong together? If any one of them be right, which is it, and how shall I know it?[1]

Young Joseph's novel approach to the problem seems strangely appealing. It appears that while reading the Bible he found a particular verse that made a very strong impression on him: 'If any of you lack wisdom, let him ask God, that giveth to all men liberally, and upbraideth not; and it shall be given him' (Jas 1:5).

The story goes on:

> At length I came to the conclusion that I must either remain in darkness and confusion, or else I must do as James directs, that is, ask God. I at length came to the determination to 'ask God' concluding that if he gave wisdom to them that lacked wisdom, and would give liberally, and not upbraid, I might venture.[2]

Despite the quaint language, the simple logic of it all is striking. Why not indeed? By now it's getting late but you want to know what happens next.

It seems that the lad went into a nearby wood, checked that he was alone and – prayed. The answer he got was more than he bargained for – more than anyone would have bargained for:

> I saw a pillar of light exactly over my head, above the bright-
> ness of the sun, which descended gradually until it fell upon
> me... When the light rested upon me I saw two Personages,
> whose brightness and glory defy all description, standing
> above me in the air. One of them spake unto me, calling me by
> name and said, pointing to the other – *This is my beloved Son.*
> *Hear Him!*[3]

The atmosphere in the room has changed. One of you looks at the other – who is totally involved in the story that is unfolding right there in your own home. You look back at your visitors convinced that the one thought in your mind must be obvious to them: which church is the true one?

The boy did ask which church he should join and your worst fears are realised when you hear the answer: 'I was answered that I must join none of them, for they were all wrong.'[4] It didn't end there though. It appears that Joseph Smith was to be instrumental in restoring the true church to the earth – a church that had been lost to the world soon after the first century. He was also to bring to the world a new message of scripture: the Book of Mormon – Another Testament of Jesus Christ.

Now it really is late and your visitors must go. But before they leave they give you a copy of the Book of Mormon with instructions to read key passages that are marked for you. You are also introduced to Moroni's promise:

> And when ye shall receive these things, I would exhort you
> that ye would ask God, the eternal Father, in the name of
> Christ, if these things are not true; and if ye shall ask with a sin-
> cere heart, with real intent, having faith in Christ, he will man-
> ifest the truth of it unto you, by the power of the Holy Ghost.[5]

Challenging you to pray as Joseph did, they reassure you that God will answer. You will recognise the answer by a warm feeling in your heart that seems to confirm all that you have heard. They call it a 'burning in the bosom'. The last thing they leave you with is their testimony: 'I know that Joseph Smith is a prophet of God and that the Book of Mormon is the word of God. I know that the Church of Jesus Christ of Latter-day Saints is the only true church on the earth today and that a prophet stands at the head of the church.'

They also leave you with an invitation to come to church on Sunday morning at 10 am. Before you know what is happening you have agreed to come, and to have them over again next week, and they are gone.

Your reaction to the above account will depend on who you are and how you understand things. To a Mormon it will be heart warming because everything is as it should be. To a committed Christian it will be incredible, even alarming. The story is not incredible however. Over 9 million people in the world today have gone on from a similar experience to put their faith in the story of Joseph Smith. Why?

The couple in the story will typically be people with little or no religious experience. At best they will have experienced only a nominal Christianity. They will be unfamiliar with the tests a lively-minded Christian would apply: is the story credible as a supernatural occurrence; is it consistent with what God has already done or revealed about himself; is the account historically accurate (did Joseph Smith exist); have others already covered the same ground and come up with different, better answers; is the Bible as unreliable as the Mormons say it is? Thrown back on their own resources, the couple are ill prepared to judge the story they will hear.

When they attend church they will find themselves in the company of very charming people who will all tell them that the church is true. These people will have gone through similar experiences to their own and will have all come to the same conclusion: God spoke to and through Joseph Smith. They will be from every strata of society, but predominantly middle class, intelligent, professional – or aspiring to those things.

The women will smile warmly and the men will shake hands firmly as our visitors are led to their seats. In a multipurpose building the chapel area is treated with considerable reverence with even the children folding their hands on their laps as the Bishop rises to address the gathered congregation. Many of the hymn tunes will be familiar, though not always the words. Sermons will sound generally Christian and will be peppered with King James English as will the prayers.

The three-hour period passes quickly; it is full of activity, with something for everyone. The feel of it all is formal but friendly, and while their senses are bombarded with new experiences, all encouraging, one theme runs through it all: Joseph Smith is a Prophet of God, the Book of Mormon is the word of God, and the church is true.

Challenged once more to test Moroni's promise – having confessed that they haven't yet prayed – our visitors leave with more than one invitation to dinner ringing in their ears. With more verses to read, a church magazine and a lot to think about, our investigators (they found themselves in the investigators' class that morning) begin to discuss and pray about this wealth of new information. Discussion is relatively easy, but praying is rather stiff and formal to begin with, as both of them feel quite self-conscious. Nothing special happens as a result of their prayers, but they are aware of an excitement, a rising hope, a sense of expectation that they had never experienced before.

On their second visit the couple's new-found friends inform them that the following Sunday is Conference Day and they are cordially invited. It is out of town at something called a stake centre. Transport will be provided and, of course, they will be accompanied on their visit so they don't feel lost or completely out of place. After another 'discussion' and a lot of encouragement (delight that they have started praying), one of them bears his testimony: 'I know that these things are true; that Joseph Smith was a prophet of God; that the Book of Mormon is the word of God and that the Church of Jesus Christ of Latter-day Saints is the only true church on the earth.'

There is an excitement about Conference. The coach hired for the occasion is not full but seems to be. People sing church songs, sometimes hymns, sometimes children's songs for the younger ones. There is a lot of talk about the visiting 'general authority' and it becomes clear that someone from church headquarters is going to be there.

On arrival the couple find themselves in a building very similar to the local church but bigger. Although more than 800 people are there, they find that seats have been kept for them near the front. The service proceeds with the familiar formula of hymn, prayer, talk (sermon) and testimony. The bulk of the time is given over to the visiting church leader who brings news of the church, tells of the importance of the youth, and speaks warmly of the 'restoration' of the gospel through Joseph Smith whom he solemnly testifies to have been a prophet, further testifying that the Book of Mormon is the word of God, and that the Church of Jesus Christ of Latter-day Saints is the only true church on the face of the earth today.

They file out, joining in the general excitement at the prospect of shaking the hand of an Apostle, for that is who the visitor is. His handshake is warm and his smile sincere as they are introduced as investigators, and he asks them if they have prayed about the Book of Mormon. They are encouraged to persevere with sincerity and faith and they will know 'as surely as I know' that 'Joseph Smith is a prophet of God, that the Book of Mormon is the word of God and this is the only true church on the earth today'.

That evening the couple talk over their recent experiences. These people seem so sincere. They also seem to get so much more out of life and out of their faith. There has developed an unspoken ambition to be like them. Up to now they have been detached. Now it's under their skin and the issues have become personal. Perhaps for the first time there is an urgency to know the truth. No longer completely on the outside asking whether they should come in, they go in prayer and meet the challenge of Moroni's promise.

The next visit is somehow different. There is a lot of encouragement and affirmation as our investigators tell how they had prayed and felt a strange warmth about it all. They feel a sense of relief now that it is settled and they 'know' as their visitors 'know'. They find they have a new status, as though they are now 'one of us'. Plans are discussed for the next step in the process – baptism into the church. Their excitement grows with their confidence and when a friend they know to be a Christian calls the next evening they are eager to share with him their new-found faith.

He doesn't seem so enthusiastic however. In fact he appears concerned, even hostile towards the church they are about to join. Clearly agitated he shares with them some things he 'knows' about Joseph Smith and what he calls his gold bible. Shocked by his words they nevertheless determine to overlook them and bear their testimony, fervently declaring that they know Joseph Smith was a prophet of God, that the Book of Mormon is the word of God, and that the Church of Jesus Christ of Latter-day Saints is the only true church on the earth today. Shaking his head he leaves saying he will pray for them.

If all this sounds a little cynical on our part it is not meant to. You see, Mormons are really nice people. They sincerely believe what they say and their warmth is usually genuine. Even the invitations to dinner will be sincere. Should you test Moroni's promise and come to know as they know that Joseph Smith is a prophet of God, the Book of Mormon is the word of God, and the church is true, they will be genuinely delighted. These people are not deceivers. They are themselves deceived.

* * *

For those who are not well versed in Scripture, the message of the Mormons fits in with the little that most people know and the vague ideas they have as to what Christianity is all about. Most people think that Christianity is about believing in God and Jesus, reading the Bible, going to church, praying, and trying hard to be good. So when the Mormons come along teaching these very things, they are not equipped to distinguish truth from error.

The Mormon story begins by playing on the 'great apostacy' and the diversity of belief among Christian denominations. They teach that after Christ's death and resurrection the leaders of the early church were gradually all killed and the pure teachings of Christ were corrupted until little remained of the original gospel. They teach that with the death of the apostles, the priesthood authority to minister in the church was also lost. The diversity of Christian belief is used as evidence of the way men have changed the gospel to suit themselves. God would not tell one man one thing and another man something different, they say. Only one church can be right. So how is the honest seeker to know which it is?

Enter Joseph Smith. He is portrayed as a young boy facing this very dilemma. Joseph Smith was inspired to seek the answer to his dilemma by reading James chapter 1, verse 5: 'If any of you lacks wisdom, he should ask God, who gives generously to all without finding fault, and it will be given to him.' The story of the 'First Vision' is introduced to share the good news that God has spoken again from heaven. He has revealed the true church of Jesus once more and restored the priesthood authority which was lost. The seeker is promised that God will answer his prayers in the same way that he answered Joseph Smith.

In introducing their gospel message they use two key scriptures, both from their own 'standard works'. The first is Moroni 10:4 from the Book of Mormon (known as Moroni's promise):

> And when ye shall receive these things, I would exhort you that ye would ask God, the Eternal Father, in the name of Christ, if these things are not true; and if ye shall ask with a sincere heart, with real intent, having faith in Christ, he will manifest the truth of it unto you, by the power of the Holy Ghost.

The second is Doctrine and Covenants 9:8,9:

> But, behold, I say unto you, that you must study it out in your mind; then you must ask me if it be right, and if it is right I will cause that your bosom shall burn within you; therefore, you shall feel that it is right.
>
> But if it be not right you shall have no such feelings, but you shall have a stupor of thought that shall cause you to forget the thing which is wrong.

They will ask you to pray and seek that 'burning in the bosom' which will show you the truth.

But should a testimony be based on feelings? Mormon missionaries present this as God's way. But if it is not God's way, why is it so convincing? It seems so open and honest to ask you to test their message 'independently'. But they have already influenced you enormously by the time they challenge you with the promise, and they leave nothing to chance because

(a) they tell you exactly what to do

(b) they tell you exactly what to expect.

Here it is:

1. Joseph Smith, confused by so many churches (just like you), turned to the Bible and found James 1:5.

2. He sought God for wisdom (just like you).

3. God spoke to Joseph and from that time he knew the truth. God will speak to you and you too can know the truth.

4. You will know the truth by means of a 'burning in the bosom'.

In short, when you seek God honestly he will confirm the truth to you by means of a feeling. This is very unreliable but most people don't question it, perhaps because it has to do with prayer, and prayer does seem to be the shortest and most reliable route to God. Mormon methods depend on you thinking this way. However, how do you know that the feeling you receive is from God, and not from Satan or from within yourself? Don't you feel warmth in your heart when you are excited about something or in anticipation of some important event?

Let us look at James chapter 1, verse 5 again in the context of the whole biblical book.

James 1:1. The epistle was written to Jewish Christians who had been scattered after the death of Stephen, so any promises contained in it are for Christians not non-Christians (Acts 8:1, 11:19).

James 1:2–17. The context of the verse is encouragement in suffering. The wisdom of James 1:5 then is for the benefit of Christians, enabling them to face suffering with 'pure joy'.

James 3:13–18. Here, James defines the wisdom he is

referring to and contrasts it with the wisdom of the world.
Clearly the issue is one of character. A worldly character full
of bitterness and selfish ambition ill equips us to deal with the
trials he refers to at the beginning of the letter. Peacemakers,
on the other hand, are equipped with the wisdom of heaven
and are able to face their trials patiently, knowing the harvest
is theirs.

The rest of the letter is teaching on the practical application
of wisdom in the Christian life (eg, Jas 2:1–4; 3:13).

James chapter 1, verse 5 is not the promise Mormons make
it out to be. If your testimony is gained on a false premise, it is
unreliable. Once you believe the Mormon church is true, then
all else follows, even if you don't understand it. The church
teaches that 'when the prophet speaks, all debate is ended'. If
he really is a prophet of God, you should not doubt or question. You are asked to accept things blindly, and rely on feelings instead of guarantees.

God's word in the Bible, however, does not depend on feelings. The promises are there in black and white, and they hold
true when you are feeling bad, or nothing at all, just as when
you feel good.

So how *does* God answer the honest seeker? What has been
the experience of others who sought truth? And how did those
who taught confirm the truth to their listeners? The Scriptures
speak for themselves. 'In these last days God has spoken to us
by his Son' (Heb 1:2). Jesus said that we are in error if we do
not know the Scriptures (Matt 22:29). The Scriptures were
written to teach us and give us hope (Rom 15:4) and in order
that we may believe in Christ (Jn 20:31). Isaiah declared that
every message should be checked out against the word of God
(Is 8:20), and that is just what the Bereans did when Paul and
Silas preached the gospel to them (Acts 17:11).

What we are not told to do is to go away and pray about it
without checking it out first. Mormons claim to substantiate
their teachings from the Scriptures, but a closer examination,
as above with James chapter 1, verse 5, will often show how
they have misused or misinterpreted them. As will be seen
in the sections of this book dealing with specific Mormon

doctrines, their proof often appears logical and convincing, but it is not.

Notes

1. Joseph Smith, History of the Church 1:10.
2. As above, 1:13.
3. As above, 1:17.
4. As above, 1:19.
5. Moroni 10:4.

Chapter 2
Structure

The Mormon church is highly and rigidly organised. Every congregation across the world duplicates the same set pattern. Teaching materials and syllabuses are prepared and distributed so that the same lesson is taught on the same day in every church. The organisation structure lays down not only the major leaders in each church, but includes the finer details such as a music director to lead the singing and a secretary to take the minutes of the meetings and keep attendance rolls.

Organisations are provided for children, young people, women and men, as well as the standard Sunday meetings for all members. Prior to 1980 these groups met during the week. Since then, the consolidated meeting schedule means that all groups meet at the same time on Sunday for instruction, with only activities during the week.

The church is a hierarchy, with the General Authorities at the top, then the regional and area leaders. The stake is the Mormon equivalent of the Anglican diocese, and each church (or parish) is called a ward. Where there are not enough members for a ward, a branch is formed. A stake will have many wards and some branches. Where there are not enough members for a stake, branches are organised into districts, supervised by the mission, which is also responsible for all missionary work. The goal of every branch is to become a ward, and of every district to become a stake. Then the goal is to grow large enough to divide.

Wards

Each ward has a chapel, built to one of several standard designs. The building consists of a chapel area, with an organ and a piano, for all religious services. There is also a recreation hall connecting onto the chapel area in such a way that screens can be opened up to extend the seating for especially large meetings. The hall is used for sports, games and dances, and has a stage for drama and concerts. The Mormon church aims to provide all recreational activities for its members, especially young people, to discourage them from going elsewhere where there may not be such high moral standards. The chapel building will also have a number of classrooms, a baptism font, offices, sometimes a library, and kitchen and toilet facilities.

The ward is presided over by a Bishop and two counsellors, with a clerk for administration. All officers are unpaid and have full-time jobs as well as their church duties. The individual organisations within the church, known as auxiliaries, are also presided over by a president and two counsellors, with a secretary for administration. In addition there are teachers, scout leaders, sports, drama and music directors, and many other responsibilities. This enables a large majority of ward members to serve in some way.

Auxiliaries

The first meeting a child will attend will be Primary. This caters for children up to twelve years of age. They meet for religious instruction on Sunday, while their parents are in their own meetings. There is a short service with children's songs and talks, and then classes for different ages, followed by an activity period. Special activity nights are held occasionally during the week. The president and counsellors of Primary are always women.

At the age of twelve the boys will go on to the Aaronic Priesthood Quorums and the girls to the Young Women's meeting. These have classes for religious instruction, with an activity night during the week. The Aaronic Priesthood Quorums are in three age groups: Deacons (twelve to fourteen years old), Teachers (fifteen to seventeen years old) and Priests (seventeen to nineteen years old). All worthy male members of the church hold the priesthood and advance according to age and worthiness. The Young Women meet in similar age groups: twelve to thirteen, fourteen to fifteen and sixteen to seventeen years old. Combined activities for Young Men and Young Women are under the direction of the Bishopric Youth Committee, assisted by the Activities Committee and the Ward Physical Activities Specialist. Special emphasis is placed on the development of talents, such as drama and speech.

The weekday activity for boys and young men is ideally Scouting. Every ward is encouraged to have its own Cub Scout pack and Scout troop where possible. At nineteen young men join the Melchizedek Priesthood Quorums, consisting of Elders, Seventies and High Priests. The majority of men are Elders. They meet for instruction in their priesthood duties and the responsibilities of fatherhood, as well as religious instruction.

At eighteen, the young women join the Relief Society, one of the oldest women's organisations in the world. Their lessons are taught on successive weeks each month: spiritual living (including testimonies), mother education, social relations and cultural refinement. In months with a fifth Sunday, home management is taught. Once a month a homemaking session is held during the week.

Aaronic Priesthood Quorums, Melchizedek Priesthood Quorums, Young Women's meetings and Relief Society are all held at the same time. Following these meetings there is a short break and then everyone goes to Sunday school where there are classes for all age groups. The Primary meeting for those under twelve continues over both sessions. The president and two counsellors of the Sunday school are always men.

At the end of the second session, including Primary, there is another short break and then the whole church meets for Sacrament meeting. This is the main religious service, in which the Sacrament of bread and water (water is used instead of wine in keeping with the church ban on alcohol) is taken. In some localities the schedule is run the other way around, with Sacrament meeting first, then Sunday school and Primary, and then the auxiliary meetings.

The whole programme takes three hours and is designed to encourage full attendance at all meetings and minimise travel. It also facilitates the double use of the church building, where two wards can use the same facilities by having one meet in the morning and one in the afternoon. Families are encouraged to 'plan and carry out appropriate Sabbath-day family activities' during the rest of the day.

Activities

Church buildings and facilities are closed on Monday evenings and no meetings are allowed to be held. Monday night is family home evening. There is an instruction manual provided by the church with lessons for families to study together, and recreational activities are also encouraged. The main emphasis is on the family being together and growing closer.

One evening other than Monday is designated as ward activity day. On this day activities for organisations or the whole ward are scheduled, where possible, to minimise travel, conserve energy resources and reduce the running costs of the building.

Special events are held by each auxiliary and the whole ward several times a year, such as socials, arts festivals, seminars, sports events, Daddy-Daughter parties and so on. Events are also held at stake level, where wards can meet together.

Training and supervision

Regular meetings are held at both ward and stake level to train and supervise the workers in the various organisations. Teacher training also takes place.

Each Mormon family is visited briefly every month by local Home Teachers. These are priesthood holders who visit a designated area in pairs. It is their responsibility to encourage those they visit to be more faithful, and to pick up on cases of need so that the church can give assistance. In addition, the women from Relief Society also visit in pairs to look after the women of the church.

Records are kept of all meetings and attendance, and correlated and sent up the line. A detailed record of each member's tithing is also kept and once a year they must attend Tithing Settlement to give an account. (Tithing involves giving one-tenth of one's annual income to the church.)

Stake

The organisation of the stake mirrors, to a large degree, that of the ward. There is a Stake President with two counsellors and a clerk. Each organisation has its president and counsellors and other workers at stake level, who supervise, train and encourage the wards, and organise stake-wide events. One difference is that under the Stake Presidency is a Stake High Council, consisting of twelve men who hold the priesthood office of High Priest. They, jointly, hold equal authority to the Stake Presidency. Their duties fall into two main categories: they assist the Stake President in administering the many quorums and auxiliary groups, and represent him in visiting wards and branches; and they have the main legislative and disciplinary powers – for example the Stake High Council are convened to excommunicate or disfellowship any priesthood holder.

The Aaronic Priesthood Quorums report directly to the ward Bishopric, but the Melchizedek Priesthood Quorums report to the Stake Presidency, and are organised at that level, even though they will also meet in their own wards on Sundays.

Another important office within the stake is that of Patriarch. Stake Patriarchs are nominated by the First Presidency and the Council of Twelve, and not by Stake Presidents. Patriarch literally means head of a family or tribe, and in the Bible there are many records of fathers bestowing special prophetic blessings on their sons. The Stake Patriarch's duty is to give special Patriarchal Blessings to the members of the stake. In order to receive your Patriarchal Blessing it is necessary to obtain a recommendation from your Bishop, following an interview for worthiness.

Regional and area representatives

All the Stakes in the church are organised into Areas, each of which has an Area Presidency. These are full time officers who generally serve for three years. The Area Presidencies are assisted by Area Authorities (a new office in the church, instituted in August 1995). The Area Authorities serve part-time, euphemistically known as 'serving on a Church-service basis', ie unpaid. A whole tier of paid, full-time, officers, known as Regional Representatives, were 'released' from office to make way for the Area Authorities, thus creating a new tier of unpaid ministry.

Presiding bishopric

These are directed by the First Presidency and the Twelve. They preside over the Aaronic Priesthood and administer various practical matters, such as membership records, tithing, budgets, ward and stake reports, and operation and maintenance of church buildings.

First Council of Seventy

This consists of seventy men, under a presidency of seven, which assists the Council of Twelve, particularly in the area of missionary work. There are also seventies in every stake, who preach the gospel.

Council of the Twelve Apostles

The Council of the Twelve is called to administer the affairs of the church under the direction of the First Presidency. They are 'prophets, seers and revelators'. Each apostle holds all the 'keys of the kingdom of God on earth', but only the President of the church actively exercises all of the keys. When the president dies, the First Presidency is dissolved, and the Council of Twelve lead the church. The president of the Twelve, who is the longest-serving member, then becomes the new Prophet.

First presidency

The President of the Church is assisted by two counsellors, and also by the Council of the Twelve. He is the Prophet, and directs all areas of the church. It is through him that God speaks to man today.

A church that provides

The church attempts to provide for the needs of its members in every area of life, and many of its programmes attract people into the church. Priesthood Home Teachers and Relief Society Visiting Teachers visit each home every month to bring a message, encourage faithfulness, and to enquire into the welfare of the family.

There is also a comprehensive welfare programme, from simple local support during times of illness or difficulty, to the provision of food and clothing, the payment of bills, the opportunity to work for assistance to preserve the dignity of the unemployed, professional counselling and an adoption agency.

Education is prized and encouraged. The church has many schools, and the prestigious Brigham Young University, Provo, Utah. There is also a Seminary and Institute programme for the study of their religion, which all young people are actively encouraged to join, and which has been opened in recent years to all members. Clearly, the church believes that it should not be necessary for its members to go outside for anything, where standards may not be so high and temptation will be greater.

Chapter 3
How It All Began

Joseph Smith Jnr, the founder of the Church of Jesus Christ of Latter-day Saints, was born on 23 December 1805 in the town of Sharon, Vermont. This is in New England, in the north-east corner of the USA, adjacent to the Canadian border. The son of a farmer, Joseph was one of nine children. In 1819 he moved with his family to Manchester, Ontario County, in the Finger Lakes area of New York State.

Although he had little formal schooling, he was an imaginative and bright child. His imagination led him into divination and treasure-seeking in his teens. He was convicted on 20 March 1826 of being 'a disorderly person and an imposter', after deceiving people that he could look into a glass seer-stone and discover buried treasure.[1] Yet he had great charisma and a strong personality. John Bernhisel lived in Joseph's home for many months, and described him in 1844 as 'a man of strong mental powers, and is possessed of much energy and decision of character, great penetration, and a profound knowledge of human nature'.[2]

It was his intelligence, imagination and deep reflection that enabled him to create the foundation of the Mormon church.

> The Prophet also left more than a hundred revelations and numerous important addresses that formed the foundation of the Church, both in its organisational structure and its doctrine. He inaugurated a vigorous missionary system to take the restored gospel to the nations of the earth. Through him, the Lord brought forth the Book of Mormon, the Doctrine and

Covenants, and the Pearl of Great Price. In addition, Joseph made significant progress toward a revision of the Bible. As a capstone, he restored the highest knowledge and blessings of God available to man, knowledge that guarantees the perpetuation of the family unit and prepares men to meet God.[3]

The incongruous marriage of great prophet and ignorant farm boy in one man is the stuff of legend. Joseph Smith was neither. Long iconised by the church, the real Joseph Smith is a stranger to today's Latter-day Saints.

First Vision

The area where he grew up was known as the 'Burned-over District' because of the number of revivals and religious campaigns it experienced. Joseph's record claims that it was a revival in 1820 that drove him to seek God. However, no revival is recorded for that area between 1817 and 1824.[4]

Joseph claimed to have had a vision in 1820, when he prayed for wisdom in a woodland glade near his home. 'I saw a pillar of light exactly over my head, above the brightness of the sun, which descended gradually until it fell on me,' he said. 'I saw two personages whose brightness and glory defy all description. One of them spake unto me, calling me by name and said, pointing to the other – "This is My Beloved Son. Hear Him!"' He asked which church he should join and records that they told him not to join any religion, because 'all their creeds were an abomination in his sight'.[5]

Like many of Joseph's visions and revelations, this amazing experience was only recorded many years afterwards. It is not even mentioned for twelve years, and there are four different versions.

An angel and a book

Joseph's second vision came on 23 December 1823 when an angel named Moroni appeared three times in one night. He told Joseph about a set of golden plates on which were inscribed a book giving an account of the early inhabitants of America. He said it contained the fullness of the everlasting gospel. Two stones in a silver bow, called Urim and

Thummim,[6] were with the plates and would enable Joseph to translate them.

He was shown in a vision a nearby hill called Cumorah where, under a large stone, he claims he found the plates. But he was forbidden to move them for four years. He was to return to the spot each year for instruction. Joseph finally obtained the plates on 22 September 1827, but was told to show them to nobody or he would be destroyed. The word got out, however, and soon many people were trying to get their hands on them. They were moved from one hiding place to another, but it became impossible for Joseph to work on them.

Joseph had married Emma Hale a short while before, so he moved to Harmony, Pennsylvania to live with his in-laws. There, with teacher Oliver Cowdery as scribe, he translated the plates. He claimed they were written in 'Reformed Egyptian', a language dismissed by experts as non-existent.[7] The record had been compiled by a prophet named Mormon, so Joseph entitled the book 'The Book Of Mormon'.

Oliver and the other scribes never saw the plates, as Joseph always dictated translations from behind a curtain. Often, Joseph did not see the plates either. He preferred to translate by looking into a hat containing a seer stone or the Urim and Thummim.[8]

On 15 May 1829, Joseph and Oliver went to the woods to pray about the doctrine of baptism. John the Baptist descended, said Joseph, and conferred the priesthood of Aaron on the two men. He promised them that they would soon receive the higher Melchizedek priesthood. Joseph and Oliver then baptised and ordained one another. Not long afterwards, near the Susquehanna River, it is claimed that the apostles Peter, James and John appeared and ordained them to the Melchizedek priesthood.

In June 1829 the work on the Book of Mormon was completed, and Joseph said that he returned the plates to the angel Moroni. Joseph took three men – Oliver Cowdery and farmers Martin Harris and David Whitmer – to the woods to pray that the men should be allowed to see the plates. The three witnesses say in the front of the Book of Mormon that they saw the gold plates in the hands of an angel who descended in a beam of light.

The witnesses, however, proved to be unreliable, so Joseph gathered another eight disciples together. They also witness in the Book of Mormon that they saw the plates. This time it was Joseph who showed them the plates, with no heavenly manifestation. All of the three witnesses, and all but three of the eight witnesses (Joseph's father and two brothers) later left or were expelled from the church.

A new church and a new bible

As word of the 'golden bible' spread, the church began to grow. The church was formally organised on 6 April 1830, with six members. It was called The Church of Jesus Christ. The phrase 'Latter-day Saints' was added later, in 1838.[9] Missionary work was immediately begun. The first Mormon conference was held in June, with twenty-seven members. By the next conference, a year later, there were 2,000 members in attendance.

In the spring of 1831, Joseph began revising the translation of the Bible.[10] He had concluded that there were errors and omissions which had changed the doctrine. He amended verses and added new sections where appropriate to back up his own teachings. He even added a verse to Genesis prophesying the coming of a seer whose name would be Joseph, after the name of his father. This translation was completed in 1833, but was not published until after his death, by which time it was the property of the Reorganised Church of Jesus Christ of Latter-day Saints.

Revelations

Following a divine revelation, Joseph moved with his followers to Kirtland, Ohio, where he ordered a temple to be built.[11] The Kirtland Temple was dedicated in March 1836, but abandoned soon afterwards due to persecution.

Joseph's scribe for the translation of the Bible was Sidney Rigdon, a Campbellite preacher, who eventually became his first counsellor in the presidency. Sidney's congregation had established a cooperative venture based on the description in

Acts of the early church having all things in common (Acts 2:44–45; 4:32).

Between 1831 and 1834 Joseph gave revelations to the church, setting out the Law of Consecration and establishing a United Order in which members consecrated all their possessions to the church and were then granted stewardships over the things they needed.[12] This was not a success. Eventually, in June 1834, Joseph gave a revelation to disband the United Order. In the revelation the Lord said, 'They have not learned to be obedient to the things which I required at their hands, but are full of all manner of evil, and do not impart of their substance, as becometh saints.'[13]

In the course of Joseph's translation of the Bible, he came to John chapter 5, verse 29 which speaks of the judgement of the dead. This was in February 1832. He and Sidney Rigdon claimed a revelation at this point which was radical in its doctrine. They stated that heaven has three degrees of glory to which men will be assigned after judgement, according to their works.[14] A year later Joseph issued the revelation which came to be known as the Word of Wisdom, which is a health law banning the use of tea, coffee, tobacco and alcohol, and advising on a healthy diet.[15]

New scripture

During this period, Joseph had issued more than sixty revelations, and it was decided to publish them for the church. The collection was called The Book of Commandments. This was later revised and enlarged with further revelations, and became the Doctrine and Covenants. This was first published in 1835 and approved by the church as scripture.[16] The revelations included the calling of the Quorum of the Twelve Apostles and Quorum of the Seventy, the organisation and duties of the priesthood, tithing, and temple work – baptism for the dead and endowments (see p. 44/45). In 1835 the church also purchased some Egyptian mummies and papyrus scrolls, which Joseph stated contained the writings of Abraham and Joseph who was sold into Egypt. The Book of Abraham was eventually published in 1842.

When Franklin D. Richards became president of the British

Mission in 1850, he collected together materials that he felt would provide valuable instruction but which were not readily available. They were published in Liverpool in 1851 as 'The Pearl of Great Price'. The next edition was revised and expanded in Utah, and was accepted as one of the church's standard works on 10 October 1880.[17] It consists of the Book of Abraham, the Book of Moses – Joseph Smith's revision of Genesis chapters 1–6, a revision of Matthew chapter 23, verse 39 and chapter 24, excerpts from Joseph Smith's History of the Church, and the Articles of Faith of the Church of Jesus Christ of Latter-day Saints.

Growth and persecution

Missionary work was a priority. Within six months of organising the church, missionaries were sent to the Indians, since the Book of Mormon reveals that they are one of the lost tribes of Israel.[18] Missionaries went into Canada very early on, and were first sent to England in 1837. Missionaries also went to Europe, Palestine and the Pacific.

This was a time of great persecution and apostasy in the church. The gathering of converts was viewed with suspicion by the local people, who feared they would be outnumbered. They were particularly worried as most of them were pro-slavery and the Mormons were not. There were political, cultural and economic differences as well as religious ones. Church members were expelled from Jackson County, Missouri by mob rule in 1833, and from the whole of Missouri in 1838–39.

The call for the saints to 'gather to Zion' was designed to strengthen the church through this time.[19] The first British members emigrated to America in 1840, and they continued to come until after the turn of the century. Eventually the church was seen to be suffering from loss of members elsewhere, and gathering was discouraged in 1894.

Temple work

The Mormons created a town for themselves in Illinois, from swamp land on the Mississippi River. They named it Nauvoo, a Hebrew word meaning 'beautiful'. A temple was also built here. In August 1840 Joseph Smith preached a sermon on 1

Corinthians chapter 15, verse 29, and introduced the doctrine of baptism for the dead. The first baptisms for the dead were performed in the Nauvoo Temple in November 1841. (Mormons believe that the gospel is preached to the dead, so they spend considerable time and money in searching out the details of their dead ancestors in order that they can be baptised on their behalf.[20] The church has microfilmed thousands of parish records and other records of birth, marriage and death, and stores them in a huge system of caves hollowed out of a mountain. Today there is an intensive programme of transferring all this data onto records for temple work.)

During this period Joseph also revealed the endowment ceremony and the doctrine of eternal marriage. The first endowments were introduced to a few trusted members in the upper room of Joseph's store, where many of the church meetings were held. Once the temple was built, these ordinances were performed there.

The rituals of the endowment were based on the Masonic rituals which Joseph learned when he joined the Freemasons. A Masonic lodge was set up in Nauvoo in 1842 and Joseph joined on 15 March.[21] Many of the secret ceremonies in Mormon temples are based on the Masonic traditions of ritual and symbolism, including the washing and anointing of naked initiates, clothing in a special undergarment and the secret handshakes and passwords in the endowment ceremony. The first endowments were given on 4 May 1842, less than two months after Joseph became a Mason.[22]

On 12 July 1843, Joseph claimed a revelation on marriage, which contained two startling new doctrines: eternal marriage and polygamy.

> 'Except a man and his wife enter into an everlasting covenant and be married for eternity, while in this probation, by the power and authority of the holy priesthood,' the Prophet says, 'They will cease to increase when they die; that is, they will not have any children after the resurrection.'[23]

Civil marriage is until death only. Joseph and the other church leaders began to teach that there is no entry into the highest degree of glory in the celestial kingdom without marriage for eternity. Thus worthy couples would be able to have spirit children in heaven and create their own worlds for them to live on.

What followed was even more amazing:

> If a man espouse a virgin and desire to espouse another, and if the first give her consent...then he is justified; he cannot commit adultery for they are given unto him.
>
> And if he have ten virgins given unto him by this law, he cannot commit adultery, for they belong to him, and they are given unto him; therefore is he justified.[24]

There was a lot of resistance to this revelation. In order to keep it, members had to break the law of the land which forbade polygamy. It is interesting to note that although it is dated for 1843, the revelation was not printed until 1852 and did not appear in the Doctrine and Covenants until 1876. Polygamy was practised only by church leaders, and originally in secret. After Joseph's death, nearly fifty women claimed to have been his plural wives, and many of them were sealed to him for eternity in the Nauvoo temple.[25] His wife, Emma, was against it, and was warned in the revelation that she would be destroyed if she resisted.[26]

Death of a Prophet

Persecution had followed the church as the town of Nauvoo grew and became a threat to the politics and economics of the neighbouring counties. Several warrants were issued for the arrest of Joseph Smith, some of which were dismissed in court. Many appeals were made to the government, mostly without avail. In an attempt to protect themselves, Joseph became a candidate for President of the United States in January 1844.[27]

A newspaper, *The Nauvoo Expositor*, was set up by apostate members. It condemned the prophet's sexual licence and false doctrines, so Joseph had the printing office burned down and the editor run out of town. A warrant was issued for the arrest of Joseph, his brother Hyrum and sixteen others. When

Joseph resisted and armed the Mormons, a civil war seemed imminent.

The militia were called out, but the Governor of Illinois persuaded Joseph to give himself up, and he was imprisoned in Carthage Jail. With him were his brother Hyrum, John Taylor and Willard Richards. There, late in the afternoon of 27 July 1844, Joseph and his brother died in a gunfight at the hands of a mob who burst into the jail and shot him.[28]

There was a bitter struggle for leadership of the church following Joseph's death. Sidney Rigdon was first counsellor in the First Presidency, and claimed that he should be caretaker of the church until God called the next Prophet. He called a special conference on 8 August to decide the matter.

Brigham Young's claim was that the keys of the kingdom resided with the Quorum of the Twelve Apostles, and he was the President of the Quorum. His claim was strengthened, and Sidney Rigdon's defeated, by a remarkable event in the special conference meeting. As Brigham Young rose to address the meeting, his face was transfigured and appeared to be Joseph Smith's.[29] A week later the Twelve sent an epistle to all the saints, stressing that they were the proper successors to Joseph Smith because they held the keys. Brigham Young led the church as President of the Quorum of the Twelve.

It was not until 5 December 1847 that the Quorum of the Twelve sustained Brigham Young as President of the Church. This was ratified on 27 December when the saints, assembled in general conference at Kanesville (Council Bluffs), Iowa, voted to sustain Brigham Young as President of the Church.[30]

Later, another faction arose. Joseph's family and many others believed that the Presidency should be hereditary, and the Presidency should fall on his son, Joseph Smith III. The split was so strong that when his claim was refused, his followers left and began what is now the Reorganised Church of Jesus Christ of Latter-day Saints. Their headquarters are in Independence, Missouri. The United States later recognised the Reorganised Church as Joseph's legitimate heirs, and granted them title to the Kirtland Temple. Their Presidents have all claimed direct descent from Joseph Smith.

The trek westward

In the face of fierce persecution, the saints resolved to move westward. Their hand was forced when, in 1846, Nauvoo's charter was revoked and mobs drove them out of the city. In the dead of winter, and ill-prepared, the great trek westward was begun. It ended with the founding of Salt Lake City, the hub of modern-day Mormonism.

During the Mormon pioneer period, 1846–68, nearly 80,000 saints crossed the plains. Following their 1,000-mile migration, the saints established, within thirty years, a commonwealth of over 300 settlements. The cornerstone of the famous Salt Lake Temple was laid on 6 April 1853 and the temple was dedicated on 6 April 1893.

The longest-serving Mormon prophet, Brigham Young, died on 29 August 1877, leaving a thriving church, seventeen wives, fifty-six children and a personal fortune of nearly 2 million dollars.

Statehood

The 'Mormon' territory of Utah was finally granted statehood in 1896. The price was high however. Bitter persecution and the confiscation of church property by the government threatened the very existence of the church. In 1890 the president of the day, Wilford Woodruff, bowed to public pressure and issued a statement bringing the practice of polygamy to an end.

With statehood, church property was returned. It was not until 1906 that the church was debt free. This paved the way for a new period of prosperity and growth. From that time church growth has been consistently impressive. Today it is one of the top fifty corporations in America and the most successful of all the traditional Christian cults.

Notes

1. Jerald and Sandra Tanner (eds), *The Changing World of Mormonism*, 1980, pp 67-74.
2. John Bernhisel, Letter to Governor Thomas Ford of Illinois, 14 June 1844, quoted in Joseph Smith, History of the Church 6:468.

3. *My Kingdom Shall Roll Forth: Readings in Church History*, manual, 1979, p 8.

4. Wesley P. Walters, *New Light on Mormon Origins from the Palmyra (NY) Revival*, Utah Christian Tract Society, 1967.

5. Joseph Smith, History of the Church.

6. See Exodus 28:30 and Numbers 27:21. 'The Urim (lights) and Thummim (shadows) were the means whereby God talked to his high priests in the Old Testament. By reading the reflections of the seven-branched candlestick on the high priest's breastplate according to a secret code, the will of Jehovah would be made known.' Abbe Fouard, *The Christ the Son of God*, 1890.

7. Jerald and Sandra Tanner (eds), *The Changing World of Mormonism*, 1980, pp 141-44.

8. Arch S. Reynolds, *How Did Joseph Smith Translate?*, Springville, Utah, 1952, p 21.

9. Doctrine and Covenants 115:4.

10. As above, 45:60-61.

11. As above, 37.

12. As above, 41:9; 42:30-34; 48; 51; 70:1-8; 72; 78; 82:11-12; 83; 85; 104:47-66.

13. As above, 104:3.

14. As above, 76.

15. As above, 104.

16. As above, 1:37-39.

17. Introductory note, The Pearl of Great Price.

18. Doctrine and Covenants 32.

19. As above, 45:64; 57:1-2; 58:56; 84:2; 101:20-22.

20. As above, 138:47,48,58,59.

21. Joseph Smith, History of the Church 4:551.

22. Jerald and Sandra Tanner (eds), *The Changing World of Mormonism*, 1980, pp 534-47.

23. Bruce R. McConkie, *Mormon Doctrine*, 1966, p 238.

24. Doctrine and Covenants 132:61-62.

25. Fawn M. Brodie, *No Man Knows My History*, pp 434-65.

26. Doctrine and Covenants 132:54-56.

27. Joseph Smith, History of the Church 6:188.

28. Doctrine and Covenants 135.

29. *My Kingdom Shall Roll Forth: Readings in Church History*, manual, 1979, pp 11-12.

30. As above, p 15.

Chapter 4
Growth in Britain

On 23 July 1837, in a chapel in Preston, the Reverend James Fielding welcomed his brother Joseph, visiting from America with some friends, and invited them to preach to his congregation. The message they brought was new and exciting, and seven days later nine of the congregation were baptised. This was the foundation for a great missionary achievement.

The membership of this new church doubled and redoubled at an amazing rate. Branches were established in over a dozen places around Preston, including Eccleston, Rochester and Clithero. The 'Cock Pit' (Temperance Hall), a large building in Preston, was rented for meetings. On Christmas Day 1837, the first conference was held. Over 300 church members were in attendance. On 1 April 1838, a second conference of the church in England was held at Preston. The church membership was then 1,500–2,000. Joseph Fielding was ordained as President of the British Mission, with Willard Richards and William Clayton as counsellors. Following the conference, Heber C. Kimball and Orson Hyde returned to America.

Is this the story of a revival? What was the message which captured the hearts of church-goers in their hundreds? This is the beginning of the British Mission of the Church of Jesus Christ of Latter-day Saints – the Mormon church.

The mission began because many of the people who had joined the church in Canada were English and they were anxious to share the Mormon gospel message with their English relatives. Two members of the Mormon Twelve Apostles, Heber C. Kimball and Orson Hyde, plus Willard Richards and four members from Canada, were called to begin this mission. Their ship arrived in Liverpool on 20 July 1837. The majority were penniless. The Reverend James Fielding was the first of many clergy to give them assistance. He soon realised, however, that he risked losing his congregation, and closed his chapel to them. They then taught in private homes, and by 6 August there were nearly fifty converts in Preston and the Preston Branch was organised.

Why were they welcomed?

In the mid-nineteenth century there was a new freedom of thought and, with it, freedom of religious expression. Since the industrial revolution there had been sweeping social and economic changes, and people felt less fettered by the past and were willing to break free from tradition and consider new ideas. It was not uncommon for a group of people to disagree with their church minister and begin meeting separately.

Prior to 1812, the Mormon missionaries could not have preached openly or held meetings without breaking the law. The Conventicle Acts of 1660 and 1670 limited the right of nonconformist ministers to preach, and forbade non-Anglicans to assemble together for religious purposes. Sharp penalties were imposed upon anyone discovered worshipping illegally, which began with excommunication and included prison and even transportation. The repeal of these Acts in 1812 meant that many branches of nonconformism flourished and the Mormons and others like them were free to preach.

There had been revivals before this, and new gospels had come over from America. In this respect the Mormons were nothing new. Lorenzo Dow led revivals with the Primitive Methodists in 1805 and 1818, Asahel Nettleton had preached with great success in 1831, and the Millerites and Campbellites would come over in the 1840s. 'But the Latter-day Saints mission of 1837 was something different: Elder Kimball and company ushered in the most spectacular and lasting of the American missionary endeavours in Britain, and the church became the fastest-growing religious body of that period.'[1]

Ministers and rectors in the south of England tried unsuccessfully to get a bill through parliament, prohibiting the Mormons from preaching in Britain. Their petition stated that one Mormon missionary had baptised 1,500 people, mostly members of the English Church, in a period of seven months.

Wilford Woodruff recorded in his journal a brief account of his efforts in southern England in 1840:

> I travelled 4,469 miles, held 230 meetings, established 53 places for preaching, and planted 47 churches and jointly organised them... The baptisms of the year were 336 persons under my own hands, and I assisted at the baptism of 86 others. I baptised 57 preachers mostly connected with the United Brethren, also two clerks of the Church of England.

This was duplicated by many of the other missionaries.

Between March and July 1840, Wilford Woodruff preached at Hill Farm in Castle Frome, the home of John and Jane Benbow, and baptised all but one of the 600 members of the United Brethren congregation. Nearly 2,000 other residents of the area joined the church in the early 1840s.

In 1841 Brigham Young arranged for richly bound copies of the Book of Mormon to be presented to Queen Victoria and Prince Albert, which are still in the Royal Library.[2]

The church's greatest success was among the working class, because of its compassion for their plight and its outspokenness in condemning the evils of British society. The call to 'gather to Zion' (for all members to move to America together to strengthen the young church) offered them hope for a better life. The response was so great that membership fell from a peak of over 30,000 in 1850 to 2,770 in 1890.

Rapid growth

The rapid increase in members resulted in a church organisation that was unique. As in America, local members were organised into 'branches', and these met together periodically in 'conferences' later renamed 'stakes'. In Britain, as the number of conferences grew, they were grouped into 'pastorates' with a pastor over each. This third tier of organisation was never used anywhere else, and was discontinued when membership fell due to emigration.

The success of the British Mission was such that by 1850 over half the members of the church were located in Britain. If the Mormons had not been encouraged to gather to the American Zion, the church today might have been considered a European rather than an American church. The first shipload of converts left Liverpool on 6 June 1840. This was the beginning of a migration movement of such magnitude that the church in America became predominantly British for the next fifty years. From 1847 to 1869, more than 32,000 British and Irish converts left for a new life in America.[3] The Perpetual Emigrating Fund was established in September 1849 to assist with the cost of emigrating. Those who had been helped would pay back the money as they could, so that others could be helped in their turn.

British contributions to the church

It is interesting to note that the apostolic mission to Britain in 1839 contained the next four Presidents of the church: Brigham Young, John Taylor, Wilford Woodruff and Lorenzo Snow. John Taylor was actually born in England. Ten Presidents have served missions in Britain, and almost all of them have British ancestry.

The rapid growth in membership created a great need for literature and teaching materials. The facilities for publishing were readily at hand, so it made good sense that most of the church publishing should be done there. New editions of the Book of Mormon, Doctrine and Covenants, and hymn books were printed. In 1840 the church began publishing the *Millennial Star*, a periodical that would have a continuous run from 1840 to 1970. It carried sermons, poetry, hymns, stories and news of the church, as well as articles of general interest such as recipes and items for children.

When Franklin D. Richards became President of the British Mission in 1850, he collected together materials that he felt would provide valuable instruction but which were not readily available. They were published in Liverpool in 1851, in a one-shilling, paper-bound pamphlet called the *Pearl of Great Price*. The next edition was revised and expanded in Utah, and was accepted as one of the church's standard works on 10 October 1880.

George D. Watt, the first British convert, emigrated to America in 1842 and learned to write in shorthand. From 1851 to 1869 he recorded many of the sermons of President Brigham Young and other church leaders. For the benefit of the British members, these were published as a sixteen-page, twice-monthly periodical, beginning on 1 November 1853. It was called the *Journal of Discourses* and eventually ran to twenty-six volumes of twenty-four issues each. It is still cited as a doctrinal resource today.

Other contributions include the founding of the church's Sunday school organisation in 1849 by Richard Ballantyne from Scotland; the first pioneer party to cross the plains included William Pitt's Brass Band from the Midlands; William Clayton from Penwortham, Lancashire, served as Joseph Smith's clerk and wrote 'Come, Come, Ye Saints', one of the best-known hymns in the church; the first conductor of the Mormon Tabernacle Choir was John Parry from Newmarket, Flintshire, and its first organist was Joseph Daynes from Norwich.[4]

England is also the site of the oldest standing Mormon meeting house in the world, at Gadfield Elm near Cheltenham. It was given to the church by the United Brethren when they were converted.

The Welsh connection

In the autumn of 1840, Brigham Young, later to become the second president of the church, and his missionary companion, Heber C. Kimball, paid a visit to Overton, Flintshire, North Wales, where they preached the message of Mormonism. They were the first two missionaries of the church to set foot in Wales.

Many were converted, and within three months the church had nearly one hundred new members in the Overton area. The work eventually spread to all parts of Wales and was greatly enhanced by the missionary zeal of Captain Dan Jones, known as the 'Welsh Prophet'. During the 1840s and 1850s over 10,000 converts were baptised.

Baptism usually meant leaving Wales, as the church leaders called for the faithful to gather to Salt Lake City in the Rocky Mountains of America. The first group of about eighty-five Welsh Mormon converts crossed the Atlantic in 1849. Their fame for singing came with them as they crossed the plains in the summer of that year. When this group reached Salt Lake Valley, President Brigham Young asked John Parry, their leader, to organise a choir to sing at a conference of the church. The choir he directed was the nucleus of what would become the world-famous Mormon Tabernacle Choir.

The Welsh pioneers, however, would do far more than sing. Their contributions to the frontier society of Utah were remarkable. They were the master masons for the temples; miners, blacksmiths and iron-workers; farmers, weavers, dressmakers, milliners and schoolteachers. These early Welsh Mormon pioneers – several thousand of them – wove their way into the fabric of Utah to the extent that by 1993 over one-fifth of the state population descended, to some degree, from Welsh ancestry.

The first chapel to be dedicated in Wales was in 1937 in Merthyr Tydfil, and the first stake, also in Merthyr Tydfil, was created on 12 January 1975. Wales also boasts the first building constructed as a Mormon chapel in Britain, dedicated in Llanelli on 28 January 1849.

The church in Scotland

The first Mormon missionaries to Scotland were two Scots from Canada: Alexander Wright of Banffshire and Samuel Mulliner of Midlothian, who had joined the church in Ontario early in the 1830s. They arrived in December 1839 at Samuel's parents in Edinburgh. Alexander walked most of the 100 miles from there to his relatives in Marnoch, Banffshire, and began the work there.

The first baptisms in Scotland were at Bishopton on 14 January 1840, when two people were baptised in the River Clyde. Results were slow initially, but by the beginning of May there were eighty converts. The first Scottish branch was organised at Paisley on 8 May 1840. Orson Pratt dedicated Scotland for the preaching of the gospel on 18 May 1840, from Arthur's Seat in Edinburgh. By the turn of the century there were over 100 branches. Most of them were in Lanarkshire, Renfrewshire, Ayrshire, and in the vicinity of Stirling, Fife, Clackmannan and Edinburgh. There were eventually four conferences in Scotland: Glasgow, Edinburgh, Dundee and Kilmarnock. There was very little success in the highlands, however, even though Peter McIntyre preached widely there in Gaelic during 1845.

Membership began to decline after 1851, due in part to the call to 'gather to Zion', but also caused by the practice of excommunicating members who were not meeting the requirements of membership. This affected membership all over Britain, but had a particularly marked effect in Scotland, where for several years there were nearly as many excommunications as baptisms. By 1875 the total membership in Scotland was 482, compared to the highest figure of 2,621.

In the bleak times that followed, a young man named David O. McKay was serving his mission in Stirling in 1897, when he saw an inscription carved into the wall of a new house. It read 'What-e'er thou art, act well thy part'. The inspiration that phrase gave him spurred him on and he eventually became President of the Church. The original stone which inspired him is now on display in the Museum of Church History in Salt Lake City.

The first stake in Scotland was created on 26 August 1962, in Glasgow.

The Irish experience

If persecution and emigration damaged the church elsewhere in Britain, their effect was by far the worst in Ireland. Not only was there general opposition to the new faith, with meetings disrupted, but many landlords and clergy conspired to threaten eviction and excommunication to anyone who helped the missionaries or even listened to them. Unlike many other places, there was virtually no violence against them, but many methods were used to disrupt meetings, such as cayenne pepper on the floor, smoke under the floor-boards, and fog-horns used in open-air meetings.

Consequently, converts to the church were slow in coming, and most of them emigrated. Social conditions in Ireland were very poor for many people, and with the catastrophe of the potato famine in the 1840s, the attraction of a new life in America was enormous.

Elder Reuben Hedlock visited Belfast for three days in May 1840, but it was in July 1840 that the first official missionaries were sent. They were Elder John Taylor, and two Irish-born converts, James McGuffie from Liverpool, and William Black from Manchester. They began their work in Newry and Lisburn. They did not stay very long, however, and many of the missionaries who followed also did not settle. By July 1841 there were fifty-one members, which rose to seventy-two a year later. The first branch was organised at Hillsborough on 1 October 1840.

The potato famine reduced the population of Ireland by half, from 8 million to 4 million. One million of those died, the rest left. Most of them went to England, especially Liverpool and Manchester, to Scotland, particularly Glasgow, and to South Wales, to Swansea, Cardiff and Newport. Although there were few converts in Ireland, a great many converts in these other areas were Irish.

The Mormon church was very public in stating that the famine was a 'sign of the times', and quoted prophecies from the Bible and its own leaders to show that the end was near. When the famine reached its peak in 1845, Elder Parley P. Pratt claimed that the awaited judgements had begun in Ireland. His editorial in the *Millennial Star* declared the following: 'And why did the potato crop...in Ireland perish and rot in a night?... Because the angel hath flown in the midst of heaven, having the everlasting gospel to preach to them that dwell on earth.'[5]

Virtually no missionary work was done in Ireland during the famine, but it began again in 1850. However, by 1854 there were only eighty-seven members. There were even fewer when missionary work ceased again in 1863.

A third missionary effort was launched in 1884, and in 1889

the first conference of the Irish Mission was held in Belfast. By 1920 there were 225 members in the Belfast Conference and approximately sixty members in the area around Dublin. The first church property in Ireland was not dedicated until 1948, and the first chapel in 1962.

Hard times

The church in Britain suffered greatly during the latter half of the nineteenth century and the beginning of the twentieth. The majority of the membership emigrated, and those who were left were often discouraged at not being able to go, and fell away.

Although opposition to the church was fairly common, there were times when it grew much more serious and violent. The announcement of polygamy led to anti-Mormon demonstrations, and mobs not only attacked missionaries but members leaving meetings, and ransacked the meeting places themselves. When the Edmunds-Tucker Act was passed in America in 1882 which made plural marriage illegal, it sparked a fresh outbreak of riots, even when the church ended polygamy in 1890.

Stories were rife about innocent young girls lured into polygamy in America by wicked Mormon missionaries. Winifred Graham wrote several novels on the theme, and magazines and newspapers competed to print the most shocking revelations. The authors remember stories still in existence as late as the early 1970s of a secret tunnel from Liverpool to America down which girls were smuggled, and down which young men were led to a life of home-made apple pies and as many wives as they wanted. Eventually complaints were made to the Home Secretary, Winston Churchill, who made enquiries and issued a report exonerating the Mormons.

In 1898, in an attempt to convey the message that Mormons were not dangerous, the church arranged for a series of eight lectures on Mormonism to be given by Dr James E. Talmage. He was the President of the University of Utah and a member of several prominent British scientific societies, so it was felt that he would be respected by both the press and the public. Contrary to expectations, halls were packed to overflowing every night, and audiences were very responsive. Even newspapers that had previously attacked the church reported the presentations very favourably.

In 1906, President Joseph F. Smith became the first President of the Church ever to visit Europe while serving as prophet. Hundreds of members heard him speak in Finsbury Town Hall and the Exchange Hall in Blackburn, and complete transcripts of his sermons given there were published in the *Millenial Star* – which reached members all over Britain. He also spoke in many other places in England and Scotland.

However, despite these attempts to win over the British public and encourage church members, anti-Mormon feeling continued to escalate. The Mission President reported 'scenes of violence and mobocracy' at places across the country, including Sunderland, Birmingham, Bristol, London and Norwich. The crusade reached its height in 1911, with an anti-Mormon rally in Liverpool led by an Anglican vicar, and newspapers competing to publish sensational stories about polygamy.

World War

The First World War saw a drastic reduction in the number of missionaries from America. By 1919 there were only thirty-one missionaries in the whole of Britain. This was a great blow, as missionaries in those days ran many of the church organisations and branches, and organised much of the regular life of the church. With so many men away, the women of the Relief Society shouldered the burden and not only aided the war effort in many ways but were called as part-time missionaries. Eventually 300 women were called to fill the gaps left by the departure of the missionaries.

One benefit which the church gained from the war was the increase in concern for spiritual matters in the general population. More people turned to prayer and looked for spiritual guidance, and church membership increased.

When the war ended, the church was shocked to find that missionaries were unable to return because the British government refused to grant them visas. The rumours about polygamy had done their work and the government was afraid that 'their presence here w[oul]d be strongly resented by large classes of the community' and 'w[oul]d certainly lend to disorder'.[6] It took over a year before the British government agreed to grant the missionaries visas. When the missionaries did arrive they were cautioned to be very careful, and street meetings were discouraged as being provocative. It was not until James E. Talmage became Mission President (1924–28) and began a campaign to win over the owners and editors of the newspapers that major opposition finally ended.

Building

In 1894 the church began to discourage emigration to America, and members were asked to 'build up Zion' in their own localities. In the 1930s the branches in Britain were encouraged to set up building-fund programmes and make plans to buy or build their own meeting houses, instead of the rented halls which they had previously used. This encouraged the members that the church really was supporting them where they were. By 1935 twelve branches had their own buildings. In 1935 the British Mission developed three major attractions to gain attention and praise for the church:

• It was the first year of organised league baseball in Britain, and two teams of Mormon missionaries participated. The London missionary team, known as the Latter-day Saints (later called the Catford Saints because they were sponsored by Catford Stadium), won the title, becoming England's first national baseball champions. The other well-known team was the Rochdale Greys, who won the North of England championship in 1936 and 1937.

• The National Basketball Association was formed in 1935 and missionary teams were prominent here also. In the 1936 season a London missionary team won the London League championship. They called themselves the Catford Saints to take advantage of the baseball team's fame.

• In 1935 a singing group called the Millennial Chorus was organised. Sixteen missionaries were originally chosen for this special assignment – evangelising by day and singing nightly at meetings. They began to give concerts in August, and by 1938 had become a polished singing group with several outstanding soloists.

Each of these developments raised the profile of the church and helped to give it a very positive image of high standards and healthy living. Later on, they were used to draw people into the church by offering them the opportunity to participate. In the summer of 1937 the church held a great celebration to mark the hundredth anniversary of the British Mission. Church President Heber J. Grant, his first counsellor, and over fifty church leaders came to England to participate in two weeks of festivities and conferences.

Second World War

At the outbreak of war all missionaries were immediately called home. Three British elders were chosen as the acting presidency of the mission, and local members took over the activities of the branches. It was the first time that the church in Britain had been totally without missionaries from America.

In 1940 there was a serious lack of priesthood holders. The British government agreed that all Mormon elders would be recognised as ministers of religion and would therefore be exempt from war duty. Since almost every adult male member was an elder, this was open to abuse, but the church operated strict controls to ensure that only district and branch presidents requested exemption. In this way the church was able to maintain and even reorganise its branches during the war.

With so many people away, some branches became very small and others suffered from lack of leadership. The mission consolidated many branches, so that the number shrank from seventy-five to twenty-nine. The bigger branches made it possible to operate a lot of organisations, but the extra travelling made members feel isolated, and many stopped going. By the end of the war over 50 per cent of the members in some areas were inactive.

As after the First World War, the church had problems bringing the missionaries back into Britain. The British government ruled that 'aliens coming to England will not be permitted to stay longer than two months'. Although the Home Office was persuaded to extend this to six months for

Mormon missionaries, it took several months before visas were granted.

In 1946 the church welfare programme was introduced into the British Mission. The church also began improvements in branch meeting facilities, and with the return of priesthood holders from the war, and new missionaries, there was a sharp increase in attendance, which continued to rise. Every method possible was used to attract people to the church, including a film, the Millennial Chorus and sports teams. The number of convert baptisms increased spectacularly, from 366 in 1949 to over 1,000 in 1951.

Great changes

The two decades between 1951 and 1971 saw greater changes for the Church in Britain than in any period since the apostolic missions of the 1830s and 1840s. Following a long night of struggle in its first century, the Church in Britain began to see the light of a new day in the 1950s, building upon the heritage it had forged through years of faithfulness in the face of persecution and sacrifice. By 1971 it had come of age as a fully developed and vital part of the world-wide Church.[7]

This is the assessment of the Mormon book *Truth Will Prevail*, and although couched in emotive and supportive language, it is true that by this time the church had become a well-respected pillar of society.

In 1951 there was only one mission in Britain, by 1971 there were seven, and for a time there had been nine. In 1951 there were no stakes, by 1971 there were nine. The first European stake was created on 17 March 1960, in Manchester, and others quickly followed. The first stake in Scotland was organised in Glasgow in 1962, the first Irish stake in Belfast in 1974, and the first Welsh stake in Merthyr Tydfil in 1975. In 1951 most branches met in rented halls or converted houses, by 1971 there were over one hundred new chapels and a temple.

These were constructed with the help of the Building Missionary Programme, in which experienced builders were called on missions to supervise the construction of new chapels, assisted by local members. All members were expected to contribute their labour, but some young men were called as local building missionaries, and later served as evangelising missionaries – becoming the first large group of British full-time missionaries.

The building of the London Temple, at Lingfield, Surrey, was announced on 1 August 1953 and was dedicated on 7–9 September 1958. Before the dedication more than 76,000 people were allowed to tour the building at an open house held from 16 August to 3 September. More than 12,000 members attended the six dedicatory sessions, including members from Scandinavia, the Netherlands, Germany and France. In 1963 the House of Lords upheld a ruling that since the Temple was not open for public worship, it was liable for tax. There was some speculation that the building would have to be closed, but the British members, with help from general church funds, were able to raise the required amount.

In 1960 Deseret Enterprises Ltd was opened in Mitcham, Surrey, to handle the distribution of church books and supplies so that each individual branch no longer needed to order from America. This eventually led to the establishment of an official church distribution centre at the end of the 1960s.

The church seeks to attract and keep its members and provide for their needs in every area of life by means of a myriad of organisations. During the 1960s in Britain, for example, the British Athletics Association, the Latter-day Saints Student Association, the Seminary and Institute home study programmes for young people (and later adults) and the Church Public Relations were all set up.

The Presiding Bishopric established administration offices in 1972, and the first Bishop's Storehouse[8] was opened in Birmingham in 1980. During the next few years a 305-acre farm was purchased, with dairy and beef cattle, and sheep. Further Bishop's Storehouses were opened in Glasgow, Sheffield, Stevenage, Bristol, Reading and Crawley, and others followed. Agricultural land is currently being purchased by the church, which is now (1995) among the top ten owners of farmland in Britain. The church's Welfare Services programmes include employment centres, professional counselling and a licensed adoption agency. These are intended to provide a complete network of support for members.

The growth in membership has slowed down since 1971, but the church has consolidated and strengthened its position. The first area general conference (anywhere in the world) was held in Manchester on 29 August 1971 when over ten thousand people attended. Britain was also the first country to hold three area conferences simultaneously, in June 1976, in London, Manchester and Glasgow. By the mid 1980s the whole of Britain was covered by stakes, with only the Republic of Ireland still served by districts within a mission. There were thirty-two stakes in England, five in Scotland, two in Wales, and one in Northern Ireland.

There are also at least thirty-three genealogical libraries in branches all over Britain, which make available copies of key records at the church's main library in Salt Lake City. Nearly half of its 8 million names are from the British Isles. Initially there was resistance from the clergy to handing over their parish records for microfilming, but in 1979 the Parochial Records Measure required parish documents to be deposited in central records offices, who had no interest in questions of doctrine and were only too happy to have an organisation offer to preserve the records.

Great strides have been made in public relations. From being hated and feared, the church is now well respected, and many church members have been given important positions in education, business, government and civic affairs. At the time of writing the following Mormons are prominent examples. Terry Rooney, MP for Bradford North; The Sheriff of York, David Halliwell; Ronald L. Gigg, Leader of East Devon District Council and chairman of the policy committee. David Rutley works as special adviser to the Rt Hon William Waldergrave MP, and former Hyde Park bishop Julian Bell works for Chris Smith MP. All are recognised for their leadership and relationship skills acquired through church programmes and service. Surveys have shown that over 95% of the news coverage of the church is positive.

Polls by British newspapers show the Mormon church to be one of the fastest-growing churches. By the 150th anniversary of the church in Britain, in 1987, there were 140,000 members and a growth rate of 5.5 per cent a year. It is also a young membership, with over fifty per cent under thirty in 1987.

The book *Truth Will Prevail*, a Mormon publication documenting the church's history in this country, ends on a triumphal note, quoting Brigham Young: 'If we will work unitedly, we can work ourselves into wealth, health, prosperity and power; and this is required of us. It is the duty of a saint of God to gain all the influence he can on this earth.'[9]

Those of us who are concerned about Mormon doctrine and the growth of a church that teaches falsehood, do not view these sentiments in the same light.

Notes

1. *Truth Will Prevail*, p 44.
2. *Encyclopaedia of Mormonism*, p 228.
3. As above, p 229.
4. As above, p 231–32.
5. *Millenial Star* 8:100 (see Revelation 14:6–7), quoted in *Truth Will Prevail*, p 342.
6. Thorp, British Government, quoted in *Truth Will Prevail*, p 342 (our brackets).
7. *Truth Will Prevail*,p 395.
8. The Bishop's Storehouse is literally a means of storing essential supplies which are used for the relief of church members who find themselves in need. It is part of the welfare programme.
9. *Journal of Discourses* 12:376, quoted in *Truth Will Prevail*, p 441.

Part Two
VISIONS, PROPHECIES AND REVELATIONS

Chapter 5
The First Vision

Freedom

The American Declaration of Independence, on 4 July 1776, signalled a great freedom of thought and action, fuelled by a population explosion and a wide, unexplored frontier in which to grow. From this rich soil sprang many religious movements, including the Mormon Church.

The first government census was taken in 1790. By 1830 the population of the United States had tripled. Most people lived on the east coast, and here the increase was modest. The biggest growth occurred along what was then the western frontier, from Maine to Georgia and across the Appalachian mountains, where the population increased nearly six times. The availability of land enabled it to spread westward.

The migrants took their churches with them, which brought stability and order to their new surroundings, but a significant shift took place. Previously, each village had only one church, and even in the bigger towns the churches were branches of the same congregation. The new societies changed all this. Hundreds of thousands of Americans broke from traditional faiths and chose a new church. Children were not automatically absorbed into the traditional church, but allowed to make their own choice. Many churches could now be found in the same area.

At the same time, information began flowing into the towns as never before. By 1850 every town of any size had its own newspaper, carrying articles copied from papers all over the country. The improved postal system brought regional or national circulation to scores of magazines and specialised periodicals. The political freedom following independence and migrations from old neighbourhoods, a variety of accessible churches and voluntary associations, and a melée of conflicting values and beliefs compelled each person to choose to a degree unknown a hundred years earlier. Freedom allowed people to ask questions, but it did not provide answers.

Questions

Among the questions which excited the minds of the people in New York State was the question of buried treasure, particularly since the area was rich in Indian relics. Hundreds of burial mounds dotted the landscape, filled with skeletons and artefacts of stone, copper and sometimes beaten silver. Money-diggers and fortune-hunters abounded, using crystals, mineral rods and various other paraphernalia. There were many tales of seer stones, ghosts, magic incantations and nocturnal excavations.

Superstition was rife in the churches as well, and this together with the desire for religious liberty brought about many new religions and schisms in the old ones. In Palmyra, New York, in 1820, the townspeople could choose among the Baptists, Methodists, Presbyterians, the Society of Friends, and the Episcopalians. The Shakers, under Ann Lee, flourished in New York State and built community halls only thirty miles from Palmyra.

Palmyra was also the centre of one revival after another. The people were constantly being challenged, not only to accept the gospel, but to decide which church to join. Competition was fierce.

Visions

Spectacular conversion stories were plentiful, many of which included visions.

In 1816 Elias Smith, a minister, published a book in which he told of his conversion.

> I went into the woods...a light appeared from heaven...My
> mind seemed to rise in that light to the throne of God and the
> Lamb...The Lamb once slain appeared to my understanding,
> and while viewing him, I felt such love to him as I never felt to
> any thing earthly...It is not possible for me to tell how long I
> remained in that situation.[1]

Alexander Campbell wrote the following on 1 March 1824, concerning a revival in the state of New York: 'Enthusiasm flourishes...This man was regenerated when asleep, by a vision of the night. That man heard a voice in the woods, saying, "Thy sins be forgiven thee." A third saw his Saviour descending to the tops of the trees at noon day.'[2]

The Wayne Sentinel published an account of a revelation by Asa Wild: 'It seemed as if my mind...was struck motionless, as well as into nothing, before the awful and glorious majesty of the Great Jehovah. He then spake...He also told me, that every denomination of professing christians had become extremely corrupt.'[3]

Similarities and inconsistencies

In the midst of this speculation a young man, Joseph Smith, was brought up. His family were poor farmers from Vermont, who moved to Palmyra in 1817, and struggled with a mortgage, debts and poor crops. In the early 1830s Joseph wrote an account of a vision he claimed to have had in 1821, when he was nearly sixteen, in which he saw the Lord of Glory – the Son of God.[4] A later account appeared in his diary for 1835–36, in which he said that he was about fourteen and saw two persons and many angels.[5] In 1855 another version appeared, in which he saw an angel who told him that none of the churches were right. These discrepancies would not be so serious were they not the foundation of the Mormon church.

The official version of what is known as the First Vision, written in 1838, did not appear until 1851, published in the Pearl of Great Price and accepted by the church as scripture. It puts Joseph in his fifteenth year and describes his concern over which church he should join, prompted by a local revival and the religious debates between the denominations:

While I was laboring under the extreme difficulties caused by the contests of these parties of religionists, I was one day reading the Epistle of James, first chapter and fifth verse: 'if any of you lack wisdom, let him ask of God, that giveth to all men liberally and upbraideth not; and it shall be given him.'

Never did any passage of scripture come with more power to the heart of man than this did at this time to mine...I reflected on it again and again, knowing that if any person needed wisdom from God, I did.

At length I came to the conclusion that I must either remain in confusion, or else do as James directs, that is, ask of God... So, in accordance with this my determination, I retired to the woods to make the attempt. It was on the morning of a beautiful, clear day, early in the spring of 1820.

Having looked around me, and finding myself alone, I kneeled down and began to offer up the desires of my heart to God. I had scarcely done so, when immediately I was siezed upon by some power which entirely overcame me, and had such an astonishing influence over me as to bind my tongue so that I could not speak. Thick darkness gathered around me, and it seemed for a time as if I were doomed to sudden destruction.

Just at this moment of great alarm, I saw a pillar of light exactly over my head, above the brightness of the sun, which descended gradually until it fell upon me. It no sooner appeared than I found myself delivered from the enemy which held me bound.

When the light rested upon me I saw two Personages, whose brightness and glory defy all description, standing above me in the air. One of them spake unto me, calling me by name, and said, pointing to the other, 'This is my Beloved Son. Hear Him!'

My object in going to inquire of the Lord was to know which of all the sects was right, that I might know which to join. No sooner, therefore, did I get possession of myself than I asked the Personages who stood above me in the light, which of all the sects was right – and which I should join.

I was answered that I must join none of them, that 'they draw near to me with their lips, but their hearts are far from me; they teach for doctrines the commandments of men, having a form of godliness, but they deny the power thereof.'[6]

If such a life-changing experience really happened, it would surely imprint itself on the mind, and the tale, however elaborated or brief, would always be essentially the same. Most church members are not aware that there are other versions of the first vision, which are all suppressed by the church.

No record for twenty years

Joseph Smith goes on to say that he shared his experience with a local Methodist preacher and was treated with contempt: 'I soon found, however, that my telling the story had excited a great deal of prejudice against me among professors of religion, and was the cause of great persecution, which continued to increase.'[7] Soon the story spread and he was subjected to 'the most bitter persecution and reviling' by 'the great ones of the most popular sects of the day'.[8] Yet no record has been found of the vision in any records of the time, or for almost twenty years afterwards.

In defending the absence of any reference to a vision until at least 1832, Milton V. Backman Jr., quotes Dean C. Jessee, research historian for the Joseph Fielding Smith Institute for Church History at Brigham Young University:

> Considering the youth of the Prophet, the frontier conditions in which he lived, his lack of academic training, the absence of any formal directive to motivate him to write, and the antagonistic reception he received upon first relating the experience, it is not strange that he failed to preserve an account of his First Vision during the decade between 1820 and 1830.[9]

Fawn M. Brodie, who published a biography of Joseph Smith in 1945, was one of the first to cast doubt upon the authenticity of the story:

> The description of the vision was first published by Orson Pratt in his Remarkable Visions in 1840, twenty years after it was supposed to have occurred. Between 1820 and 1840 Joseph's friends were writing long panegyrics; his enemies were defaming him in an unceasing stream of affidavits and pamphlets, and Joseph himself was dictating several volumes of Bible-flavored prose. But no one in this long period even intimated that he had heard the story of the two gods. At least, no such

intimation has survived in print or manuscript...The first published Mormon history, begun with Joseph's collaboration in
1834 by Oliver Cowdery, ignored it altogether...Joseph's own
description of the first vision was not published until 1842,
twenty-two years after the memorable event.

If something happened that spring morning in 1820, it
passed totally unnoticed in Joseph's home town, and apparently
did not even fix itself in the minds of members of his own family. The awesome vision he described in later years may have
been the elaboration of some half-remembered dream stimu-
lated by the early revival excitement and reinforced by the rich
folklore of visions circulating in his neighborhood. Or it may
have been sheer invention, created some time after 1834 when
the need arose for a magnificent tradition to cancel out the stories of his fortune-telling and money-digging.[10]

James B. Allen, who now serves as assistant church historian, admits that 'none of the available contemporary writings
about Joseph Smith in the 1830s, none of the publications of
the Church in that decade, and no contemporary journal or
correspondence yet discovered mentions the story of the first
vision.' Dr Allen goes on to state that in the 1830s 'the general
membership of the Church knew little, if anything, about it'.[11]

In view of the religious and social conditions of the time,
and the many stories of visions which were circulating, it
would have been a simple matter to invent such a story in
response to questions as to where the church came from, and
to give Joseph Smith the status he needed as leader of the
church.

Church explanations

As recently as 1944 the church insisted that there was only
one version of the first vision: 'Joseph Smith lived a little more
than twenty-four years after this first vision. During this time
he told but one story.'[12] However, in January 1985, *Ensign* magazine published an article entitled 'Joseph Smith's Recitals of
the First Vision', in which Milton V. Backman Jr. attempted to
reconcile the different versions of the first vision. This was, no
doubt, in response to the publishing of the different versions
by Jerald and Sandra Tanner of the Utah Lighthouse Ministry.

He begins by asserting that in a court of law, a witness whose story is always word perfect is suspected as having made it up. 'In an important way, the existence of these different accounts helps support the integrity of the Latter-day Saint Prophet. It indicates that Joseph did not deliberately create a memorised version which he related to everyone.'[13]

He goes to great lengths to compare examples of differing accounts in the Bible, for example the differences between the four Gospels. He says that the differences are not important: 'It is the great reality that is important, not the somewhat differing perceptions of it.'[14] He attempts to apply this to the different versions of the first vision, trying to say that we should concentrate on the central message.

> While describing his sacred experience of 1820, he sometimes emphasised one theme and at other times concentrated on other major concepts. Although the precise wording of what he learned from the Savior is different in all the accounts, the same basic message was included in all except the 1835 recital – that God's true church was not upon the earth in 1820. Of utmost importance was not the specific language in which the truths were unfolded but the truths themselves.[15]

Yet in the same quote he admits that the very truth which he holds to be central is missing from one of the accounts.

Acknowledging that the 1832 version of the story has a different date from the official account, he explains: 'Since Joseph was describing an event in 1832 that occurred twelve years earlier, it may have been difficult for him to remember certain details, such as the exact date of this vision.'[16] He even goes so far as to speculate that the handwriting is very bad, and the insertion that the event occurred in his sixteenth year could actually read fifteenth.

The same 1832 version mentions only one personage. 'This does not mean that in 1832 Joseph said that *only* one personage appeared or in any way disclaimed that the appearance of two personages,' insists Milton Backman.[17] He continues: 'Joseph focused on the message which the Saviour unfolded to him'.[18] Surely if God the Father had also appeared, it would not be overlooked in the telling! These arguments are plainly grasping at straws.

The 1835 account refers to two personages (unnamed) and 'many angels'. The explanation he gives for this is that because of persecution 'apparently, in his discussions with some nonmembers, the Prophet hesitated to identify the personages who had appeared to him.'[19] He also attempts to prove that 'God' and 'Angel' can be used interchangeably, by referring to Genesis 48:15–16. The *NIV Study Bible* has this to say: 'As the Lord's personal messenger who represented him and bore his credentials, the angel could speak on behalf of (and so be identified with) the One who sent him.'[20] This footnote refers specifically to the Angel of the Lord. Joseph did not identify any of the personages who appeared to him as the Angel of the Lord.

The 1838 account is the one printed in The Pearl of Great Price. As it was intended to be part of the official church history, 'this account was undoubtedly more carefully considered than either of the first two'.[21] 'If there is a contradiction in these accounts, then the 1838 account should be considered as the more reliable history. The young Joseph Smith, like many others then and now, was possibly not precise in his use of all words.'[22]

Here, as in many places in the article, he attempts to gloss over the differences. It is interesting that in many cases the differences between the accounts are mentioned in passing, but no explanation is offered. The explanations which are there are weak, and boil down to the argument that the differences do not matter, it is the message that is important.

Yet he also says that the 1832 account contains important details which are not in the officially accepted version.

> By way of summary, the 1832 account is the only known recital of the First Vision in which Joseph told of (a) his prolonged quest for religious truth, (b) his earnest desire to secure a forgiveness of sins, (c) his utmost concern because of the sins of mankind, (d) his learning about the nature of the Atonement and the reality of the Second Coming, and (e) his rejoicing following his spiritual experience.[23]

It is simply not possible to select the helpful parts of the three accounts and brush away the differences. The stories are so different as to destroy their credibility. Did God the Father and Jesus Christ appear to Joseph Smith, or only Jesus, or two unnamed personages and lots of angels? Was he told that God's true church was not on the earth or not?

How firm a foundation?

Despite the differences in the accounts, the church has said that it stands or falls on the reality of the first vision:

> Mormonism, as it is called, must stand or fall on the story of Joseph Smith. He was either a prophet of God, divinely called, properly appointed and commissioned, or he was one of the biggest frauds this world has ever seen.[24]
> The Church of Jesus Christ of Latter-day Saints, the Church which is founded and grounded on the testimony that Joseph Smith saw God and was in literal reality chosen to be his mighty latter-day Prophet.[25]

In 1855 Brigham Young, the second president of the church, preached a sermon in which he referred to the first vision:

> But as it was in the days of our Savior, so was it in the advent of this new dispensation...The Lord did not come with the armies of heaven, in power and great glory...But He did send His angel to this same obscure person, Joseph Smith, jun.[26]

Since the church places such store by the vision which began it all, it cannot so lightly dismiss the discrepancies which it has for so long sought to hide.

Notes

1. *The Life, Conversion, Preaching, Travels, and Sufferings of Elias Smith*, Portsmouth, NH, 1816, pp 58–59.
2. *The Christian Baptist*, Vol. 1, pp 148–49.
3. *The Wayne Sentinel*, 22 October 1823.
4. Described in *Brigham Young Studies*, Spring 1969, p 281.
5. Described in *Dialogue: A Journal of Mormon Thought*, Spring 1971.
6. Joseph Smith, History of the Church 1:11–19.
7. As above, 1:22.
8. As above, 1:23.
9. Dean C. Jessee, 'The Early Accounts of Joseph Smith's First Vision', *Brigham Young University Studies*, Vol. 9, Spring 1969, p 294, quoted in 'Joseph Smith's Recitals of the First Vision', *Ensign* magazine, January 1985.
10. Fawn M. Brodie, *No Man Knows My History*, 1945, pp 24–25.
11. *Dialogue: A Journal of Mormon Thought*, Autumn 1966, pp 29–45.
12. Preston Nibley, *Joseph Smith the Prophet*, 1944, p 30.
13. Milton V. Backman Jr, 'Joseph Smith's Recitals of the First Vision', *Ensign* magazine, January 1985, p 8.
14. As above, p 10.
15. As above, p 17.
16. As above, p 13.
17. As above, p 13.
18. As above, p 13.
19. As above, p 14.
20. Footnote to Genesis 16:7 cross-referenced from Genesis 48:16, *New International Version Study Bible*.
21. Milton V. Backman Jr, same source, p 14.
22. As above, p 15.
23. As above, p 13.
24. Joseph Fielding Smith, *Doctrines of Salvation*, Vol. 1, 1954, p 188.
25. Bruce R. McConkie, *Mormon Doctrine*, p 287.
26. *Journal of Discourses*, Vol. 2, p 171.

Chapter 6

Joseph Smith, False Prophet

It seems appropriate to take a look at what Mormons of today think about Joseph Smith. Unlike the Jehovah's Witnesses who barely mention Charles T. Russell these days, the Mormons revere their founder and first prophet. His legacy is a mixed blessing, however, and there must be times when they wish they could ignore him.

The Mormon reverence for Joseph Smith is perhaps best and most remarkably illustrated in the fact that a hymn of the church was written in the last century to praise his exploits. All over the world today church members sing:

> Praise to the man who communed with Jehovah!
> Praise to his memory...

> Long shall his blood, which was shed by assassins,
> Plead unto heav'n while the earth lauds his fame.

> Great is his glory...

> Mingling with Gods, he can plan for his brethren.[1]

Note the phrase 'Long shall his blood...plead unto heaven' which we will look at shortly.

Greater than Jesus

If the above sounds over the top it should be realised that it is perfectly in keeping with what the prophet had to say about himself.

I combat the errors of the ages; I meet the violence of the mobs; I cope with illegal proceedings from executive authority; I cut the gordian knot of powers, and I solve mathematical problems of universities, with truth diamond-truth; and God is my 'right hand man.'[2]

If they want a beardless boy to whip all the world, I will get on the top of a mountain and crow like a rooster; I shall always beat them...I have more to boast of than any man had. I am the only man that has been able to keep a whole church together since the days of Adam. A large majority of the whole have stood by me. Neither Paul, John, Peter nor Jesus ever did. I boast that no man ever did such a work as I. The followers of Jesus ran away from Him, but the Latter-day saints never ran away from me yet.[3]

Exalted forebears

Brigham Young, Joseph's successor as President of the Church, said of him:

The Lord had his eye upon him, and upon his father, and upon his father's father, and upon his progenitors clear back to Abraham, and from Abraham to the flood, from the flood to Enoch, and from Enoch to Adam. He has watched that family and that blood as it has circulated from it's fountain to the birth of that man.[4]

Eminent teachers

In a recent article, Robert L. Millet, Dean of Religious Education at Brigham Young University, stated:

Save Jesus Christ only, the world has never known a more competent scriptural authority than Joseph Smith. It is one thing to read a book of scripture and quite another to be personally instructed by its authors. Who among the world's scholars and religious leaders can lay claim to having stood face to face with Adam, Enoch, Noah, Moses, Elijah, John the Baptist, Peter, James and John?[5]

Mediator of the restored covenant

In the same article Robert Millet says:

The life of Joseph Smith was in some degree patterned after that of his Master, Jesus Christ. That pattern holds true even when extended to its tragic conclusion. Like his Master, Joseph Smith also shed his blood in order that the final testament, the re-establishment of the new covenant, might be in full effect (see Heb 9:16).

Hebrews 9:16 is a reference to the death of Jesus releasing to those who trust in him 'the promised eternal inheritance' (Heb 9:15), thus making him 'the mediator of a new covenant' (Heb 9:15). Mormon theology teaches that such benefits were lost in apostasy (a complete falling away from the truth) before the end of the second century. Therefore, it was necessary for blood to be shed again in order to re-establish what had been lost. The blood of Joseph was deemed sufficient to achieve that for which the blood of Christ alone was once thought sufficient. Joseph, then, becomes the mediator of the restored covenant.

No other name under heaven?

The above enhances our understanding of the following statements made by Joseph Smith's successor Brigham Young:

> No man or woman in this dispensation will ever enter into the celestial kingdom of God without the consent of Joseph Smith...He reigns there as supreme a being in his sphere, capacity and calling, as God does in Heaven.[6]
> I am an Apostle of Joseph Smith...all who reject my testimony will go to hell.[7]
> I will now give my scripture – Whosoever confesseth that Joseph Smith was sent of God...that spirit is of God, and every spirit that does not confess that God has sent Joseph Smith...is of Anti-christ.[8]

The record of such a person would have to be compelling reading. His conduct both as a prophet and as a man would surely be remarkable and his legacy to the church inestimable.

Joseph Smith and prophecy

There is much more to being a prophet than just predicting the future. Indeed, much of a prophet's work is in bringing the word and the will of the Lord to his people here and now. When a prophet does predict future events, however, the Lord himself has given us a means by which we can test that prophet.

> But a prophet who presumes to speak in my name anything I have not commanded him to say, or a prophet who speaks in the name of other gods, must be put to death.
> You may say to yourselves, 'How can we know when a message has not been spoken by the Lord?' If what a prophet proclaims in the name of the Lord does not take place or come true, that is a message the Lord has not spoken. That prophet has spoken presumptuously. Do not be afraid of him. (Deut 18:20–22.)

The penalty for false prophets is severe. But speaking in the name of God is a serious business. Does Joseph Smith pass the test?

Civil war

Charge any Mormon with following a false prophet and he will likely refer you to Joseph Smith's prophecy of the American civil war as a proof of his divine calling. Given on 25 December 1832, a full twenty-eight years before that conflict began, it is an apparently impressive pronouncement:

> Verily, thus saith the Lord concerning the wars that will shortly come to pass, *beginning at the rebellion of South Carolina,* which will eventually terminate in the death and misery of many souls;
> And the time will come that *war will be poured out upon all nations, beginning at this place.*
> For behold the Southern States shall be divided against the Northern States, and *the Southern States will call on other nations, even the nation of Great Britain, as it is called, and they shall also call upon other nations, in order to defend themselves; and then war shall be poured out upon all nations.*

And it shall come to pass, after many days, *slaves shall rise up against their masters,* who shall be marshalled and disciplined for war.

And it shall come to pass also that *the remnant who are left of the land will marshall themselves,* and shall become exceedingly angry, and shall vex the Gentiles with a sore vexation.[9]

The key points of the revelation have been italicised. These are the things that should be tested.

Yesterday's news

To have predicted the war at all a full twenty-eight years before the event seems impressive – until you look at the historical background. It is a fact, for example, that: 'On July 14, 1832, Congress passed a tariff act which South Carolina thought was so bad, she declared the tariff null and void. President Andrew Jackson alerted the nation's troops.'[10] The troops were on alert fully five months before the prophecy. It was common knowledge that rebellion was in the air and many newspapers of the day carried articles predicting the conflict. Indeed, for thirty years leading up to the American civil war, the anticipation of conflict was never far from the public mind. The fact that war broke out twenty-eight years later works rather against Joseph Smith who, reflecting the thinking of his day, thought war imminent. This much is clear from his words 'beginning at the rebellion of South Carolina'. That rebellion, which we have seen had already occurred, did not in fact end in war. Another twenty-eight years passed before war broke out.

Nor was war 'poured out upon all nations, beginning at this place', as history clearly shows. Neither did the Southern States involve other nations, from which involvement war was to be 'poured out upon all nations' as history also clearly attests. There was not an orchestrated uprising of slaves as the prophecy seems to suggest, and 'the remnant', identified by Orson Pratt as the native Indians, while often in conflict with 'the Gentiles', could hardly be said to have been a sore vexation.[11] The chaos that was to have followed the beginning of hostilities never occurred.

The second coming

It is inevitable that someone in Joseph Smith's position should attempt to predict the time of the Lord's coming. Scripture clearly tells us that 'no-one knows about the day or the hour, not even the angels of heaven, nor the Son, but only the Father' (Mt 24:36).

The parable of the ten virgins (Mt 25:1–13) makes it clear that we always need to be prepared and waiting for his coming precisely because we do not know when it will be. Such divine instruction, however, has never deterred the prophet who is determined to make his mark.

The church's own history records that in 1835:

> President Smith then stated...it was the will of God that those who went to Zion, with a determination to lay down their lives, if necessary, should be ordained to the ministry, and go forth to prune the vineyard for the last time, or the coming of the Lord, which was nigh – even fifty-six years should wind up the scene...There are those of the rising generation who shall not taste death till Christ come.[12]

In a diary entry for 1843 we find: 'I prophecy in the name of the Lord God – and let it be written: that the Son of Man will not come in the heavens till I am eighty-five years old forty-eight years hence or about 1890.'[13] It hardly seems necessary to point out that 1890 has come and gone relatively uneventfully.

Zion established

In September 1832, Joseph Smith was in Kirtland, Ohio. These were the very early days of the church and, despite opposition (Joseph Smith had been tarred and feathered earlier that same year), expectations were high. The saints were defiant of the mob and determined to persevere. Church members had been arriving in hundreds at the frontier town of Independence, Missouri, which had been identified in an earlier revelation as the centre place of Zion.[14]

It was against this background that, on 22 and 23

September 1832, Joseph Smith gave a revelation concerning the establishment of Zion:

> Yea, the word of the Lord concerning his church, established in the last days for the restoration of his people...for the gathering of his saints to stand upon Mount Zion, which shall be the established city of New Jerusalem.
>
> Which City shall be built, beginning at the temple lot, which is appointed by the finger of the Lord, in the western boundaries of the State of Missouri.
>
> Verily this is the word of the Lord, that the city New Jerusalem shall be built by the gathering of the saints, beginning at this place, even the temple lot, which temple shall be reared in this generation.
>
> For verily this generation shall not pass away until an house shall be built unto the Lord.
>
> Which house shall be built unto the Lord in this generation, upon the consecrated spot as I have appointed.[15]

In the early months of 1839 the Mormons were driven from Missouri, no temple having been built. For many years they held to the hope that they would return to fulfil the prophecy. Even as late as 1935, ninety-six years after the expulsion and over a hundred years since the revelation, Joseph Fielding Smith said: 'I firmly believe that there will be some of that generation who were living when this revelation was given who shall be living when this temple is reared.'[16] More recently, however, he has said: 'It is also reasonable to believe that no soul living in 1832, is still living in mortality on the earth.'[17]

Although there are Mormons in Missouri again (about thirty-six thousand or six per cent of the population), the site referred to in the 1832 revelation is owned by the Church of Christ (Temple Lot), a break-away group, and remains empty.

Joseph Smith and the Word of Wisdom

Doctrine and Covenants, section 89 is known as the Word of Wisdom, and was given in 1833. It is a health law for the church and, although originally understood as a principle rather than an instruction, it soon took on the nature of a commandment. The law forbids the use of hot drinks (which modern church members interpret to mean tea and coffee), alcohol and tobacco. It also gives detailed instruction regarding the use of various staples like meat, fruit and grain.

Mormons are known for their 'peculiar' abstention from tea and coffee, but most people outside the church are unaware of the full extent of the revelation. This is not surprising since the greater part of the commandment, which speaks of the importance of sensible eating habits, is effectively ignored. When interviewed for office, church members are quizzed regarding their worthiness, which includes the strict keeping of the Word of Wisdom. There is never any mention, however, of dietary habits, the emphasis being on abstention. A Mormon can eat themselves into an early grave and still hold office, but a cup of tea disqualifies.

Breaking the Word of Wisdom bars a member from holding office in the church or going to the temple. Joseph Fielding Smith went so far as to say that a cup of tea can keep a member out of heaven:

> SALVATION AND A CUP OF TEA...my brethren if you drink
> coffee or tea, or take tobacco, are you letting a cup of tea or a
> little tobacco stand in the road and bar you from the celestial
> kingdom of God...? There is not anything so little in this world
> in the aggregate. One cup of tea, then it is another cup of tea
> and another cup of tea, and when you get them all together,
> they are not so little.[18]

It is generally accepted among church members that Joseph Smith must have kept the Word of Wisdom. Sadly this is not the case. If Joseph Smith were alive today he would be barred from the temple and likely barred from office in the church. Consider the following taken from Joseph Smith's own history dated May 1843: 'Wednesday, 3. – Called at the office and drank a glass of wine with Sister Jenetta Richards, made by her mother in England.'[19]

Jerald and Sandra Tanner, in their book *The Changing World of Mormonism*, point out that official church history has been rewritten to cover up the fact that Joseph Smith regularly broke the Word of Wisdom.

In one instance, Joseph Smith asked 'Brother Markham' to get 'a pipe and some tobbacco' for Apostle Willard Richards. These words have been replaced with the word 'medicine' in recent printings of the *History of the Church*.

At another time Joseph Smith related that he gave some of the 'brethren' a 'couple of dollars, with directions to replenish' their supply of 'whisky'. In modern editions of the *History of the Church*, twenty-three words have been deleted from this reference to cover up the fact that Joseph Smith encouraged the 'brethren' to disobey the Word of Wisdom.[20]

Joseph Smith, publican

In *The Saint's Herald* (22 January 1935) Joseph Smith's son tells how his father had a new home built for his family in 1842. The main room contained 'a bar, with counter, shelves, bottles, glasses and other paraphernalia customary for a fully-equipped tavern bar, and Porter Rockwell in charge as tender.' When challenged by his wife over such impropriety, 'he reminded her that all taverns had their bars at which liquor was sold or dispensed.'

As Mayor of Nauvoo, Joseph Smith passed an ordinance in 1843 stating: 'The Mayor of the city be and is hereby authorized to sell or give spirits of any quantity as he in his wisdom shall judge to be for the health and comfort or convenience of such travellers or other persons as shall visit his house from time to time.'[21]

Joseph Smith and polygamy

We have already seen that Joseph Smith practised polygamy. Since the 1890 Manifesto was passed, he would, if he were alive today, be considered completely apostate. The situation that prevails in the church today with regard to polygamy is the same as that which prevailed for most of Joseph Smith's own lifetime – it was forbidden. But this did not stop him practising polygamy and thereby breaking the law of the land and the tenets of his own twelfth Article of Faith: 'We believe in being subject to kings, presidents, rulers, and magistrates, in obeying, honoring, and sustaining the law.'

As soon as the early 1830s there were charges of

fornication against the church. These charges prompted the revelation known as Doctrine and Covenants, Section 101. The fourth verse emphatically stated that one man should have one wife. But Joseph was already involved with other women and, by the time the revelation on polygamy was given in 1843, he had taken at least twenty-seven other wives.

Joseph Smith was indeed a remarkable man. More remarkable, however, is the skill with which the Mormon church has hidden the true Joseph from his followers. The Joseph Smith of popular Mormonism never existed. The Joseph Smith of history dare not exist.

Notes

1. *Hymns*, 1985, No. 27.
2. Joseph Smith, History of the Church, Vol. 5, p 467.
3. As above, Vol. 6, pp 408–09.
4. *Discourses of Brigham Young*.
5. *Ensign*, June 1994, p 20.
6. *Journal of Discourses*, Vol. 14, p 203.
7. As above, Vol. 7, p 289.
8. As above, Vol. 8, p 176.
9. Doctrine and Covenants 87:1–5.
10. Larry S. Jonas, *Mormon Claims Examined*, p 52.
11. *The Seer*, p 242.
12. Joseph Smith, same source, Vol. 2, p 182.
13. Jerald and Sandra Tanner (eds), *The Changing World of Mormonism*, 1981, p 419.
14. Doctrine and Covenants 57.
15. As above, 84:2–5,31.
16. Joseph Fielding Smith, *The Way to Perfection*, 1935, p 270.
17. *Answers to Gospel Questions*, Vol. 4, p 112.
18. *Doctrines of Salvation*, Vol. 2, p 16.
19. Joseph Smith, same source, Vol. 2, p 369.
20. Jerald and Sandra Tanner (eds), same source, p 471.
21. Joseph Smith, same source, Vol. 6, p 111.

Chapter 7

Revelations of Convenience

Constant change is here to stay

Essential to Mormon thinking is the belief that the heavens have been opened once more, and that God, through his servants the prophets, directs and guides the affairs of his people. From the First Vision to the present day, continuing revelation is understood to be the lifeblood of the church. The earliest church members did not hold such a view. For them what is looked upon today as a great commencement was a grand conclusion.

From 1820, the time of the 'first vision', until 1830 Joseph Smith received revelations to guide him in the establishment and organisation of the church. During that time the Book of Mormon was brought forth, priesthood authority was restored, men were called to high office, and the order of heaven was established. The culmination of all this activity was the official forming of the church on 6 April 1830.

David Whitmer, one of the three witnesses to the Book of Mormon, informs us:

> After the translation of the Book of Mormon was finished, early in the spring of 1830, before April 6th, Joseph gave the stone to Oliver Cowdery and told me as well as the rest that he was through with it, and he did not use the stone anymore. He said he was through the work God had given him the gift to perform, except to preach the gospel. He told us that we would have to depend on the Holy Ghost hereafter to be guided into truth and obtain the will of the Lord.[1]

Official church history also informs us that:

> In the Latter part of 1831, it was decided by a council of Church
> leaders to compile the revelations concerning the origin of the
> Church and its organisation. The collection was to be called the
> 'Book of Commandments'. Such a collection was made and pre-
> sented to a conference of the Priesthood at Hiram, Ohio,
> November 1, 1831. On the first day of the conference Joseph
> Smith received a revelation which was made the preface for the
> new volume and is now Section 1 of the Book of Doctrine and
> Covenants. In this preface we read:
>
>> 'Search these commandments, for they are true and faithful,
>> and the prophecies and promises which are in them shall all
>> be fulfilled.'
>
>> On the second day of the conference the brethren arose in
>> turn and bore witness to the divine origin of the revelations in
>> the collection...After accepting the collection as scripture it
>> was voted to print 10,000 copies.[2]

Chapter 4, verse 2 of the Book of Commandments reads:
'And he has a gift to translate the book, and I have commanded
him that he shall pretend to no other gift, for I will grant him
no other gift.'

It seems then that by 1831 the work of Joseph Smith in re-
establishing the 'true church' was complete. A record of that
work had been compiled for publication and all that was left to
do was to 'preach the gospel'. From now on the church was to
depend, not on a prophet but on the Holy Ghost.

In the spring of that year, however, Joseph Smith had begun
what is now known as 'The Inspired Translation of the Bible'.
This was not actually a translation but rather a revision. This
work, we are told, was undertaken 'at the command of the
Lord and while acting under the spirit of revelation'.[3]

In July 1835, Joseph Smith came into possession of the
papyrus from which he translated the Book of Abraham, now
one of the standard works of the church. By 1835, then,
Joseph had gone beyond what God had commanded. To
accommodate this, a revelation that had been given by God,

ratified by a conference of priesthood leaders, declared to be scripture and published to the world – was changed.

Where the original 1833 version read: 'And he has a gift to translate the book, and I have commanded him that he shall pretend to no other gift, for I will grant him no other gift.' The 'revised' 1835 version, published in the newly produced Book of Doctrine and Covenants, read: 'And you have a gift to translate the plates; and this is *the first gift that I bestowed upon you*; and I commanded that you should pretend to no other gift, *until my purpose is fulfilled in this*; for I will grant unto you no other gift *until it is finished.*'

This is the earliest and perhaps most significant in a series of changes, amendments and fresh revelations designed to accommodate the changing fortunes and policies of the church. The Christian writer Floyd McElveen refers to them as 'revelations of convenience' in his book of the same name.[4] A precedent had been set and the church was to follow it from time to time up to the present day.

Plural marriage

In the same 1835 edition of the Doctrine and Covenants we read:

> Inasmuch as this church of Christ has been reproached with the crime of fornication, and polygamy: we declare that we believe, that one man should have one wife; and one woman, but one husband, except in the case of death, when either is at liberty to marry again.[5]

This is in conformity with the Book of Mormon teaching on the subject:

> Behold David and Solomon truly had many wives and concubines which thing was abominable before me, saith the Lord... Wherefore my brethren, hear me, and hearken to the word of the Lord: For there shall not any man among you have save it be one wife.[6]

It is notable that the revelation was given because 'this church...has been reproached with the crime of fornication and polygamy'. It is no wonder that such reproach was brought to bear because there is evidence that as soon as 'the early or mid-1830s' Joseph Smith may have entered into plural marriage with one 'Nancy Johnson'.[7]

On 12 July 1843, Joseph Smith was given a revelation which was to become Doctrine and Covenants, section 132 – perhaps the most controversial of all his teachings. It was a revelation of such importance, however, that those who disobeyed it would be damned: 'For behold, I reveal unto you a new and an everlasting covenant; and if ye abide not that covenant, then are ye damned; for no one can reject this covenant and be permitted to enter into my glory.'

Obedience, on the other hand, would bring nothing less than godhood:

> And again, verily I say unto you, if a man marry a wife by my word, which is my law, and by the new and everlasting covenant...they shall pass by the angels, and the gods, which are set there, to their exaltation.
> Then shall they be gods.

The nature of the covenant is that:

> If any man espouse a virgin, and desire to espouse another, and the first give her consent, and if he espouse the second, and they are virgins, and have vowed to no other man, then he is justified; he cannot commit adultery for they are given unto him; for he cannot commit adultery with that that belongeth unto him and to no one else.
> *And if he have ten virgins given unto him by this law, he cannot commit adultery,* for they belong to him, and they are given unto him; therefore is he justified.

Although this revelation was given in 1843 it was not added to the Doctrine and Covenants until 1876. It was at that time that the original revelation, Doctrine and Covenants 101:4, was removed. This means that between 1843 and 1876 church leaders entered into polygamy in spite of the fact that until 1876 their own published scriptures forbade it.

When it is realised that, by the church's own admission,

Joseph Smith was probably married to at least twenty-seven women prior to the 1843 revelation, one begins to realise the possible reason for the change in official doctrine. And, as though to confirm our worst suspicions, we read in the same revelation:

> And let mine handmaid, Emma Smith, receive all those that *have been given* unto my servant Joseph, and who are virtuous and pure before me; and those who are not pure, and have said they were pure, shall be destroyed, saith the Lord God.
>
> And I command mine handmaid, Emma Smith, to abide and cleave unto my servant Joseph...But if she will not abide this commandment she shall be destroyed, saith the Lord.[8]

The old has gone, the new has come. The order has been changed by means of a 'new and everlasting covenant'. But what about the Book of Mormon? The church, we have said, started in conformity with its teachings:

> Behold David and Solomon truly had many wives and concubines which thing was abominable before me, saith the Lord... Wherefore my brethren, hear me, and hearken to the word of the Lord: For there shall not any man among you have save it be one wife.

To this day these verses stand unaltered in the Book of Mormon.

In the Doctrine and Covenants, however, there is an altogether different account of events:

> David also received many wives and concubines, and also Solomon and Moses my servants...*and in nothing did they sin* save in those things which they received not of me.
>
> David's wives and concubines were *given unto him of me*, by the hand of Nathan, my servant, and other prophets who had the keys of this power; *and in none of these things did he sin against me* save in the case of Uriah and his wife.[9]

When challenged to reconcile these statements, Apostle Legrand Richards, author of *A Marvelous Work and a Wonder*,

said: 'I am afraid I can't adequately reconcile these two statements. If the one in the Doctrine and Covenants had omitted
the names of David and Solomon, then I think I could reconcile the two statements.'[10]

The manifesto

The church suffered intense persecution as a direct result of
their polygamy doctrine. They stuck to their convictions however, suffering great privations and loss rather than give up
the 'order of heaven'. But there was a further development in
1890 when Church President Wilford Woodruff issued a 'manifesto' putting a stop to the practice. Pressure from the outside
world had become unbearable and the president of the church
realised that the Mormons stood to lose everything if they
continued to defy not only public opinion but the law of the
land. The official church line is that it 'suspended the general
practice of it in the Church, while still retaining it as a doctrine'.[11]

This is a remarkable turn around in light of the essential
nature, not only of the doctrine, but also of the practice of
polygamy to the salvation of Mormons. Consider that it has
been said: 'When that principle [of plural marriage] was
revealed to the Prophet Joseph Smith...an Angel of God, with
a drawn sword, stood before him and commanded that he
should enter into the practice of that principle or he should be
utterly destroyed.'[12]

Heber C. Kimball was once told by Joseph Smith that if he
did not practice polygamy 'he would lose his apostleship and
be damned'.[13] Heber C. Kimball went on to state that:

> The principle of plurality of wives never will be done away
> with.[14] You might as well deny 'Mormonism' and turn away
> from it, as to oppose the plurality of wives...[15] I speak of the plu-
> rality of wives as one of the most holy principles that God ever
> revealed to man, and all who exercise an influence against it,
> unto whom it is taught...will be damned...the curse of God will
> be upon them.[16]

Brigham Young clearly taught that 'the only men who

become Gods, even Sons of God, are those who enter into polygamy'.[17]

The order changed back again when President Woodruff, in a statement now known as Official Declaration 1, declared:

> There is nothing in my teachings to the Church or in those of my associates...which can be reasonably construed to inculcate or encourage polygamy; and when any Elder of the Church has used language which appeared to convey any such teaching, he has been promptly reproved. And I now publicly declare that *my advice to the Latter-day Saints is to refrain from contracting any marriage forbidden by the law of the land.*[18]

The first seven presidents of the Mormon church practised polygamy, the last being Heber J. Grant who served as President from 1918 until 1945. He was convicted in 1899 of unlawful cohabitation, nine years after the Manifesto, and in 1903 fled the country to avoid arrest. In 1906 President Joseph F. Smith was convicted of the same offence and fined 300 dollars. This was sixteen years after the Manifesto.[19]

Today the Mormon church struggles to persuade tens of thousands of Mormon 'fundamentalists' in Utah to comply with church doctrine and the law of the land. In the face of such hypocrisy among leaders of an earlier generation, the struggle seems doomed to failure. The Mormon Apostle Bruce R. McConkie has said: 'Any who pretend or assume to engage in plural marriage in this day...are guilty of gross wickedness. They are living in adultery, have already sold their souls to Satan and...they will be damned in eternity.'[20] Early church leaders clearly taught that those who opposed polygamy would be damned. Today's leaders teach the exact opposite. It seems you're damned if you do and damned if you don't!

Early church leaders taught that polygamy was essential to exaltation. Today's leaders say, 'Plural Marriage is not essential to salvation or exaltation.'[21] Polygamy is a doctrine they can neither embrace nor reject. To do the former would be to go against the teachings of the Prophet who brought them the word of God through the Manifesto. To follow the latter course they would have to reject the Prophet who taught them polygamy, the founder of their faith, and cast doubt on everything else he ever did. The result either way would be catastrophic. It remains, therefore, a 'principle' of the gospel while its practice continues to be frowned upon.

Racism and the Mormon church

The most pernicious and offensive doctrine of the Mormon church must be that which for almost 150 years barred people from full participation on the basis of skin colour. In 1966, a time when civil rights was high on the agenda of American activists, the following was being written about the Mormon church:

> The Negro Mormon can hold no office whatsoever in a church which offers some office to every one of its male members at some time in his life. A gray-haired Negro Mormon who may have spent his adult life in the careful practice of all the complicated and demanding rules set down by the LDS church stands disenfranchised before the altar where a youth whose beard is just beginning to fuzz may preside. A twelve year old boy may become a member of the Aaronic priesthood, more than this Negro man has been able to achieve through a lifetime of devotion. To hold office, a Mormon must be a member of the priesthood.[22]

From the time of the establishment of the church in 1830 until 1978, Negroes were denied the priesthood. On 9 June 1978, church leaders announced a remarkable change in doctrine that removed this prohibition. Today blacks of African lineage are given 'all the privileges and blessings which the gospel affords'.[23]

The ongoing success of the Mormon church is attributable in no small measure to such 'political' decisions. As with polygamy, leaders can present the image of a church that sticks to its principles despite unpopularity, while at the same time, because of the illusion of ongoing revelation, it can conveniently tap God for a way out of any corner that its principles might paint it into.

The decision to allow Negroes to hold priesthood office has

opened up a whole new mission-field for the church. Between
1935 and 1965 church membership in South Africa increased
by 3,500 members. Between 1965 and 1993 the increase was
over 17,000. In less than thirty years a growth of 362% –
growth directly attributable, by the church's own admission,
to the announcement of 9 June 1978.

In 1979, the year following the announcement, President
Spencer Kimball rededicated South Africa. 1985 saw the dedication of the Johannesburg Temple and by 1990 Africa was
made a separate Area with headquarters in Johannesburg. In
East Africa the first Kenyan to join the church was baptised in
1980. Uganda saw its first baptisms in the late 1980s and one
of the first baptisms in Tanzania took place in 1990.[24]

Overall church growth of over 150% in the last twenty years
is in no small part attributable to the influx of Africans, or people of African descent, into the church all over the world. The
strengthening of the church by this means has been so effective that one wonders why the decision to admit Negroes was
not made earlier. And thereby hangs a tale. The history of this
aspect of church policy makes one wonder why the decision
was made at all if not for the sake of expediency.

Inferior birthright

A cynic once said that all men are born equal but some are
born more equal than others. This has certainly been the case
in the Mormon church. A church that taught, unashamedly,
for almost 150 years that the Negro is born 'of an inferior race',
and that his 'black covering [is] emblematic of eternal darkness'.[25]

Such extreme views stem from the Mormon doctrine
known as pre-existence of human spirits before the creation of
the world. The Book of Abraham tells us:

> Now the Lord had shown unto me, Abraham, the intelligences
> that were organised before the world was; and among all these
> there were many of the noble and great ones;
> And God saw these souls that they were good, and he stood in
> the midst, and he said: These I will make my rulers.[26]

What made these noble and great was their valour in the war in heaven (see chapter 9). Apostle Mark E. Petersen frankly declares:

> Is there any reason then why the type of birth we receive in this life is not a reflection of the worthiness or lack of it in the pre-existent life?...We cannot escape the conclusion that because of performance in our pre-existence some of us are born as Chinese, some as Japanese, some as Latter-day Saints. These are rewards and punishments.[27]

Besides the noble and great ones were those who were less valiant. In Mormon theology, as we will show, a dark skin is a mark of inferiority. At the bottom of the scale is the Negro. The least valiant in that conflict, he was fortunate to be born at all. Apostle Bruce R. McConkie explains it this way:

> Though he was a rebel and an associate of Lucifer in pre-existence, and though he was a liar from the beginning whose name was Perdition, Cain managed to attain the privilege of mortal birth...he came out in open rebellion, fought God, worshipped Lucifer, and slew Abel.
>
> As a result of his rebellion, *Cain was cursed with a dark skin; he became the father of the Negroes,* and those spirits who were not worthy to receive the priesthood are born through his lineage.[28]

Mormons teach that the 'mark of Cain' was continued through the wife of Ham, son of Noah. John Taylor said:

> And after the flood we are told that the curse that had been pronounced upon Cain was continued through Ham's wife, as he had married a wife of that seed. And why did it pass through the flood? Because it was necessary that the devil should have a representation upon the earth as well as God.[29]

To Mormons, the Negroes' black skin is an emblem of eternal darkness and a representation of the devil upon earth. Being inferior, they were not entitled to the full blessings of the gospel, denied the priesthood and barred from the temple.

Curse of the Lamanites

The earliest example of this doctrine in the church is to be found in the simple story of the Nephites and the Lamanites in the Book of Mormon. The Lamanites, having rebelled, were cursed with a dark skin.

> As they were white, and exceeding fair and delightsome, that they might not be enticing unto my people the Lord God did cause a skin of blackness to come upon them.
>
> And thus saith the Lord God: I will cause that they shall be loathsome unto thy people, save they shall repent of their iniquities.
>
> And because of their cursing which was upon them they did become an idle people, full of mischief and subtlety.[30]

The Book of Mormon, however, predicts that through repentance the curse will be lifted and the Lamanites will be white again. Clearly they are further up the scale from the Negroes.

> And then shall they rejoice; for they shall know that it is a blessing unto them from the hand of God; and their scales of darkness shall begin to fall from their eyes; and many generations shall not pass away among them, save they shall be a white and delightsome people.[31]

Spencer W. Kimball, the twelfth President of the Church, told members in 1960 that there was evidence of that prophecy coming true in the current generation of Lamanites (native Americans).

> I saw a striking contrast in the progress of the Indian people today...they are fast becoming a white and delightsome people...For years they have been growing delightsome, and they are now becoming white and delightsome, as they were promised...The children in the home placement program in Utah are often lighter than their brothers and sisters in the hogans on the reservations.[32]

Current editions of the Book of Mormon show a change to

the prophecy in 2 Nephi (note 31). Where earlier editions prophesied that the Lamanites would become 'a white and delightsome people' current editions refer to 'a pure and delightsome people'.[33] Could this be because native Americans are obviously staying their native colour?

Prejudice in practice

The result of this doctrine is clearly demonstrated by Bruce R. McConkie who said that 'the gospel message of salvation is not carried affirmatively to [Negroes]'.[34]

Throughout the history of the church the strongest language has been used in relation to the Negro. Joseph Smith, who condoned slavery, said, 'I can say, the curse is not yet taken off the sons of Canaan, neither will it be until it is affected by as great a power as caused it to come.'[35] Brigham Young went so far as to say, 'Shall I tell you the law of God in regard to the African race? If the white man who belongs to the chosen seed mixes his blood with the seed of Cain, the penalty, under the law of God, is death on the spot. This will always be so.'[36]

John Taylor, the third President of the Church, has said that the Negro is the representative of Lucifer on the earth, and as recently as 1966, Joseph Fielding Smith, the church's tenth President, said, 'It would be a serious error for a white person to marry a Negro, for the Lord forbade it.'[37] In that same year, one church leader was reported to have said that 'any red-blooded American doesn't want his children to marry Negroes'.[38]

Not while time endures

Brigham Young made it clear that Negroes would not receive priesthood blessings until after the resurrection: 'The Lord told Cain that he should not receive the blessings of the priesthood nor his seed...until the redemption of the earth.'[39] John L. Lund, a Mormon writer, stipulated in 1967 two conditions that were to be met before Negroes could receive the priesthood:

The first requirement relates to time. The Negroes will not be allowed to hold the priesthood during mortality, in fact, *not until after the resurrection of all of Adam's children*...The last of Adam's children will not be resurrected until *the end of the millennium*. Therefore, the Negroes will not receive the Priesthood until after that time.

The second major stipulation is that...Abel marry, and then be resurrected, and ultimately exalted in the highest degree of the Celestial Kingdom so that he can have a continuation of his seed. It will then be necessary for Abel to create an earth for his spirit children to come to an experience of mortality. These children will have to be 'redeemed' or resurrected. After the resurrection or redemption of Abel's seed, Cain's descendants, the Negroes, will then be allowed to possess the Priesthood.[40]

President Joseph Fielding Smith said in 1935:

Not only was Cain called to suffer, but because of his wickedness he became the father of an inferior race. A curse was placed upon him and that curse has been continued through his lineage and must do so while time endures.[41]

Protests, prophets and polygamy revisited

In 1963 Richard Riley, the twenty-five-year-old president of the branch of the church in Eccles, resigned from his calling 'quite simply [because of the] colour bar.[42] This was typical of the type of protest that eventually led to the change of policy announced in 1978.

The church and its educational establishments were increasingly ostracised by universities, political and religious groups, and individuals. Local Mormon church leaders were even known to have 'ordained' Negroes as a protest and in an attempt to force the church leaders' hands. Ordinary members risked ex-communication to voice their growing disquiet over the issue. Finally, on 9 June 1978, the First Presidency announced that:

We have pleaded long and earnestly in behalf of these, our faithful brethren, spending many hours in the upper room of the Temple supplicating the Lord for divine guidance.

He has heard our prayers, and by revelation has confirmed
that the long promised day has come when every faithful, worthy man in the church may receive the holy priesthood, with
power to exercise its divine authority, and enjoy with his loved
ones every blessing that flows therefrom, including the blessings of the temple. Accordingly, all worthy male members of
the church may be ordained to the priesthood without regard
for race or color.[43]

Fundamentalists protested, and many left the church, as
was the case with polygamy. However, the majority of church
members breathed a sigh of relief along with innumerable
concerned groups and individuals all over the world.

Questions remain however. As with polygamy, in the face of
the clearest teaching expressed in the strongest language the
church has reversed its policy. In 1935 Joseph Fielding Smith
said, 'Not while time endures.' In 1978 Spencer W. Kimball said,
'The time has come.'

What of the Negro priesthood holder today? Was he really
less valiant in the pre-existence? Is he still a member of an inferior race and a representative of Satan on earth? The Mormon
teaching on the pre-existence remains intact on these issues.
Black skin is still the mark of Cain according to the Book of
Mormon, a sign of God's disfavour. Colour and race are still
looked upon as an indication of rewards and punishments for
choices made in a pre-existent life. The Book of Abraham is
the only Mormon scripture to explain this doctrine of pre-existence. Since 1967, when the original manuscript from which it
was 'translated' was rediscovered, it has been common knowledge among students of Mormonism that that book is dis-
credited (see chapter 18). The more things change, the more
they stay the same.

Notes

1. David Whitmer, *An Address to All Believers in Christ*, p 32, quoted in
   Jerald and Sandra Tanner (eds), *The Changing World of Mormonism*,
   1981, p 111.
2. William E. Berret, *The Restored Church*, 1969, p 102.
3. Bruce R. McConkie, *Mormon Doctrine*, 1958, pp 351–52.

4. Floyd McElveen, *Mormon Revelations of Convenience*, Bethany Fellowship, 1978.
5. Doctrine and Covenants 101:4.
6. Jacob 2:24,27.
7. John J. Stewart, *Brigham Young and His Wives*, p 31, quoted in Jerald and Sandra Tanner (eds), same source, p 215.
8. Doctrine and Covenants 132:4,19,20,61,62,52,54.
9. As above, 132:38,39.
10. Letter from Legrand Richards to Morris L. Reynolds, 14 July 1966, quoted in Jerald and Sandra Tanner, *Mormonism: Shadow or Reality?* 1982, p 205.
11. John J. Stewart, same source, pp 29–30, quoted in Jerald and Sandra Tanner (eds), *The Changing World of Mormonism*, p 269.
12. Joseph Fielding Smith, *Journal of Discourses*, Vol. 20, pp 28–31, our brackets.
13. Life of Heber C. Kimball, p 336, quoted in Jerald and Sandra Tanner (eds), same source, p 258.
14. *Deseret News*, 7 November 1855, quoted in Jerald and Sandra Tanner (eds), same source, p 263.
15. Joseph Fielding Smith, same source, Vol. 5, p 203.
16. As above, Vol. 11, p 211.
17. As above, Vol. 11, p 269.
18. Official Declaration, Doctrine and Covenants, 1982, pp 291–92, our italics.
19. Jerald and Sandra Tanner (eds), same source, p 284.
20. Bruce R. McConkie, same source, pp 522–23, quoted in Jerald and Sandra Tanner (eds), same source, p 287.
21. Bruce R. McConkie, same source, p 523, quoted in Jerald and Sandra Tanner (eds), same source, p 289.
22. Wallace Turner, *The Mormon Establishment*, pp 243–44, quoted in Jerald and Sandra Tanner (eds), same source, p 292.
23. *Deseret News*, 9 June 1978.
24. *Ensign* magazine, February 1993 and October 1994.
25. Joseph Fielding Smith, *The Way to Perfection*, 1935, pp 101–02, our brackets.
26. Abraham 3:22–23.
27. Mark E. Petersen, Race Problems – As They Affect the Church, quoted in Jerald and Sandra Tanner (eds), same source, p 294.
28. Bruce R. McConkie, same source, p 102, our italics.
29. Joseph Fielding Smith, *Journal of Discourses*, Vol. 22, p 304.
30. 2 Nephi 5:21–24.
31. 2 Nephi 30:6, The Book of Mormon, 1959 edition.
32. *Improvement Era*, December 1960, pp 922–23.
33. 2 Nephi 30:6, The Book of Mormon, 1982 edition.
34. Bruce R. McConkie, same source, p 477, our brackets.
35. Joseph Smith, History of the Church, Vol. 2, p 438.
36. Joseph Fielding Smith, *Journal of Discourses*, Vol. 10, p 110.

37. Joseph Fielding Smith, Letter to Morris L. Reynolds, 9 May 1966.
38. Reported by David L. Brewer in a PhD dissertation, quoted in Jerald and Sandra Tanner, *Mormonism: Shadow or Reality?* 1982, p 267.
39. Brigham Young Addresses, Latter-day Saints church historical department, quoted in Jerald and Sandra Tanner (eds), *The Changing World of Mormonism*, 1981, p 312.
40. John L. Lund, The Church and the Negroe, 1967, pp 45–49, our italics.
41. Joseph Fielding Smith, *The Way to Perfection*, 1935, p 101.
42. UPI report, Exeter, as quoted in Jerald and Sandra Tanner (eds), same source, p 312, our brackets.
43. *Deseret News*, 9 June 1978, pla.

Part Three

BELIEFS AND PRACTICES

Chapter 8
Blinded by Faith

When one considers the facts against Mormonism, and the fallacious arguments put forward to defend it one would expect that any Mormon shown the errors in that faith would immediately leave it. This is plainly not the case. There are, of course, emotional, social and cultural reasons which make leaving difficult. It means a drastic change in lifestyle, a loss of friends (and sometimes loved ones) and giving up the security brought by membership of a tightly-knit group. But there is more to it than that. Even those with few ties will not move. Mormons will not listen, will not even concede that the points made against their beliefs are valid. Why? Because they are blinded by faith.

When you investigate the Mormon church, you are taught their gospel and the stories of Joseph Smith and the Book of Mormon. You are invited to follow Joseph's example and find out for yourself whether these things are true by asking God. They use three scriptures:

1. From the Bible. 'If any of you lacks wisdom, he should ask God, who gives generously to all without finding fault, and it will be given to him' (Jas 1:5).

This is the verse which inspired Joseph Smith to ask God for wisdom. You are encouraged to do the same, and promised that God will give you the answer.

2. From the Book of Mormon. 'And when ye shall receive these things, I would exhort you that ye would ask God, the Eternal Father, in the name of Christ, if these things are not

true; and if ye shall ask with a sincere heart, with real intent, having faith in Christ, he will manifest the truth of it unto you by the power of the Holy Ghost. And by the power of the Holy Ghost ye may know the truth of all things' (Moroni 10:4,5).

This is known as Moroni's Promise. You are encouraged to try the promise, and you will know that what you have been told is true.

3. From Doctrine and Covenants – 'But behold, I say unto you, that you must study it out in your mind; then you must ask me if it be right, and if it is right I will cause that your bosom shall burn within you; therefore, you shall feel that it is right' (Doctrine and Covenants 9:8).

This is the way you will know the truth – by a burning in the bosom.

The anticipation which all this searching raises is enough to create the glow of excitement which can be taken as confirmation that the church is true. The Mormon gospel has been logically explained to you, and you now have your own personal miracle – a revelation from God – to confirm it.

Compare this with some investigators of the early church. In Acts chapter 17 we meet the Bereans. Paul came and preached the gospel to them. But they did not go away and pray about it – they searched the Scriptures to see if what they had been taught was in agreement with God's word: 'They received the message with great eagerness and examined the Scriptures every day to see if what Paul said was true' (Acts 17:11). Jesus also encouraged his hearers to search the Scriptures. 'You diligently study the scriptures because you think that by them you possess eternal life. These are the scriptures that testify about me' (Jn 5:39). We have shown elsewhere, in discussing the Mormon testimony, that James chapter 1, verse 5 is not aimed at non-Christians seeking the truth of the gospel. The promise it contains does not apply in this situation, and the results it brings are unreliable.

Once you have decided that the things you have been taught by the Mormons are true, you are told that the next step is to join the church through baptism. You are baptised 'into the church'. Compare this with the response of the Christian church when someone professes faith. The

Christian invitation is to be baptised into Christ, to enter into a personal relationship with Jesus. This relationship is life-giving and enabling, supplying saving grace and the power to live the godly life. Joining an organisation will give you rules to live by, encouragement and support, but you must conform by your own strength.

A typical Mormon testimony is not about relationship and power, but about things. This is hardly surprising when you consider how it is gained. Such a testimony says: 'I know that the Church of Jesus Christ of Latter-day Saints is the only true church on earth today, that Joseph Smith was a prophet of God, and that the Book of Mormon is the word of God.' With this as a foundation, it then follows that everything taught by the church, the prophet and the Book of Mormon must be true. 'When the prophet speaks, all debate is ended.' Doctrines which would not be accepted in the cold light of day, are received without question in the warm glow of the Mormon testimony gained by the 'burning in the bosom'.

To a Mormon, feelings are of paramount importance. They are more reliable than mere evidence and are a sure indication of truth. This is not to say that Mormons never use conventional methods, or present evidence arrived at by conventional means. However, the way they feel about the evidence is more important than what the evidence tells them. Truth is arrived at by a series of personal revelations, or 'burning in the bosom' experiences, and these always take precedence over mere facts. In other words, it is right because it 'feels' right.

While it is true that knowledge by the Holy Spirit lifts our understanding above the academic, to a Mormon it precludes the academic. Indeed, a Mormon may sometimes appear to distrust completely any knowledge arrived at by conventional means. This explains the Mormon appeal to the argument 'that is just your interpretation'. A Mormon will often say this when faced with Bible truths that clearly, and incontrovertibly, contradict Mormon teaching. Rather than change their world view in light of the evidence, they question the means (interpretation) by which the presented conclusion was arrived at. The 'interpretation' is clearly unreliable if it contradicts their feelings.

Surely, though, if we only accept what feels good we are sitting in the comfortable pew. If we are not simply to accept what is comfortable then we must have a means of measuring truth that is independent of our feelings. For Christians, this means is the Bible. The words of Scripture are true however we 'feel' and whatever the discomfort it causes us or the challenges it presents to our preconceptions. When Christians are met with an argument which challenges their faith, they ask, 'Can the argument be borne out in Scripture and experience?' Like the Bereans, they examine the Scriptures to see what God has already revealed that will shed light on the question. The Mormon criteria in facing a challenge to their faith is 'does this agree with the church?'

For example, James chapter 2, verses 17 and 18 appears to teach that salvation is by works which prove your faith. This challenges the Christian belief that salvation is by faith alone. The Christian reaction to this scripture is that the belief in salvation by actions does not fit with the bulk of gospel teaching in the rest of the New Testament (see Romans 4 and 5; Galatians 3; Ephesians 2:8–10; Philippians 2:13), nor with the rest of the teaching within the book of James (see James 2:14–26). Nor does it fit with Christians' experience of being saved through no effort of their own.

The challenge of salvation by faith, not works, is met by Mormons with the reaction that the church is true and therefore its teachings must be right. The Book of Mormon claims that the Bible has been corrupted over the years:

> For behold, they have taken away from the gospel of the Lamb many parts which are plain and most precious; and also many covenants of the Lord have they taken away. And all this have they done that they might pervert the right ways of the Lord, that they might blind the eyes and harden the hearts of the children of men.[1]

The eighth Article of Faith states: 'We believe the Bible to be the word of God as far as it is translated correctly.' Joseph Smith said that the Book of Mormon is 'the most correct of any book on earth, and the keystone of our religion, and a man would get nearer to God by abiding by its precepts, than by any other book.'[2]

If you start with the assumption that Mormonism is true and all things Mormon are 'most correct', the only way to handle criticism is to deny and denigrate all authority outside the church no matter how reliable or trustworthy. Typically, Mormons see all their critics as at best deceived, and more often pernicious and incapable of fully honourable motives. It is a given that the church is right and all others wrong; the church is pure and true and all others corrupt and false; the church is fully reliable and its detractors predictably unsound.

In the mind of the Mormon there is always something beyond mere facts that explains attacks on the church. So Mormons can, with impunity, criticise whole chunks of the Bible as being incomplete or translated incorrectly without having a shred of evidence or even the first idea of what they are talking about. But if the Bible contradicts the church, this is the only possible conclusion.

As in many cults, doubt is sin. If you are unhappy with some of the teachings of the 'only true church on earth today', then there must be something wrong with you.

> Apostasy usually begins with question and doubt and criticism...They who garnish the sepulchres of the dead prophets begin now by stoning the living ones. They return to the pronouncements of the dead leaders and interpret them to be incompatible with present programs. They convince themselves that there are discrepancies between the practices of the deceased and the leaders of the present...They allege love for the gospel and the Church but charge that leaders are a little 'off the beam'!...Next they say that while the gospel and the Church are divine, the leaders are fallen. Up to this time it may be a passive thing, but now it becomes an active resistance, and frequently the blooming apostate begins to air his views and to crusade...He now begins to expect persecution and adopts a martyr complex, and when finally excommunication comes he associates himself with other apostates to develop and strengthen cults.[3]

Critics are branded as, knowing or unknowing, conspirators against the truth. This fear is understandable when one realises that it is something beyond mere facts which puts Mormons into such an untenable position in the first place – feelings.

Notes

1. 1 Nephi 13:26,27.
2. Joseph Smith, History of the Church 4:461.
3. The Teachings of Spencer W. Kimball, Salt Lake City: Bookcraft, 1982, quoted by Elder L. Aldin Porter of the Presidency of the Seventy, in *Ensign* magazine, General Conference issue, November 1994, p 63.

Chapter 9

The Plan of Salvation

The basic Mormon gospel is laid down in the Plan of Salvation (see below).

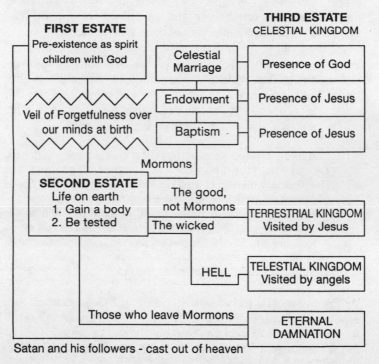

The plan of salvation

114 MORMONISM: A GOLD PLATED RELIGION

The story begins before life on earth, when everyone lived as spirit children of God. The God that we know is one of many gods, and is called Elohim. He has many wives, and they gave birth to all his spirit children.

> There is not a person here today but what is a son or daughter of that Being. In the spirit world their spirits were first begotten and brought forth, and they lived there with their parents for ages before they came here.[1]

God's first-born son is Jesus, and his second son is Lucifer. Thus God is our literal Father, and Jesus and Lucifer our elder brothers. In God's presence we learned and grew. However, since God has a physical body[2] and grew to be God through obedience and worthiness, his spirit children could not progress unless given the same opportunity. 'And a difference there is between our Father and us consists in that he has gained his exaltation, and has obtained eternal lives.'[3]

As the head of the gods, our God called a great council in heaven to decide the future of all his spirit children. 'According to that which was ordained in the midst of the Council of the Eternal God of all other gods before this world was.'[4] He proposed to create an earth where they might receive physical bodies and be tested for obedience.

> And there stood one among them that was like unto God, and he said unto those who were with him: We will go down, for there is space there, and we will take of these materials, and we will make an earth whereon these may dwell;
>
> And we will prove them herewith, to see if they will do all things whatsoever the Lord their God shall command them;
>
> And they who keep their first estate shall be added upon; and they who keep their second estate shall have glory added upon their heads for ever and ever.[5]

The pre-mortal life as spirit children of God is called the first estate. Those who prove themselves worthy are allowed to come to earth to gain physical bodies and be tested. This is the second estate. Those who are faithful and obedient in this life receive eternal glory.

God called for someone to become their saviour. Lucifer offered to be the saviour, but wanted to force everyone to be saved and so claim the glory for himself. Jesus wanted to give mankind freedom of choice, and give the glory to God. The vote in the council was for Jesus, which infuriated Lucifer. He rebelled against God and persuaded many of the spirit children to follow him. When the revolt was defeated, Lucifer became Satan, and he and his followers were cast out of heaven onto the earth.

> And I, the Lord God, spake unto Moses, saying: That Satan, whom thou hast commanded in the name of mine Only Begotten, is the same which was from the beginning, and he came before me, saying – Behold, here am I, send me, I will be thy son, and I will redeem all mankind, that one soul shall not be lost, and surely I will do it; wherefore give me thine honor.
>
> But, behold, my Beloved Son, which was my Beloved and Chosen from the beginning, said unto me – Father, thy will be done, and the glory be thine forever.
>
> Wherefore, because that Satan rebelled against me, and sought to destroy the agency of man, which I, the Lord God, had given him, and also, that I should give unto him mine own power; by the power of mine Only Begotten. I caused that he should be cast down.[6]

Those who were not cast down were promised physical bodies and the opportunity to prove themselves worthy of future blessings. Some, however, had not been so valiant in the battle, waiting to see who would win, and they would not be allowed such great blessings on earth. They were marked by being born with a dark skin – which is the Mormon explanation for the Negroes. Until 1978 anyone with Negro blood was not allowed to hold the Mormon priesthood.

> There is a reason why one man is born black and with other disadvantages, while another is born white with great advantages. The reason is that we once had an estate before we came here, and were obedient, more or less, to the laws that were given us there. Those who were faithful in all things there

received greater blessings here, and those who were not faithful received less.[7]

When we are born on earth, we do not remember our life
before, because a 'veil of forgetfulness' is drawn across our
minds. This is so that we can obey God by our own free
choice, and not because we remember him and his plan for us.

> I want to tell you, each and every one of you, that you are well
> acquainted with God our Heavenly Father, or the great Elohim.
> You are all well acquainted with him, for there is not a soul of
> you but what has lived in his house and dwelt with him, when
> the fact is, you have merely forgotten what you did know.[8]

According to the Book of Moses, God has said, 'For behold,
this is my work and my glory, to bring to pass the immortality
and eternal life of man.'[9] In Mormon theology there is a difference between immortality and eternal life. Because Christ
conquered death, all mankind will be resurrected and become
immortal: 'and all men become incorruptible, and immortal,
and they are living souls.'[10] This is the free gift of God through
Jesus Christ. Eternal life – or exaltation – is the reward given
to those who are worthy and have been obedient to all the
'laws and ordinances of the gospel' as laid down by the
Mormon church. 'O then, my beloved brethren, repent ye, and
enter in at the strait gate, and continue in the way which is narrow, until ye shall obtain eternal life.'[11]

Christ's atonement paid for Adam's sin, so that all people
are born sinless. 'We believe that men will be punished for
their own sins, and not for Adam's transgression.'[12] The atonement opens the way for mankind to be forgiven of their sins
and work for their salvation.

> We believe that through the Atonement of Christ, all mankind
> may be saved, by obedience to the laws and ordinances of the
> gospel.[13]
> For we know that it is by grace that we are saved, after all we
> can do.[14]

> For I remember the word of God which saith by their works
> ye shall know them; for if their works be good, then they are
> good also.[15]

The first requirement is for membership of the Mormon church, through baptism. All the commandments must be obeyed, including the Word of Wisdom (a health law banning tea, coffee, alcohol and tobacco) and the payment of tithes and offerings. Tithing is giving 'one-tenth of all their interest annually'.[16] It is a requirement for worthiness, and strict records are kept to check how much is paid. Mormons are promised that 'he that is tithed shall not be burned at his [the Son of Man's] coming'.[17] In addition, members are expected to fast for two meals once a month and pay the money saved as 'fast offering' for the welfare of those in need. Also, regular contributions are encouraged towards the local church budget, and building, welfare and missionary funds.

The Mormon gospel is said to be the 'fulness of the gospel' and is called 'the new and everlasting covenant':

> When we accept the new and everlasting covenant, we agree to
> repent, to be baptized, to receive the Holy Ghost, to receive our
> endowments, to receive the covenant of marriage in the temple
> and to live righteously to the end of our lives. We must keep all
> our covenants with exactness. If we do, our Heavenly Father
> promises us that we will receive exaltation in the celestial
> kingdom.[18]

Exaltation in the next life, and blessings in this, are ours by right when we are obedient. 'For all who will have a blessing at my hands shall abide the law which was appointed for that blessing, and the conditions thereof, as were instituted from before the foundation of the world.'[19] 'I, the Lord, am bound when ye do what I say.'[20]

The next stage is to be counted worthy and ready to go to the temple. Two ordinances are performed there for living church members, in addition to work which is done there for the dead. These are the endowment and celestial marriage – marriage for time and eternity.

The ceremony of the endowment is preceded by ritual washings and anointings, to make the recipients clean in readiness for the 'further light and knowledge' which will be revealed to them. The endowment reveals the secrets of creation, the fall and the plan of salvation, and teaches the secret signs and passwords by which to enter heaven. At the same time, solemn vows are made of chastity, loyalty and dedication of all you possess to the furtherance of the church.

> It is a wonderful thing to come into the Church, but you cannot receive an exaltation until you have made covenants in the house of the Lord and received the keys and authorities that are there bestowed and which cannot be given in any other place on the earth today.[21]

When a couple marry, they marry 'until death do us part'. The Mormon church claims that they have the priesthood authority given to Peter by Jesus: 'I will give you the keys of the kingdom of heaven; whatever you bind on earth will be bound in heaven' (Mt 16:19). In the temple, couples are married for time and eternity so that they can continue their relationship in the celestial kingdom.

> If a man marry a wife by my word, which is my law, and by the new and everlasting covenant, and it is sealed unto them by the Holy Spirit of promise, by him who is anointed, unto whom I have appointed this power and the keys of this priesthood;...it shall be done unto them in all things whatsoever my servant hath put upon them, in time, and through all eternity; and shall be of full force when they are out of the world.[22]

It is not possible for anyone to enter the highest level of the celestial kingdom without celestial marriage. 'In the celestial glory there are three heavens or degrees; And in order to obtain the highest, a man must enter into this order of the priesthood [meaning the new and everlasting covenant of marriage].[23]

When Mormons die, they go to paradise to await the judgement.

And then it shall come to pass, that the spirits of those who are righteous are received into a state of happiness, which is called paradise, a state of rest, a state of peace, where they shall rest from all their troubles and from all care, and sorrow.[24]

After the judgement they go to the celestial kingdom. The celestial kingdom is where God lives, but it is divided into three levels. Those Mormons who have not been worthy enough, or who have not received the rituals within the temple, will inherit the lower levels. Those Mormons who inherit the highest degree of glory expect to become gods. Each god will have many goddess wives and they will have their own spirit children. They will create and rule over their own planet, and the cycle will begin again.

Which glory shall be a fulness and a continuation of the seeds forever and ever.

Then shall they be gods, because they have no end;...then shall they be above all, because all things are subject unto them. Then shall they be gods, because they have all power, and the angels are subject unto them.[25]

Mormons believe that those who have been righteous, but not members of the Mormon church, will go to spirit prison when they die. There the gospel will be preached to them, and they will accept it. After judgement, they will go to the terrestrial kingdom, where they will be visited by Christ.

And again, we saw the terrestrial world...

Behold, these are they who died without the law;

And also they who are the spirits of men kept in prison, whom the Son visited, and preached the gospel unto them, that they might be judged according to men in the flesh;

Who received not the testimony of Jesus in the flesh, but afterwards received it.

These are they who are honorable men of the earth, who were blinded by the craftiness of men.

These are they who receive of the presence of the Son, but not of the fulness of the Father.[26]

Those who have been wicked will spend their time in hell, but after the judgement they will go to the telestial kingdom, where they will be visited by angels.

> And again, we saw the glory of the telestial...
> These are they who received not the gospel of Christ...
> These are they who are thrust down to hell.
> These are they who shall not be redeemed from the devil until the last resurrection.[27]

Those who have once been Mormons and have turned away from the faith will go to eternal damnation with Satan and his angels.

> Who glorifies the Father, and saves all the works of his hands, except those sons of perdition who deny the Son after the Father has revealed him.
> Wherefore he saves all except them – they shall go away into everlasting punishment, which is endless punishment, which is eternal punishment, to reign with the devil and his angels in eternity, where their worm dieth not, and the fire is not quenched, which is their torment –
> And the end thereof, neither the place thereof, nor their torment, no man knows.[28]

Notes

1. *Discourses of Brigham Young*, p 50.
2. 'The Father has a body of flesh and bones as tangible as man's', Doctrine and Covenants 130:22.
3. *Discourses of Brigham Young*, p 50.
4. Doctrine and Covenants 121:32.
5. Abraham 3:24–26.
6. Moses 3:1–3.
7. Joseph Fielding Smith, *Doctrines of Salvation*, Vol. 1, p 61.
8. *Discourses of Brigham Young*, p 50.
9. Moses 1:39.
10. 2 Nephi 9:13.
11. Jacob 6:11.
12. Articles of Faith 2.
13. Articles of Faith 3.
14. 2 Nephi 25:23.
15. Moroni 7:5.
16. Doctrine and Covenants 119:4.
17. Doctrine and Covenants 64:23.
18. *Gospel Principles Manual*, p 92.
19. Doctrine and Covenants 132:5.
20. As above, 82:10.
21. Joseph Fielding Smith, same source, Vol. 2, p 253.
22. Doctrine and Covenants 132:19.
23. As above, 131:1,2.
24. Alma 40:12.
25. Doctrine and Covenants, 132:19,20.
26. As above, 76:71–75,77.
27. As above, 76:81,82,84,85.
28. As above, 76:43–45.

Chapter 10

The Godhead and God

On first examination, Mormons believe in a triune Godhead, with a Heavenly Father who created the universe, Jesus Christ his Son, the Saviour of mankind, and the Holy Ghost who is the comforter and the revealer of truth. However, as we have pointed out elsewhere, it is essential to define your terms when speaking to Mormons, because their doctrine is only 'Christian' on the surface. So what do we find when we scratch the surface of Mormon beliefs on the Godhead?

One, two or three?

The first thing we find is that Mormon theology has 'developed' over the years, and what Joseph Smith taught in the beginning is not what the church believes today. Mormon scholar Melanie Moench Charles has researched the differences:

> Like the Book of Mormon, Mormonism before 1835 was largely modalistic, making no explicit distinction between the identities of the Father and the Son. Yet Mormonism gradually began to distinguish among different beings in the Godhead. This means the christology of the Book of Mormon differs significantly from the christology of the Mormon church after the 1840s.
>
> The current theology that most Mormons read back into the Book of Mormon is tritheism: belief in three Gods. Joseph Smith and the church only gradually came to understand the

Godhead in this way. When he translated the Book of Mormon, Smith apparently envisioned God as modalists did: he accepted Christ and Christ's father as one God. In his first written account of his 'first vision' in 1832 Smith told of seeing 'the Lord' – one being.

Later, in 1844, Smith said, 'I have always declared God to be a distinct personage – Jesus Christ a separate and distinct personage from God the Father, the Holy Ghost was a distinct personage and or Spirit, and these three constitute three distinct personages and three Gods'...Mormon history does not support Smith's claim about what he taught earlier. Documents from early Mormonism reflect that Smith went from belief in one god to belief in two and later three gods forming one godhead.[1]

In fact, the Testimony of Three Witnesses, printed in the front of every copy of the Book of Mormon, finishes with the sentence: 'And the honor be to the Father, and to the Son, and to the Holy Ghost, which is one God. Amen.'

In the Book of Mormon we find:

I would that ye should understand that God himself shall come down among the children of men, and shall redeem his people.

And because he dwelleth in flesh he shall be called the Son of God, and having subjected the flesh to the will of the Father, being the Father and the Son.

And they are one God, yea, the very Eternal Father of heaven and of earth.[2]

Christ the Son, and God the Father, and the Holy Spirit, which is one Eternal God.[3]

These verses certainly do not agree with Joseph Smith's statement of 1844, quoted above, in which he said that they were three distinct personages and three Gods. Yet it is to this later statement which Mormon theology conforms.

Most members of the Mormon church today are not aware of this development. They are taught that the eternal truths of the gospel were restored to the earth through Joseph Smith, and have stood since then in their purity. The teaching today is supported by reference to the baptism of Jesus and the promise of the Holy Spirit. At the baptism of Jesus, while Jesus was in the water, the voice of God was heard from heaven, and the Holy Spirit descended in the form of a dove. At the end of his ministry, Jesus promised that the Holy Spirit would be sent from the Father. These instances are used to prove that the Godhead must be three separate individuals, as one cannot be in three places at one time. Immediately, Mormons have limited God. They cannot accept the mystery that these three individuals can be one God, and insist that the Godhead must therefore consist of three gods.

Many gods

'And then the Lord said: Let us go down. And they went down at the beginning, and they, that is the Gods, organised and formed the heavens and the earth.'[4] Thus begins the creation account recorded in the Book of Abraham in The Pearl of Great Price. It mirrors the account in Genesis, except for the phrase 'the Gods', which occurs in almost every verse. Mormons believe that there are many gods, but only one 'God with whom we have to do'.[5]

Not only are there many gods on a par with our God, but our God has a god of his own. The Mormon Apostle Orson Pratt explained: 'We were begotten by our Father in Heaven; the person of our Father in Heaven was begotten on a previous heavenly world by His Father; and again, He was begotten by a still more ancient Father.'[6]

Contrast this with the Bible, where God says, 'Is there any God besides me? No, there is no other Rock; I know not one' (Is 44:8). Once again, the development of ideas is in evidence when we look at the Book of Mormon:

> And Zeezrom said unto him: Thou sayest there is a true and living God?
> And Amulek said: Yea, there is a true and living God.
> Now Zeezrom said: Is there more than one God?
> And he answered, No.
> Now Zeezrom said unto him again: How knowest thou these things?
> And he said: An angel hath made them known unto me.[7]

Mormons believe that God is omniscient (all-knowing), yet insist there are other gods. Either there are no other gods, or God is lying!

Physical body

> The Father has a body of flesh and bones as tangible as man's; the Son also; but the Holy Ghost has not a body of flesh and bones, but is a personage of Spirit. Were it not so, the Holy Ghost could not dwell in us.[8]
>
> Our Heavenly Father has a glorified body of flesh and bone, inseparably connected with His spirit.[9]

Mormon theologians quote the many statements in the Bible which say that men and women were made in the image of God. They also use verses that refer to parts of the body in speaking of God. For example: 'your eyes saw my unformed body' (Ps 139:16), 'it was your right hand, your arm, and the light of your face' (Ps 44:3), and 'every word that comes from the mouth of the Lord' (Deut 8:3). Such verses, they say, prove that God must have a physical body. This, however, falls down when we add references like 'He will cover you with his feathers, and under his wings you will find refuge' (Ps 91:4) which must therefore prove that God is a chicken!

The reasoning is often very shallow, as in the books *A Marvelous Work and a Wonder*: 'The Father must have had a voice or he could not have spoken',[10] and *The Articles of Faith* (referring to the Church of England's view): 'We affirm that to deny the materiality of God's person is to deny God; for a thing without parts has no whole, and an immaterial body cannot exist.'[11] These books are accepted as standard reference works by the church today.

The Concise Dictionary of Christian Tradition points out: 'Human words and images are all that we possess to describe God, and if they are used correctly, they are perfectly proper.'[12] It is quite obvious that every reference to a part of the human body in relation to God is describing his activity, not his physical form. For example, 'every word that comes from the mouth of the Lord' (Deut 8:3) is a reference to God's communicating with us, which he does in many ways.

The idea that God has a physical body is also a foundational part of the Mormon Plan of Salvation. The teaching goes: as spirit children of God, we wanted to be like him. We could not grow to be like him without obtaining a physical body. This is one of the reasons we came to earth. The Bible clearly states that 'God is Spirit' (Jn 4:24) and, interestingly enough, so does the Book of Mormon:

> And then Ammon said: Believest thou that there is a Great Spirit?
> And he said, Yea.
> And Ammon said: This is God.[13]

Exalted man

Not only do Mormons teach that God has a physical body, but that he is an exalted man. Joseph Smith said, 'God himself was once as we are now, and is an exalted man, and sits enthroned in yonder heavens.'[14] Mormon Apostle Orson Pratt went even further:

> The Gods who dwell in the Heaven have been redeemed from the grave in a world which existed before the foundations of this earth were laid. They and the Heavenly body which they now inhabit were once in a fallen state...they were exalted also, from fallen men to Celestial Gods to inhabit their Heaven forever and ever.[15]

The Mormon Plan of Salvation teaches that those who live worthy lives and fulfil all the ordinances of the church can become gods one day. This is an endless cycle: God was once a man and lived worthily enough to become a god. He created an earth to hold his spirit children so that they in their turn could follow him. Mormon Apostle Legrand Richards wrote a letter to Morris Reynolds on 14 July 1966, in which he said: 'There is a statement often repeated in the Church, and while it is not in one of the Standard Church Works, it is accepted as

Church doctrine, and this is: "As man is, God once was; as God is, man may become.'"

This teaching belittles God and reduces him to our level. It also goes against every scripture in the Bible which speaks of God as unchanging. For example: 'For I am the Lord, I change not' (Mal 3:6). Once again the Book of Mormon would agree: 'For I know that God is not a partial God, neither a changeable being; but he is unchangeable from all eternity to all eternity.'[16]

Heavenly mother

The Mormon Plan of Salvation teaches that we are all spirit children of God, and lived with him before we were born on earth. Mormon Apostle Bruce R. McConkie adds another interesting twist: 'Implicit in the Christian verity that all men are the spirit children of an Eternal Father is the usually unspoken truth that they are also the offspring of an Eternal Mother.'[17] This is confirmed in a modern Mormon hymn:

> In the heavens are parents single?
> No, the thought makes reason stare!
> Truth is reason; truth eternal
> Tells me I've a mother there.[18]

President Joseph Fielding Smith said:

> The fact that there is no reference to a mother in heaven either in the Bible, Book of Mormon or Doctrine and Covenants, is not sufficient proof that no such thing as a mother did exist there.[19]

Adam-God doctrine

Of all the Mormon beliefs about God, the one which has caused the most controversy, and is least known among modern-day members, is known as the Adam-God doctrine.

On 9 April 1852, Brigham Young, the second prophet of the Mormon church, publicly proclaimed that God had revealed to him that Adam was 'the only God with whom we have to do':

Now hear it, O inhabitants of the earth, Jew and Gentile, Saint and sinner! When our father Adam came into the garden of Eden, he came into it with a celestial body, and brought Eve, one of his wives, with him. He is Michael, the Arch-angel, the Ancient of Days! about whom holy men have written and spoken – He is our Father and our God, and the only God with whom we have to do.[20]

This doctrine was hard for some people to accept, but church leaders insisted upon it. The *Millenial Star* made it very clear that it was indeed a doctrine which had to be accepted:

Concerning the item of doctrine alluded to by Elder Caffall and others, viz., that Adam is our Father and God, I say do not trouble yourselves...If, as Elder Caffall remarked, there are those who are waiting at the door of the Church for this objection to be removed, tell such, the prophet and Apostle Brigham Young has declared it, and that it is the word of the Lord.[21]

This continued to be taught until at least 1889 when George Q. Cannon, a member of the First Presidency, was still teaching that 'Jesus Christ is Jehovah' and that 'Adam is still His Father and our God'.[22]

It does not seem to have occurred to anyone that if Adam was God, then he disobeyed himself when he took the apple from Eve! This doctrine was a source of great embarrassment to the Mormon church. Over the years it was gradually buried, until in a speech given on 1 June 1980, Mormon Apostle Bruce R. McConkie declared that the 'devil keeps this heresy alive...anyone who has received the temple endowment and who yet believes the Adam-God theory does not deserve to be saved'. Members of the church who continued to believe it were actually excommunicated.

However, the doctrine would not stay buried. The book *Mormonism: Shadow or Reality?* by Jerald and Sandra Tanner produced so much evidence on the subject that Apostle Bruce R. McConkie was forced to admit that they were right:

This may be the most important letter you have or will receive...

Yes, President Young did teach that Adam was the father of our spirits, and all the related things that the cultists ascribe to him...He expressed views that are out of harmony with the gospel. But, be it known, Brigham Young also taught accurately and correctly, the status and position of Adam in the eternal scheme of things. What I am saying is, that Brigham Young, contradicted Brigham Young, and the issue becomes one of which Brigham Young we will believe...Brigham Young erred in some of his statements on the nature and kind of being that God is and as to the position of Adam in the plan of salvation, but Brigham Young also taught the truth in these fields on other occasions...he was a great prophet and has gone on to eternal reward. What he did is not a pattern for any of us. If we choose to believe and teach the false portions of his doctrines, we are making an election that will damn us...it is my province to teach to the Church what the doctrine is. It is your province to echo what I say or to remain silent.[23]

So, when we scratch the surface of Mormon doctrine, we do not find the Christian God at all, but one who is so demeaned that he was once a man who grew to be God among many other gods. He has a wife (or many wives) in heaven, who are continually pregnant with all his spirit children. He created a world for them to live in, and began it all himself by coming down as Adam. The inconsistencies in these beliefs, and the fact that there is no support for them in the Bible, does not faze Mormons at all. However, it makes the rest of us stare in amazement.

Notes

1. *New Approaches to the Book of Mormon*, 1993, quoted in the *Salt Lake City Messenger*, November 1994, p 4.
2. Mosiah 15:1,2,4.
3. Alma 11:44.
4. Abraham 4:1.
5. Joseph Fielding Smith, *Journal of Discourses*, Vol. 1, p 51.
6. *The Seer*, September 1853, p 132, quoted in the *Salt Lake City Messenger*, November 1994, p 6.
7. Alma 11:26–31.
8. Doctrines and Covenants 130:22.
9. Elder Russell M. Nelson of the Quorum of the Twelve Apostles, *Ensign* magazine, General Conference issue, November 1993, p 33.
10. Legrand Richards, *A Marvelous Work and a Wonder*, 1979, p 20.
11. James E. Talmage, *The Articles of Faith*, 1977, p 48.
12. *The Concise Dictionary of Christian Tradition*.
13. Alma 18:26–28.
14. *The Teachings of the Prophet Joseph Smith*, 1976, p 345.
15. *The Seer*, January 1853, p 23, quoted in the *Salt Lake City Messenger*, November 1994, p 6.
16. Moroni 8:18.
17. *Mormon Doctrine*, 1979, p 516.
18. Hymns, 1985, No. 292.
19. *Answers to Gospel Questions*, Vol. 3, p 142.
20. Joseph Fielding Smith, *Journal of Discourses*, Vol. 1, p 50.
21. *Millenial Star*, Vol. 16, p 534, quoted in the *Salt Lake City Messenger*, November 1994, p 12.
22. Daily Journal of Abraham H. Cannon, Vol. 11, p 39, quoted in the *Salt Lake City Messenger*, November 1994, p 13.
23. Letter from apostle Bruce R. McConkie to Eugene England, 19 February 1981, quoted in Jerald and Sandra Tanner, *Mormonism: Shadow or Reality?*, 1982.

Chapter 11

Jesus Christ and the Atonement

Jesus warned his followers to beware of false Christs and false prophets (Mk 13:21–23). We need to examine the Mormon Jesus carefully to see if he is 'the One...or should we expect someone else?' (Lk 7:19).

As with many of their beliefs, on the surface Mormons appear to teach the Jesus of the Bible.

> We revere the Son of God as our Savior, our Redeemer, and our Master. He came into the world to do the will of His Father. He died for us and was resurrected from the tomb. His triumph over death brings the blessings of resurrection and immortality to all mankind. Our adoration for Him is typified in this passage from the Book of Mormon:
> 'We talk of Christ, we rejoice in Christ, we preach of Christ, we prophesy of Christ,...that our children may know to what source they may look for a remission of their sins' (2 Ne 25:26).[1]

No Christian would quarrel with this statement. However, a deeper look reveals a Jesus who is not God, but our elder brother and the brother of Satan. He was conceived by physical sexual intercourse between God and Mary, and was married and had children. His atonement for the sin of the world was not complete, as there are sins which it will not cover.

Jesus demoted

We have already seen how Mormons believe that we are all spirit children of God, and lived with him before we came to earth. They believe that God's first-born son was Jesus Christ, and so he is literally our elder brother. 'Among the spirit-children of Elohim the firstborn was and is Jehovah or Jesus Christ to whom all others are juniors.'[2]

God's second son was Lucifer, which makes him our elder brother too, and the brother of Christ.

> The appointment of Jesus to be the Savior of the world was contested by one of the other sons of God. He was called Lucifer, son of the morning. Haughty, ambitious, and covetous of power and glory, this spirit-brother of Jesus desperately tried to become the Savior of mankind.[3]

This means that Jesus is superior to us, but not different. He began as the same kind of being as ourselves. He had a beginning because he was born as a spirit child of God.

Mormons do not accept Jesus as God, only as 'a God'.[4] The Jews understood very well who Jesus claimed to be. After he said 'I and the Father are one' they attempted to stone him 'for blasphemy, because you, a mere man, claim to be God' (Jn 10:30–33). Even the preface of the Book of Mormon states that the purpose of the book is 'to the convincing of the Jew and Gentile that Jesus is the Christ, the Eternal God'. Obviously, the early Mormon church still believed that Jesus was God.

Yet the Mormon Prophet, Joseph Fielding Smith, said, 'Jesus is greater than the Holy Spirit, which is subject unto him, but his Father is greater than he!'[5] When Thomas saw the resurrected Christ, Thomas said, 'My Lord and my God!' (Jn 20:28). The modern-day Mormon Jesus would have corrected him, because he was calling Jesus 'God'. The Jesus of the Bible, however, accepted his worship and praised him for his belief.

Mormons believe that although Jesus was the eldest son, his role as Saviour was only decided upon in the council in heaven where God presented his Plan of Salvation and asked for volunteers to be the Saviour. As we have already seen,

Lucifer volunteered to save everyone by taking away their freedom of choice, but he wanted the glory for himself. Jesus wanted to preserve free agency, and offered the glory to God, so he was chosen. 'In that august council of the angels and the Gods, the Being who later was born in flesh as Mary's Son, Jesus, took prominent part, and there was He ordained of the Father to be the Savior of mankind.'[6] As one of the spirit children of God, Jesus is demoted to a secondary position, not equal with God. His place as Saviour was only given to him after Satan's offer was rejected.

Only begotten

The Bible refers to Jesus as God's only begotten son (Jn 3:16). Mormons claim that this is because Jesus is not only the son of God in the spirit, like the rest of us, but is also the son of God in the flesh. Since God has a physical body,[7] Jesus was conceived by physical sexual intercourse between God and Mary. This meant that he inherited his mortality from his mother and his divinity from his Father.

> The Only Begotten of the Father. (Moses 5:9). These name titles all signify that our Lord is the only Son of the Father in the flesh. Each of the words is to be understood literally. Only means *only*; Begotten means *begotten*; and Son means *son*. Christ was begotten by an Immortal Father in the same way that mortal men are begotten by mortal fathers.[8]
>
> When the time came that his First-born, the Savior, should come into the world and take a tabernacle, the Father came himself and favored that Spirit with a tabernacle instead of letting any other man do it. The Savior was begotten by the Father and his Spirit, by the same Being who is the Father of our spirits, and that is all the organic difference between Jesus Christ and you and me.[9]

The Mormon writer Carlfred B. Broderick made these comments:

> There are two basic elements in the Gospel view of sexuality as I interpret it from the scriptures. The first is that sex is good –

that sexuality, far from being the antithesis of spirituality, is actually an attribute of God.

In the light of their understanding that God is a procreating personage of flesh and bone, latter-day prophets have made it clear that despite what it says in Matthew 1:20, the Holy Ghost was not the father of Jesus...The Savior was fathered by a personage of flesh and bone, and was literally what Nephi said he was, 'Son of the Eternal Father.'[10]

Mormon theologians make no attempt to reconcile this belief with the statement in their own scriptures that Mary was a virgin.[11]

Married with children?

Some of the early church leaders had even more strange ideas about Jesus Christ. Several of them claimed that he was a polygamist.

I said, in my lecture on Marriage, at our last Conference, that Jesus Christ was married at Cana of Galilee, that Mary, Martha, and others were his wives, and that he begat children.[12]

The Messiah chose to take upon himself his seed; and by marrying many honorable wives himself, show to all future generations that he approbated the plurality of wives under the Christian dispensation.[13]

There may have been two reasons for these beliefs. First, they substantiated the revelation which introduced polygamy to the church as an essential part of salvation. Since Jesus is our role model, he must have been obedient in this way too. Secondly, the revelation on the degrees of glory in heaven states that only married couples sealed together for eternity can inherit the celestial kingdom.[14] This was clearly explained by the Prophet Joseph Fielding Smith: 'There can be no exaltation to the fulness of the blessings of the celestial kingdom outside of the marriage relation.'[15] For Jesus to receive exaltation in the celestial kingdom, he would therefore have to be married. There was even a rumour that Joseph Smith claimed direct descent from Jesus Christ. These teachings were, however, an embarrassment, and are not spoken of today.

Blood atonement

The Book of Mormon teaches that the atonement had to be an infinite one:

> because man became fallen they were cut off from the presence of the Lord. Wherefore, it must needs be an infinite atonement – save it should be an infinite atonement this corruption could not put on incorruption. Wherefore, the first judgement which came upon man must needs have remained to an endless duration.[16]

Joseph Smith, however, disagreed, which was strange considering his familiarity with the Book of Mormon:

> Joseph Smith taught that there were certain sins so grievous that man may commit, that they will place the transgressors beyond the power of the atonement of Christ. If these offenses are committed, then the blood of Christ will not cleanse them from their sins even though they repent. Therefore their only hope is to have their own blood shed to atone, as far as possible, in their behalf.[17]

In 1958, Apostle Bruce R. McConkie explained: 'As a mode of capital punishment, hanging or execution on a gallows does not comply with the law of blood atonement, for the blood is not shed.'[18] This is no longer practised by the Mormon church, who nevertheless still struggle over it with the occasional breakaway fundamentalist group. But the laws of the state of Utah are founded on Mormon philosophy, and as recently as 1977 we find them allowing an appeal for execution by firing squad. 'Utah State Prison – A last-minute court decision cleared the way today for the execution of Gary Mark Gilmore, 36, and moments later, the condemned killer was shot to death here by a firing squad.'[19]

Should we expect someone else?

Having examined the true beliefs of the Mormon church regarding Jesus Christ and his atoning sacrifice, we do indeed find that we need to look elsewhere for the true Saviour who will reconcile us to God.

Notes

1. Elder Russell M. Nelson of the Quorum of the Twelve Apostles, 'Combatting Spiritual Drift: Our Global Pandemic', *Ensign* magazine, November 1993, p 104.
2. James E. Talmage, *Articles of Faith*, p 471.
3. Milton R. Hunter of the First Quorum of the Seventy, Gospel through the Ages, 1945, p 15.
4. Elder Robert D. Hales of the Quorum of the Twelve Apostles, *Ensign* magazine, May 1994, p 79.
5. *Doctrines of Salvation*, Vol. 1, p 18.
6. James E. Talmage, *Jesus the Christ*, 1976, p 9.
7. Doctrine and Covenants 130:22.
8. Bruce R. McConkie, *Mormon Doctrine*, pp 546–47.
9. Brigham Young, *Journal of Discourses* 4:218.
10. *Dialogue: A Journal of Mormon Thought*, Autumn 1967, pp 100–01.
11. 1 Nephi 11:13–18; Alma 7:10.
12. Apostle Orson Hyde, *Journal of Discourses*, Vol. 2, p 210.
13. Apostle Orson Pratt, *The Seer*, p 172.
14. Doctrine and Covenants 132:19–20.
15. Joseph Fielding Smith, *Doctrines of Salvation*, Vol. 2, p 65.
16. 2 Nephi 9:6–7.
17. Joseph Fielding Smith, same source, Vol. 1, p 135.
18. Bruce R. McConkie, same source, 1958, p 314.
19. *Salt Lake Tribune*, 17 January 1977.

Chapter 12

The Holy Spirit and the Gifts

A personage or not a personage?

When the Doctrine and Covenants was first published, it contained the Lectures on Faith. These were originally delivered before a class of the elders in Kirtland, Ohio. They were considered authoritative because Joseph Smith helped to prepare them and revised them before they were published.[1]

In 1921 they were removed from the Doctrine and Covenants and have not been seen since. Since these lectures were about seventy pages long, this amounted to a major deletion. One of the reasons given was that their teachings were not complete regarding the Godhead. What this actually means is that their teachings disagree with modern Mormon theology. Once again, most Mormons today have no idea that the church has ever taught anything other than what they are taught now.

A case in point is the doctrine concerning the Holy Spirit.

Q.   How many personages are there in the Godhead?
A.   Two: the Father and the Son.
Q.   How do you prove that there are two personages in the Godhead?
A.   By the Scriptures.
Q.   Do the Father and the Son possess the same mind?
A.   They do.
Q.   What is this mind?
A.   The Holy Spirit.
Q.   Do the Father, Son and Holy Spirit constitute the Godhead?

A. They do.
Q. Does the foregoing account of the Godhead lay a sure foun-
dation for the exercise of faith in him unto life and salvation?
A. It does.[2]

In 1835 the Holy Spirit (or Holy Ghost as he is usually called
by Mormons) was part of the Godhead, but only as the mind
of the Father and the Son. He was not a personage in his own
right. Contrast that with today's doctrine, taken, strangely
enough, also from the Doctrine and Covenants: 'The Father
has a body of flesh and bones as tangible as man's; the Son
also; but the Holy Ghost has not a body of flesh and bones, but
is a personage of Spirit.'[3]

Heber C. Kimball, who was a member of the First
Presidency, said, 'The Holy Ghost is a man; he is one of the
sons of our Father and our God.'[4] So although he is part of the
Godhead, he cannot be equal with God because, like Jesus, he
is one of God's sons.

How to become a god

This raises an interesting question: if the Holy Spirit is one of
God's sons, he must have gained his godhood in the same way
as everyone else – through obedience to the 'laws of the
gospel'. These laws include baptism and celestial marriage,
which require a physical body. In fact, the first purpose of our
coming to the earth, according to the Mormon Plan of
Salvation, was to gain a physical body. But the Holy Spirit is 'a
personage of Spirit' and does not have a body. So how did he
get to be a god?

Mormon leaders are unable to explain how the Holy Spirit
became a god without a physical body. They have simply tried
to explain it away:

> In this dispensation, at least, nothing has been revealed as to
> his origin or destiny; expressions on these matters are both
> speculative and fruitless.[5]
> I have never troubled myself as to whether the Holy Ghost
> will have a body or not because it is not in any way essential to
> my salvation.[6]

Christians understand from Scripture that God is Spirit (Jn 4:24). Mormon leaders have always spoken derisively of the Christian creed in relation to God's nature:

> We affirm that to deny the materiality of God's person is to deny God; for a thing without parts has no whole, and an immaterial body cannot exist. The Church of Jesus Christ of Latter-day Saints proclaims against the incomprehensible God, devoid of 'body, parts, or passions,' as *a thing impossible of existence.*[7]

Clearly, the Holy Spirit of the Mormon church does not, by the church's own definition of God, exist.

Laying on of hands

Mormons believe that the Holy Spirit can inspire people who are seeking the truth, but will not stay with them. The way to have the constant companionship of the Holy Spirit is to have the gift of the Holy Spirit bestowed upon one 'by the laying on of hands by those in authority'. This is part of the baptism service, and is done immediately following the baptism. It is also done by proxy for the dead, when baptisms for the dead are performed in the temples. While the laying on of hands is a Christian practice and the Holy Spirit is sometimes bestowed by this means, for the Mormon it is part of a ritualistic process inexorably connected with priesthood.

> True it is that honest seekers come to know of the truth and divinity of the Lord's work by the power of the Holy Ghost: they receive a flash of revelation telling them that Jesus is the Lord, that Joseph Smith is his prophet, that the Book of Mormon is the mind and will and voice of the Lord, that the Church of Jesus Christ of Latter-day Saints is the only true and living church upon the face of the whole earth. They gain a testimony before baptism. But it is only after they pledge their all in the cause of Christ that they receive the gift of the Holy Ghost, which is the heavenly endowment of which Jesus spoke. Then they receive a fulfillment of promise: 'by the power of the Holy Ghost ye may know the truth of all things' (Moro 10:5). Then

they receive 'the spirit of revelation,' and the Lord tells them in their heart and in their mind whatsoever he will (D&C 8:1–3).[8]

The presence of the Holy Spirit to guide the faithful Mormon is one more thing for which they have to work and sacrifice. The gifts of the Spirit are 'always predicated upon obedience to law'.[9]

Gifts

Supernatural phenomena are to be found in many religions and pagan practices around the world, and they are attributable to many causes. Just because there are miracles does not authenticate the faith nor prove it is true. When Moses appeared before Pharaoh, the Egyptian magicians did the same miracles that Moses did (Exod 7:11).

Claiming to be Christian, the Mormon church uses the New Testament model in its statement of faith concerning spiritual gifts: 'We believe in the gift of tongues, prophecy, revelation, visions, healing, interpretation of tongues, and so forth.'[10] The Mormon church believes in all the gifts of the Spirit, as recorded in the Bible (1 Cor 12:7–10, 27–31) and the Christian would be hard pressed to find anything in their teaching with which to disagree. However, the practice does not match the theory.

Each father is told that, as the priesthood holder for the home, he is entitled to revelation for his family. Bishops are entitled to revelation for the ward, and so on. But only the Prophet is entitled to have revelation for the church. No lowly member can presume to speak for God in an area in which he does not 'hold the keys'. True revelation, visions and prophecy are never seen among ordinary members, but only announced from church headquarters.

Even this practice is suspect, with only four sections being added to the Doctrine and Covenants since the death of Joseph Smith. The revelation which gave Negroes the priesthood in 1978 has never been published. All the church has seen is a statement by the first presidency which says that a revelation has been received. If God did speak, we should be allowed to see his words for ourselves, in a statement which begins, 'Thus saith the Lord.'[11]

Paul quite clearly laid out for the Corinthian church how the gifts should be used:

> When you come together, everyone has a hymn, or a word of instruction, a revelation, a tongue or an interpretation. All of these must be done for the strengthening of the church. If anyone speaks in a tongue, two – or at the most three – should speak, one at a time, and someone must interpret. If there is no interpreter, the speaker should keep quiet in the church and speak to himself and God.
>
> Two or three prophets should speak, and the others should weigh carefully what is said. And if a revelation comes to someone who is sitting down, the first speaker should stop. For you can all prophecy in turn so that everyone may be instructed and encouraged. (1 Cor 14:26–31.)

Many Mormons can testify of promptings they have received from the Holy Spirit in their personal lives, but no one would presume to stand up in a church meeting and prophesy.

But Paul expected that the gifts should be manifested by every member, and should be in evidence in every meeting. When he lists the gifts earlier in the same letter, he says: 'Now to each one the manifestation of the Spirit is given for the common good' (1 Cor 12:7).

Stories about the gift of tongues and interpretation in the Mormon church are apocryphal, but always about General Authorities of the church. There are stories such as speaking to foreign saints in English who understood in their own language, or correcting a translator at a service. Missionaries who learn a foreign language very quickly are said to have the gift of tongues. In all our years in the Mormon church, we never knew anyone who had witnessed such phenomena, and the gift of tongues for praising God was unknown.

Mormons follow the admonition of James: 'Is any one of you sick? He should call for the elders of the church to pray over him and anoint him with oil in the name of the Lord. And the prayer offered in faith will make the sick person well; the

Lord will raise him up' (Jas 5:14–15). Whenever someone is ill, a priesthood holder will anoint them with consecrated oil and pray for them. Priesthood holders are instructed to carry consecrated oil with them so that they are always prepared. The ordinary Mormon will know of and have experienced the healing of minor ailments like headaches. But all the spectacular healings come by report from the general authorities, and are never documented.

It is not possible to include part of the New Testament in a statement of faith, and then ignore another part. Either the New Testament is a model for the church or it is not. Either the gifts are operating today or they are not. And if they are, they should conform to the model. The Mormon church pays only lip service to this principle. The gifts of the Holy Spirit are not in regular use in their church services.

Notes

1. Joseph Fielding Smith, *Doctrines of Salvation*, Vol. 3, p 195.
2. Doctrine and Covenants, 1835 edition, pp 52, 53, 55, 57, 58.
3. Doctrine and Covenants 130:22.
4. *Journal of Discourses*, Vol. 5, p 179.
5. Bruce R. McConkie, *Mormon Doctrine*, p 329.
6. Joseph Fielding Smith, same source, Vol. 1, p 39.
7. James E. Talmage, *Articles of Faith*, 1968, p 48, our italics.
8. Bruce R. McConkie, *The Mortal Messiah* 4:98–99.
9. Bruce R. McConkie, *Mormon Doctrine*, p 314.
10. James E. Talmage, same source, 7.
11. Jerald and Sandra Tanner (eds), *The Changing World of Mormonism*, pp 325–28.

Chapter 13
Creation and the Fall

For centuries only one account [of the creation] has been available to the world – the record now preserved in the Bible. But with the Restoration have come three others. Each of these four accounts offers valuable insight into the process and purposes of the Creation.

1. The Genesis Account (Gen 1 – 2). This is the common account shared by all Bible readers. Latter-day Saints regard it as the remnant of an account originally given to Moses.

2. The Book of Moses Account (Moses 1 – 3); Joseph Smith Translation Gen 1 – 2). After Joseph Smith had translated the Book of Mormon and learned that many plain and precious truths had been taken from the Bible, the Lord commanded him to 'translate' the Bible. In doing so, he used neither Hebrew nor Greek documents but drew upon revelation and inspiration as the source of the text.

3. The Book of Abraham Account (Abr 3 – 5). This account was recorded by Abraham. A form of it was discovered in an Egyptian tomb and later sold to the Latter-day Saints. By revelation, the Prophet Joseph Smith produced the text of the Book of Abraham.

4. The Temple Account. Using the power of drama and group participation, this account teaches, so far as possible within the limits of dramatic structure, the various steps involved in the

Creation, the sequence of events, and the roles of those involved.[1]

Thus begins an article in the Mormon church magazine the *Ensign*, comparing the four accounts of the creation. The explanation as to how the non-biblical accounts were received should already have alerted the reader that the Mormon beliefs will differ from those of the Bible. This is heightened by the description of the Genesis account as a 'remnant' of another account.

Spiritual creation

The Book of Moses adds to the biblical account that there were two creations – a spiritual and a physical. 'For I, the Lord God, created all things, of which I have spoken, spiritually, before they were naturally upon the face of the earth.'[2] Mormons claim that this explains why there are two conflicting accounts of creation in the first two chapters of Genesis. It also substantiates their belief in a pre-existence where we all lived as spirit children with God. This also appears in the Book of Abraham: 'Now the Lord had shown unto me, Abraham, the intelligences that were organised before the world was.'[3]

Scholars have long debated concerning the two accounts of creation in Genesis chapters one and two, but at no time has anyone suggested that there was a spiritual and a physical creation. The most common theory among the critics is that they are two different accounts which have been inexpertly edited together.[4] However, it is not difficult to reconcile them:

> (The) technique of recapitulation was widely practiced in ancient Semitic literature. The author would first introduce his account with a short statement summarizing the whole transaction, and then he would follow it up with a more detailed and circumstantial account when dealing with matters of special importance.
>
> To the author of Genesis 1, 2 the human race was obviously the crowning or climactic product of creation, and it was only to be expected that he would devote a more extensive treatment to Adam after he had placed him in his historical setting (the sixth creative day).[5]

Materials for creation and purpose of creation

The Book of Abraham also reveals that God did not create out of nothing, but rather organised materials that were already in existence. 'We will go down, for there is space there, and we will take of these materials, and we will make an earth whereon these may dwell.'[6]

Joseph Smith went further than this, in a revelation recorded in 1833: 'Man was also in the beginning with God. Intelligence, or the light of truth, was not created or made, neither indeed can be.'[7] This is in direct conflict with the Bible, which states: 'Through him all things were made; without him nothing was made that has been made' (Jn 1:3). If God made everything, there cannot be anything which already existed before creation, or which was not created.

The Abraham account goes on to explain the purpose of creation.

> And we will prove them herewith, to see if they will do all things whatsoever the Lord their God shall command them; And they who keep their first estate shall be added upon;...and they who keep their second estate shall have glory added upon their heads for ever and ever.[8]

This supports the Mormon belief in salvation by works.

Who created

It is interesting to note that the Moses account mirrors Genesis in attributing the creation to 'I, God'. The Abraham account, however, builds on the Mormon belief in a plurality of gods by stating that 'the Gods' created all things.[9] Not only does Abraham disagree with Moses and with the Bible, it also disagrees with the Book of Mormon: 'Now Zeezrom said: Is there more than one God? And he answered, No.'[10]

The sole contribution of the Temple account is to reveal that Adam is Michael, the archangel who helped in the creation: 'And the Lord appeared to them, and they rose up and blessed Adam, and called him Michael, the prince, the archangel.'[11] 'It is true that Adam helped to form this earth. He labored with our Savior Jesus Christ.'[12]

In Joseph Smith's diary, under 21 January 1836, he recorded a revelation: 'The heavens were opened upon us and I beheld the celestial kingdom of God...I saw father Adam, and Abraham and Michael and my father and mother, my brother Alvin.'[13] This caused some embarrassment. How could Joseph see Adam *and* Michael, if Adam *is* Michael? When the revelation was accepted as scripture in 1976, it became section 137 of the Doctrine and Covenants. There it is printed without the words 'and Michael', which neatly solves the problem.

The fall

> Some people believe that Adam and Eve committed a serious sin when they ate of the tree of knowledge of good and evil. However, latter-day scriptures help us to understand that their fall was a necessary step in the plan of life and a great blessing to all mankind. Because of the fall, we are blessed with physical bodies, the right to choose between good and evil, and the opportunity to gain eternal life. None of these privileges would have been ours had Adam and Eve remained in the garden.[14]

Once again the Mormon church has twisted Scripture to its own ends. The Fall of Adam is shown to be part of God's plan for his children, rather than a rebellion against God: 'Death hath passed upon all men, to fulfil the merciful plan of the great Creator.'[15] Joseph Fielding Smith, the tenth president of the church, actually said that Adam did not sin, but merely transgressed: 'It is not always a sin to transgress a law... Adam's transgression...was in accordance with law.'[16]

This is simply playing with words. *The Concise Dictionary of Christian Tradition* defines 'transgression' as: 'The failure to obey the law of God and thus a manifestation of human sin.'[17] The Old Testament prophet Hosea said that Adam broke a covenant and was unfaithful (Hosea 6:7), and Paul clearly told the Romans that Adam committed a sin and was disobedient (Rom 5:12–19). This does not sound like obedience to a prearranged plan.

The Book of Mormon tells us that 'Adam fell that man might be; and men are, that they might have joy.'[18] Far from it being a blessing to us, Paul says that 'the result of one trespass was condemnation for all men' (Rom 5:18). The nature of that condemnation was clearly portrayed in another of Paul's letters, when he described us as 'without hope and without God in the world' (Eph 2:12).

The best summary of Mormon beliefs about Adam and the fall comes from Sterling W. Sill, a member of the First Quorum of Seventy: 'Adam fell, but he fell in the right direction. He fell toward the goal...Adam fell, but he fell upward.' How can someone fall upward? And since the Bible teaches that Jesus Christ reversed the effects of the fall, which way are we all going now?

Notes

1. Keith Meservy, an associate professor of Ancient Scripture at Brigham Young University and a member of the Gospel Writing Committee, *Ensign* magazine, January 1986, pp 50–53.
2. Moses 3:5.
3. Abraham 3:22.
4. Josh MacDowell and Don Stewart, *Answers to Tough Questions*, Campus Crusade for Christ, 1980, pp 170ff.
5. Gleason Archer Jr, Introduction in *A Survey of the Old Testament*, Chicago: Moody Press, 1974, p 118.
6. Abraham 3:24.
7. Doctrine and Covenants 93:29.
8. Abraham 3:25–26.
9. Compare Moses 2 and Abraham 4.
10. Alma 11:28–29.
11. Doctrine and Covenants 107:54.
12. Joseph Fielding Smith, *Doctrines of Salvation*, Vol. 1, p 75.
13. Joseph Smith's Diary, 21 January 1836, p 136.
14. *Gospel Principles Manual*, 1981, p 31.
15. 2 Nephi 9:6.
16. Joseph Fielding Smith, same source, Vol. 1, p 114.
17. Douglas, Elwell & Toon, *The Concise Dictionary of Christian Tradition*, Marshall Pickering, 1989, pp 383.
18. 2 Nephi 2:25.
19. *Deseret News*, Church Section, 31 July 1965, p 7.

Chapter 14
Salvation: Immortality and Eternal Life

The Mormon understanding of salvation is encapsulated in the third Article of Faith of the church: 'We believe that through the Atonement of Christ, all mankind may be saved, by obedience to the laws and ordinances of the gospel.' Compare this with Paul's description of salvation in Romans 6:23: 'For the wages of sin is death, but the gift of God is eternal life in Christ Jesus our Lord.' The contrast between these two statements will be the main theme of this chapter as we investigate what Mormons mean when they use such familiar Christian terms as 'atonement', 'grace' and 'salvation'.

Fallen man

Essential to salvation is a true understanding of the position of man as a result of the fall of Adam. Without a clear understanding of our need for redemption we will not look for a redeemer.

We have already seen that, according to Mormon thinking, Adam fell upwards – towards the goal. The implications of such a doctrine cannot be overstated here. If it is true, then the state of man as a result of the fall must be better than it was before. Leading Mormon commentators confirm this:

> When Adam was driven out of the Garden of Eden, the Lord passed a sentence upon him. Some people have looked upon that sentence as being a dreadful thing. It was not.

The fall of man came as a blessing in disguise, and was the means of furthering the purposes of the Lord in the progress of man, rather than a means of hindering them.[1]

Brigham Young said:

It is fully proved in all the revelations that God has ever given to mankind that they naturally love and admire righteousness, justice and truth more than they do evil. It is, however, universally received by professors of religion as a Scriptural doctrine that man is naturally opposed to God. This is not so. Paul says, in his Epistle to the Corinthians, 'But the natural man receiveth not the things of God.' but I say *it is the unnatural 'man that receiveth not the things of God.'*[2]

Such a clear contradiction of Scripture is supported by the third president of the Mormon church, John Taylor, who said that 'it is not natural for men to be evil'.[3]

This doctrine is not only opposed to the teaching of Paul, but directly contradicts the teaching of the Book of Mormon which says:

For the natural man is an enemy to God, and has been from the fall of Adam, and will be, forever and ever, unless he yields to the enticings of the Holy Spirit, and putteth off the natural man and becometh a saint through the atonement of Christ the Lord.[4]

Mormon leaders still insist, however, that:

Our doctrine is positive and life affirming...We refuse to believe, with some churches of Christendom, that the biblical account of the fall of man records the corruption of human nature or to accept the doctrine of original sin. We do not believe that man is incapable of doing the will of God, or is unable to merit the reward of Divine approval; that he is therefore totally estranged from God and that whatever salvation comes to him must come as a free and undeserved gift.[5]

The plan

If man is not corrupted in his nature as a result of the fall of Adam, it seems reasonable to ask where sin comes into the picture. Mormons do speak of atonement and redemption. Where is the sin for which our Saviour atoned if not in the nature of man? From what are we to be redeemed if not ourselves?

It was all in the plan. To Mormons this life is a testing ground where they are to prove their worthiness to go on to eternal glory in the celestial kingdom of God:

> Did they [Adam and Eve] come out in direct opposition to God and to His government? No. But they transgressed a command of the Lord, and through that transgression sin came into the world. The Lord knew that they would do this, and he had designed that they should.[6]
>
> In order for mankind to obtain salvation and exaltation it is necessary for them to obtain bodies in this world, and pass through the experiences and schooling that are found only in mortality.[7]

The Psalmist declares, 'Surely I was sinful at birth, sinful from the time my mother conceived me' (Ps 51:5). Mormon scripture seems to agree with this conclusion: 'Thy children are conceived in sin' (Moses 6:55). The Mormon understanding of these verses, however, is very different to what you might expect:

> This being 'conceived in sin' [Moses 6:55], as I understand it, is only that they are in the midst of sin. They come into the world where sin is prevalent, and it will enter into their hearts, but it will lead them 'to taste the bitter that they may know to prize the good.'[8]

The Mormon understanding of the fall, then, is that according to God's plan, Adam fell up and into a condition that was 'absolutely necessary to our exaltation'.[9] This life is a probationary period in which we may prove ourselves worthy of exaltation with God, and sin is the test of our faithfulness. It is an external force that entered into the world, but not into humanity, and which we are to 'resist and overcome'.[10]

Man inherits from Adam mortal suffering and physical death. Born innocent, he is subject to temptation, and it is only as he succumbs that he sins and suffers spiritual death.[11] It is then that sin becomes personal to him:

> All have sinned. Each person is therefore unclean *to the extent to which he has sinned*, and because of that uncleanness is banished from the presence of the Lord so long as the effect of *his own wrongdoing* is upon him.[12]

This goes a long way to explaining the second Article of Faith of the church which says: 'We believe that men will be punished for their own sins, and not for Adam's transgression.'

The atonement

The atonement is designed to reverse the twin effects of the fall and also has a twofold effect itself. The first result of the atonement is that physical death is conquered and all men will, *unconditionally*, be resurrected. The second is that '*conditionally*, through repentance we may come into the presence of God and thereby inherit eternal life'.[13] John Taylor explains it like this:

> Transgression of the law brought death upon all the posterity of Adam, the restoration through the atonement restored all the human family to life...so that all men...may be placed upon the same footing, and that all men may have the same privilege...of accepting the conditions of the great plan of redemption provided by the Father.[14]

What are the conditions upon which man's eternal inheritance depends? They are in the third Article of Faith referred to earlier: 'We believe that through the Atonement of Christ, all mankind may be saved, *by obedience to the laws and ordinances of the gospel*' (our italics). By means of the atonement the whole human family is put on the same footing: we are all given an opportunity to earn or, as Hugh B. Brown put it, merit our exaltation. As we have all given in to temptation we have a need for forgiveness. The provision for this is described by Joseph F. Smith:

> Men cannot forgive their own sins; they cannot cleanse themselves from the consequences of their sins. Men can stop sinning and can do right in the future, *and so far their acts are acceptable before the Lord and worthy of consideration.* But who shall repair the wrongs they have done to themselves and to others? By the atonement of Jesus Christ, the sins of the repentant shall be washed away.[15]

Mormon grace means the washing away of the sins we commit, while leaving in place the good deeds that gain us merit in God's eyes. These deeds, free of the encumbrance of individual sins, gain us entrance into God's highest heaven – provided we are faithful enough, for long enough, in enough things.

Salvation

Salvation, in Mormon thinking, is universal. It is the redemption of all mankind from the dead. All are saved in that all are redeemed from the first effect of Adam's transgression. This does not, however, get them into God's presence. It merely gives them immortality.

Exaltation, to a Mormon, is the ultimate goal and describes existence in the presence of God in the highest heaven. This is quite different from immortality and is known as eternal life, denoting a quality of existence. James E. Talmage explains:

> Some degree of salvation will come to all who have not forfeited their right to it; exaltation is given to those only who by active labors have won a claim to God's merciful liberality by which it is bestowed.[16]

The final state of every man and woman is an immortal, but the place and quality of that immortal existence is determined by faithful obedience to the 'laws and ordinances' of the Mormon church.

Mormons, Hebrews and the apostle Paul

> If anyone else thinks he has reasons to put confidence in the
> flesh, I have more: circumcised on the eighth day, of the peo-
> ple of Israel, of the tribe of Benjamin, a Hebrew of Hebrews; in
> regard to the law, a Pharisee; as for zeal, persecuting the
> church; as for legalistic righteousness, faultless. (Phil 3:4–6.)

Such were the credentials of Paul, God's apostle to the gentiles. If ever a man lived who 'may be saved, by obedience to
the laws and ordinances of the gospel' that man was Paul. Yet
this same Paul went on to say:

> But whatever was to my profit I now consider loss for the sake
> of Christ. What is more, I consider everything a loss compared
> to the surpassing greatness of knowing Christ Jesus my Lord,
> for whose sake I have lost all things. I consider them rubbish,
> that I may gain Christ and be found in him, not having a right-
> eousness of my own that comes from the law, but that which is
> through faith on Christ – the righteousness that comes from
> God and is by faith. (Phil 3:7–9.)

What was it Paul found that effected such a change? It
seems that the rest of his life was devoted to telling what he
had discovered about the purposes of God from Adam to
Christ. Let us take the key statements of the Mormon church
regarding the 'gospel' and compare them with Paul's account
of his own discoveries.

General or conditional?

The Mormon idea of salvation is a form of universalism. They
believe that the atonement effects a general salvation for all
mankind bringing them to a state of immortality: 'the restoration through the atonement restored all the human family to
life' (John Taylor).

Paul declared to the Ephesian saints, 'For it is by grace you
have been saved, through faith' (Eph 2:8). It is clear that salvation is conditional upon faith in the one through whom it
comes. While it is true that resurrection comes to all (1 Cor
15:22), resurrection cannot be equated with salvation which

comes by faith. It is that faith which determines whether we are resurrected to life (Rev 20:6), or to condemnation (Rev 20:15).

Not by law

In the Mormon plan, man, having gained a certain footing, must now meet 'the conditions of the great plan of redemption provided by the Father' (John Taylor). Those conditions are 'obedience to the laws and ordinances of the gospel' (Third Article of Faith).

God's right and perfect law is succinctly stated by Paul in his letter to the Romans:

> [God] will give to each person according to what he has done. To those who by persistence in doing good seek glory, honour, and immortality, he will give eternal life. But for those who are self-seeking and who reject the truth and follow evil, there will be wrath and anger (Romans 2:6–8, our brackets).

The Mormon argument is that 'men can stop sinning and can do right in the future, and so far their acts are acceptable before the Lord and worthy of consideration' (Joseph F. Smith). But, having shown God's law to be just, what did Paul find?

He points out that 'the wrath of God is being revealed from heaven against all the godlessness and wickedness of men' (Rom 1:18), and that those who have God's law and pass judgement on others are themselves condemned 'because you who pass judgement do the same things' (Rom 2:1). He goes on to say: 'What shall we conclude then? Are we any better? Not at all! We have already made the charge that Jews and Gentiles alike are under sin. As it is written: 'There is no-one righteous, not even one' (Rom 3:9–10).

God's law is perfect and reflects the perfect nature of God. It is also one law and reflects the oneness of God. James put it like this: 'Whoever keeps the whole law and yet stumbles at just one point is guilty of breaking all of it. For he who said, "Do not commit adultery," also said, "Do not murder." If you do not commit adultery but do commit murder, you have become a law breaker' (Jas 2:10–11).

It is not true, then, that our good acts 'so far...are acceptable before God and worthy of consideration'. One sin makes us law-breakers and unacceptable before a God who demands that we keep the whole law. Paul discovered that 'no-one will be declared righteous in his sight by observing the law' (Rom 3:20).

Mormons will argue that Paul is speaking of the Jewish law, the Old Testament code, and that it was superceded by 'the law of the gospel'. The New Testament, however, contains no references to any other law. Indeed, Paul says, 'If a law had been given that could impart life, then righteousness would certainly have come by the law. But the scripture declares that the whole world is a prisoner of sin, so that what was promised, being given through faith in Jesus Christ, might be given to those who believe' (Gal 3:21–22).

Law was never the problem. There is absolutely nothing wrong with God's law. The problem is sin: it holds us prisoners. The law cannot impart life, not because it is incapable of doing so but because we are incapable of obeying it and thus meriting the life it imparts, for it is on merit that the law rewards or punishes. This is justice and we cannot argue with it – but neither can we meet its demands.

Fallen man

Sin and death, in the Mormon plan, are the twin consequences of the fall. They are treated separately, death coming upon all men and sin affecting men only as they succumb to temptation. Paul, however, discovered that 'sin...entered the world through one man, *and death through sin,* and in this way death came to all men, because all sinned' (Rom 5:12, our italics).

Death and sin are inseparable from the beginning. The consequence of sin is twofold – death and judgement: 'many died by the trespass of one man...The judgement followed one sin and brought condemnation...The result of one trespass was condemnation for all men (Rom 5:15,16, 18). Death, judgement and condemnation come to all men as the result of Adam's transgression. Adam did not fall up towards the goal;

he fell the way all men fall when they do fall – down. This was not a blessing in disguise. It was a disaster for all mankind.

The state of man after the fall is starkly described by Paul: 'They have become filled with every kind of wickedness, evil, greed, and depravity. They are full of envy, murder, strife, deceit and malice' (Rom 1:29). The Book of Mormon says, 'The natural man is an enemy to God' (Mosiah 3:19). This is the man that Brigham Young declares 'naturally love[s] and admire[s] righteousness, justice and truth more than they do evil'.

The key words in the above passage are 'filled' and 'full'. It is instructional that Jesus said:

> Nothing that enters a man from the outside can make him 'unclean'. For it doesn't go into his heart but into his stomach, and then out of his body...What comes out of a man makes him 'unclean'. For from within, out of men's hearts, come evil thoughts, sexual immorality, theft, murder, adultery, greed, malice, deceit, lewdness, envy, slander, arrogance and folly. All these things come from inside and make a man 'unclean'. (Mark 7:18–23.)

As the Psalmist says, 'Surely I was sinful at birth, sinful from the time my mother conceived me' (Ps 52:5). This is not coming 'into the world where sin is prevalent'; this is sinful by nature. This is the original sin that Hugh B. Brown refused to believe in.

The nature of sin needs to be clearly understood here. Sin is not simply what you *do*, it is what you *are*. In writing to the Ephesians, Paul spoke of the condition of the saints before they were saved: 'As for you, you were dead in your transgressions and sins, in which you used to live when you followed the ways of this world...Like the rest, we were *by nature* objects of wrath' (Eph 2:1–3, our italics).

As already shown, Hugh B. Brown stated, 'We do not believe that man is incapable of doing the will of God.' Speaking from his own experience, however, Paul said, 'For I have the desire to do what is good, but I cannot carry it out. For what I do is not the good I want to do; no, the evil I do not want to do – this I keep on doing' (Rom 7:18–19). Why? 'Now if I do what I do not want to do, it is no longer I who do it, but it is *sin living in me* that does it' (Rom 7:20, our italics). Paul realised that 'nothing good lives in me, that is, in *my sinful nature*' (Rom 7:18, our italics).

But, it might be argued, surely there is some merit in moving towards the goal; something to be gained by striving to do good works and please God. But it is not simply what we do that is judged but what we are, because what we do comes out of what we are. Furthermore, God's judgement is exact. One sin in thought or deed totally disqualifies us (Jas 2:10–11). Isaiah says: 'All of us have become like one who is unclean, all our righteous acts are like filthy rags' (Is 64:6).

Well might we cry with Paul, 'What a wretched man I am! Who will rescue me from this body of death?' (Rom 7:24). We might also ask with Jesus' disciples, '"Who then can be saved?" Jesus looked at them and said, "With man this is impossible, but with God all things are possible"' (Mt 19:25–26).

The plan of salvation

Mormons believe that outside their own circle there is no consistent and unified 'plan of salvation' in Christian thinking. As recently as August 1995, an article appeared in a church magazine which credited Joseph Smith with being the first to identify this problem and come up with a God-inspired solution. The writer suggested that:

> without knowledge restored through the Prophet Joseph Smith, theologians relying solely on their own interpretations of the Bible face difficult questions of faith like the following...How can we say that God has an eternal plan of salvation when, according to traditional Christian theology, Jesus Christ brought a new way of salvation which the ancients did not know? Did earlier generations actually know the divine plan of salvation, or did God mislead them by giving them a law that was both preparatory and transitory? If, however, the ancients could, in fact, be saved by the law they knew, what was the need for Jesus Christ? Did God think of a better plan after his first one failed?[17]

The Mormon answer to these questions – a plan that was presented in the council of the gods and was known in every detail by the ancients – ignores almost entirely the evidence of the Bible. As we have already seen, that plan is clearly unbiblical in its diagnosis of man's fundamental problem – sin. Its proposed solution is equally untenable as we shall see.

Hebrews chapter 11, that great chapter on faith, refers to prophets, kings and ordinary folk whose faith is commended to us as an example. From Abel, Moses and Rahab to David and beyond, they were people who lived by faith – even when they died. Faith in what?

> They did not receive the things promised; they only *saw them from a distance.* And they admitted that they were aliens and strangers on earth. People who say such things show that they are looking for a country of their own. If they had been thinking of the country they had left, they would have had opportunity to return. Instead, they were longing for a better country – a heavenly one. Therefore God is not ashamed to be called their God, *for he has prepared a city for them.* (Hebrews 11:13–16, our italics.)

They knew God's promises and, more important, they knew the God who keeps his promises. On the strength of that they lived by faith, looking for God to provide and the plan to work out. In the words of Job: 'I know that my redeemer lives, and that in the end he will stand upon the earth. And after my skin has been destroyed, yet in my flesh I will see God; I myself will see him with my own eyes – I, and not another. How my heart yearns within me' (Job 19:25–27).

A redeemer – that is the provision of God! From before the foundations of the earth a redeemer was planned: 'He was chosen before the creation of the world, but was revealed in these last days for your sake' (1 Pet 1:20). From the time of the fall a redeemer was promised: 'And I will put enmity between you and the woman, and between your offspring and hers; he will crush your head, and you will strike his heel (Gen 3:15). Through the time of the prophets a redeemer was expected: 'For to us a child is born, to us a son is given, and the

government will be on his shoulders. And he will be called
Wonderful Counsellor, Mighty God, Everlasting Father,
Prince of Peace' (Is 9:6).

When that redeemer came he said, 'You diligently study the
scriptures because you think that by them you possess eternal
life. These are the scriptures that testify of me' (Jn 5:39). On
the road to Emmaus, 'beginning with Moses and the Prophets,
he explained to them what was said in all the scriptures concerning himself' (Lk 24:27).

Jesus fulfilled the plan by his death on the cross:

> Concerning this salvation, the prophets who spoke of the grace
> that was to come to you, searched intently and with the great-
> est care, trying to find out the time and circumstances to which
> the Spirit of Christ in them was pointing when he predicted the
> sufferings of Christ and the glories that would follow. It was
> revealed to them that they were not serving themselves but
> you, when *they spoke of the things that have now been told you by
> those who have preached the gospel* to you by the Holy Spirit sent
> from heaven. (1 Peter 1:10–12, our italics.)
>
> Yet none of them received what had been promised. God had
> planned something better for us so that only together with us
> would they be made perfect. (Hebrews 11:39–40.)

It is significant that Jesus was the fulfilment of a promise
(Acts 13:23). A promise that, as Paul pointed out, preceded the
law. The promise was: 'I will make you into a great nation and
I will bless you; I will make your name great, and you will be a
blessing. I will bless those who bless you, and whoever curses
you I will curse; *and all peoples on earth will be blessed through
you*' (Gen 12:2–3, our italics).

The clause in italics is quoted in Acts 3:25 where Peter is
addressing Abraham's descendants:

> Indeed *all the prophets* from Samuel on, as many as have spo-
> ken, *have foretold these days*. And you are heirs of the prophets
> and of the covenant God made with your fathers. He said to
> Abraham, 'through your offspring all peoples on earth will be
> blessed.' When God raised up his servant, he sent him first to

you to bless you by turning each of you from your wicked ways. (Our italics.)

And again in Galatians chapter 3 where Paul is writing to the gentiles: 'The scripture foresaw that God would justify the Gentiles by faith, and *announced the gospel in advance to Abraham:* "All nations will be blessed through you"' (Gal 3:8, our italics).

Jew and Gentile alike are heirs of God's promise to Abraham through faith in the Lord Jesus Christ. The law came along 430 years after the promise was made. Paul explains it like this:

> The law, introduced 430 years later, does not set aside the covenant previously established by God and thus do away with the promise. For if the inheritance depends on the law, then it no longer depends on a promise; but God in his grace gave it to Abraham through a promise.
>
> *What then, was the purpose of the law?* It was added because of transgressions until the seed to whom the promise referred had come. The law was put into effect through angels by a mediator. A mediator, however, does not represent just one party; but God is one.
>
> Is the law, therefore, opposed to the promises of God? Absolutely not! For if a law had been given that could impart life, then righteousness would certainly have come by the law. But the scripture declares that the whole world is a prisoner of sin, so that what was promised, being given through faith in Jesus Christ, might be given to those who believe.
>
> Before this faith came, we were held prisoners by the law, locked up until faith should be revealed. *So the law was put in charge to lead us to Christ, that we might be justified by faith.* Now that faith has come, we are no longer under the supervision of the law. (Gal 3:17–25, our italics.)

Atonement

If the law has done its job well, then, it has made us 'conscious of sin' (Rom 3:20). This sin holds us trapped and renders us incapable of meeting the law's demands. Only as we understand our totally powerless state can we begin to appreciate the gift of God's grace. Justice demands that a price be paid for sin – a price we cannot pay ourselves because we are powerless. The demands of justice were met fully in Jesus Christ who 'bore our sins in his body on the tree, so that we might die to sins and live in righteousness; by his wounds you have been healed' (1 Pet 2:24).

Consider the process being described by Peter. First, Christ bore our sins. Isaiah describes graphically what is meant here: 'But he was pierced for our transgressions, he was crushed for our iniquities; the punishment that brought us peace was upon him' (Is 53:5). God does not turn a blind eye to our sins. He deals with them by punishing his own Son on our behalf that we might not have to face punishment. 'Christ redeemed us from the curse of the law by becoming a curse for us' (Gal 3:13). Paul says that all who 'have been justified through faith...have peace with God' (Rom 5:1).

Secondly, Peter says that through faith in Jesus we die to sin and live a new, righteous life. We are cut off from sin because in Jesus, sin and death are conquered. Paul describes it like this:

> Don't you know that all of us who were baptised into Christ Jesus were baptised into his death? We were therefore buried with him through baptism into death in order that, just as Christ was raised from the dead through the glory of the Father, we too may live a new life...We know that our old self was crucified with him so that the body of sin might be done away with, and we should no longer be slaves to sin – because anyone who has died has been freed from sin. (Romans 6:3–7.)

Through faith in Christ we are 'born again'. Our original birth was as descendants of Adam, who fell, and 'the result of one trespass was condemnation for all men' (Rom 5:18). Our 'new birth' (1 Pet 1:3) makes us children of God and we 'received the Spirit of sonship' (Rom 8:15).

Speaking of his own experience of coming from law to grace, Paul wrote to the Philippian church of 'not having a righteousness of my own that comes from the law, but that which is through faith in Christ – the righteousness that

comes from God and is by faith' (Phil 3:9). We have said that
the prophets testified to this righteousness that is to be had by
faith, apart from law. They also enjoyed, by faith, the benefits
of that righteousness for 'by faith Noah, when warned about
things not yet seen, in holy fear built an ark to save his family.
By his faith he condemned the world and became heir of the
righteousness that comes by faith' (Heb 11:7).

Speaking of his fellow Jews, Paul lamented their blindness
to the truth, saying, 'I have great sorrow and unceasing
anguish in my heart. For I could wish that I myself were
cursed and cut off for the sake of my brothers, those of my
own race' (Rom 9:2–3). We yearn, as did Paul, for the salvation
of our brothers and sisters – in our case, Mormons – and
observe with him:

> That the Gentiles, who did not pursue righteousness, have
> obtained it, a righteousness that is by faith; but Israel, who pur-
> sued a law of righteousness, has not attained it. Why not?
> Because they pursued it not by faith but as if it were by
> works...
>
> Brothers my heart's desire and prayer to God for the
> Israelites is that they may be saved. For I can testify that they
> are zealous for God, but their zeal is not based on knowledge.
> Since they did not know the righteousness that comes from
> God and sought to establish their own, they did not submit to
> God's righteousness. *Christ is the end of the law so that there
> may be righteousness for everyone who believes.* (Romans
> 9:30–32; 10:1, our italics.)

It has been said that Mormons out-Hebrew the Hebrews in
their pursuit of righteousness by 'the law of the gospel'.
Fervently believing that their efforts gain them eternal
rewards, they work the treadmill of obedience never knowing
the certain hope of the normal Christian life. Tragically, they
fail to see that the 'celestial' quality of life for which they strive
is a gift of God: 'For the wages of sin is death, but the gift of
God is eternal life in Christ Jesus our Lord' (Rom 6:23).

New life and James chapter 2

The objection that is always raised at this point is: 'But what about our works? Surely we have to be obedient. You make it sound as if you can do as you like.' Paul deals with this very question: 'What then? Shall we sin because we are not under the law but under grace?' (Rom 6:15). He eloquently explains that it is as if we were all married to the law (Rom 7:1–3) and goes on to tell us that we 'died to the law through the body of Christ, that you might belong to another, to him who was raised from the dead, in order that we might bear fruit for God' (Rom 7:4).

Through trusting in Christ and his death for us on the cross, we are released from that relationship with the law in order that we might enter into a relationship with Jesus and so bear fruit for God. 'When we were controlled by the sinful nature...we bore fruit for death' (Rom 7:5), but 'by dying to what once bound us, we have been released from the law so that we serve in the new way of the Spirit, and not in the old way of the written code' (Rom 7:6).

There are two positions then. We are either married to the law or to Christ; we are either controlled by the sinful nature or by the Spirit; we either bear fruit for death or for God. When we are controlled by sin we can no more help sinning than we can breathing. By the same token, when we are controlled by the Spirit we cannot help but be righteous. Peter points out that through the glory and goodness of God, 'he has given us his very great and precious promises, so that through them you may participate in the divine nature and escape the corruption in the world caused by evil desires' (2 Pet 1:4). Once we tried in our own strength to please God, striving to obey every part of the code – and failing. Now by faith in Christ 'it is God who works in you to will and to do according to his good purpose' (Phil 2:13).

When we fail in our obedience we need to go to the root of the problem which is not what we do but in whom we have believed. It is significant that when Jesus was asked, 'What must we do to do the works God requires?' 'Jesus answered,

"The work is this: to believe in the one he has sent'" (Jn 6:28–29).

In the light of all this, what are we to make of James' teaching on works? 'What good is it my brothers, if a man claims to have faith but has no deeds? Can such faith save him?' (Jas 2:14). The whole of James chapter 2 is about faith not works. James is comparing the kind of faith that leads to action with the kind that is only intellectual. He says, 'Can *such faith* save him?' or, 'Could *that sort of faith* save anyone's soul?' (*Philips Modern English Bible*, our italics). The King James Bible, which Mormons favour, is singularly unhelpful at this point, asking the question, 'Can faith save him?' This suggests to a Mormon that faith is being contrasted with deeds.

However, James goes on to say, 'Show me *your faith* without deeds, and I will show you *my faith* by what I do' (Jas 2:18, our italics). James is comparing the kind of faith that saves you with the kind of faith that does not. Using the example of Abraham he says, 'You see that his faith and his actions were working together, and *his faith* was made complete by what he did' (Jas 2:22, our italics).

Although James says, 'You see that a person is justified by what he does and not by faith alone' (Jas 2:24), he is not saying that works save us or gain us favour in God's sight. True faith is not indolent but leads to works: the fruit of the right kind of faith – saving faith.

Using the same example of Abraham, Paul clarifies the matter:

> We have been saying that Abraham's faith was credited to him as righteousness. Under what circumstances was it credited? Was it after he was circumcised or before? It was not after, but before! And he received the sign of circumcision, a seal of the righteousness that he had *by faith* while he was still uncircumcised. (Romans 4:9–11, our italics.)

Abraham was counted righteous in God's sight because he believed, long before he obeyed. His obedience was a seal on what he already owned – a righteousness he had *by faith*. This faith led to good works, but it was the faith that saved him, not the works. As J.I. Packer said, 'What saves is faith alone, but that faith that saves is never alone.'

Consider God's judgement: 'The Lord does not look at the things man looks at. Man looks at the outward appearance, but the Lord looks at the heart' (1 Sam 16:7). When it comes to works, it is humanity that looks at them. God does not need to see us do things in order to judge us. He already knows us in our hearts – from where our actions come. When we turn to Christ in faith our hearts are put right within us and we are judged righteous 'not by works, so that no-one can boast. For we are God's workmanship, created in Christ Jesus [the new birth] to do good works which God prepared in advance for us to do' (Eph 2:9–10). With Paul we may say, 'I have been crucified with Christ and I no longer live, but Christ lives in me. The life I live in the body, I live *by faith* in the Son of God, who loved me and gave himself for me (Gal 2:20, our italics).

Notes

1. Joseph Fielding Smith, *Doctrines of Salvation*, Vol. 1, pp 13–14.
2. *Journal of Discourses*, Vol. 9, p 305, our italics.
3. As above, Vol. 10, p 50.
4. The Book of Mormon, Mosiah 3:19.
5. Hugh B. Brown, April 1964 General Conference.
6. *Discourses of Brigham Young*, p 103, our brackets.
7. Joseph Fielding Smith, same source, Vol. 1, pp 113–14.
8. George Q. Morris, Conference Report, April 1958, p 38.
9. Joseph Fielding Smith, same source, Vol. 1, p 91.
10. George Q. Morris, Conference Report, April 1958, p 39.
11. *Gospel Essential Manual*, 1979, p 15.
12. Marion G. Romney, *Ensign* magazine, May 1982, pp 8–9, our italics.
13. *Gospel Essentials Manual*, 1979, p 15, our italics.
14. John Taylor, *Mediation and Atonement*, pp 178,181.
15. Joseph Fielding Smith, Conference Report, October 1899, p 41, our italics.
16. James E. Talmage, *The Articles of Faith*, 1977, p 91.
17. Edwin O. Haroldson, *Ensign* magazine, August 1995, p 10.

Chapter 15
The Book of Mormon

The Book of Mormon claims to be an account of three major civilisations of ancient America. The earliest civilisation was called the Jaredite. These people came from the lands of the Tower of Babel to America shortly after the Tower was destroyed. The second civilisation was called the Nephite. This group left Jerusalem in about 600 BC. Their record comprises the majority of the book. The third civilisation was called the Mulekite. This group left Jerusalem in approximately 588 BC.

The Book of Mormon was written by many ancient prophets of these people. They were commanded to keep a record of their ministry, their teachings of Christ, and the religious history of their people. They kept the record on metal plates and handed it down from one generation to the next. After Christ's death, resurrection and ascension, the Book of Mormon records that he visited the ancient inhabitants of America and taught them the same things he had taught in Israel, including the Sermon on the Mount. During his visit he appointed twelve apostles and organised his church. He then ascended to his Father in heaven.

By the year 421 AD, the dark-skinned people, known as Lamanites, had destroyed all the white Nephites in a number of great battles. The prophet Mormon abridged the major portion of the plates into a single record. The record, on gold plates, was buried by his son Moroni, the last living Nephite, in the hill Cumorah. In 1827 Joseph Smith claimed to have uncovered these same gold plates near his home in upstate New York. Their hiding place had been revealed to him by Moroni, who appeared to him as an angel. With the plates was a breastplate with two stones, called the Urim and Thummim, which enabled Joseph to translate the record on the plates. This record was published as the Book of Mormon in 1830.

The true source

Every poor farmer in upstate New York believed there was buried treasure in his land which would rescue his family from their deprivation. Joseph Smith was well known for seeking it out, and was even paid by some people to help them find it. Like many money-diggers he used a peep-stone and various other 'tools of the trade'. His family's farm was mortgaged, and payments were increasingly difficult to meet.

The area was dotted with ancient burial mounds, filled with skeletons and artefacts of stone, copper and, sometimes silver. There was much speculation as to who they were and why they had been buried in such mass graves. The theory was that the people in the mounds were a race of farmers and metalworkers who had been exterminated by a bloodthirsty race that was the ancestor of the American Indians.

Joseph, with his fertile imagination, loved to invent stories about them. His mother wrote:

> He would describe the ancient inhabitants of this continent, their dress, mode of travelling, and the animals upon which they rode; their cities, their buildings, with every particular; their mode of warfare; and also their religious worship. This he would do with as much ease, seemingly, as if he had spent his whole life with them.[1]

A Palmyra newspaper reported in 1821 that diggers on the Erie Canal had unearthed several brass plates, along with skeletons and fragments of pottery. The *Wayne Sentinel*, 1 June 1827, published an account of a discovery of a Mexican manuscript in hieroglyphics, which was considered proof that originally the Mexicans and Egyptians 'had intercourse with each other, and...had the same system of mythology'.[2]

It is likely that Joseph Smith thought that he could publish his stories and perhaps make enough money to save the mortgage on the family farm. His claim that it was a translation from an ancient record on metal plates, written in hieroglyphics, would add to the excitement and attraction of the book. The idea that the language was a form of Egyptian was clever because at the time Egyptian was thought to be indecipherable. The grammar from the Rosetta stone was not published until 1837.

The Bible

The Book of Mormon is claimed to be a companion to the Bible and another testament of Jesus Christ. 'It is the American volume of scripture and is just as sacred and inspired as is the Bible, which contains the sacred records of the Hebrew race on the Eastern Hemisphere.'[3]

Where the two volumes disagree, the Book of Mormon is accepted over the Bible.

> The Book of Mormon contains a number of quotations from the ancient Jewish scriptures...In the case of such passages there is no essential difference between Biblical and Book of Mormon versions, except in instances of probable error in translation – usually apparent through inconsistency or lack of clearness in the Biblical reading.[4]

Fullness of the gospel

Joseph Smith said that the Book of Mormon is 'the most correct of any book on earth, and the keystone of our religion, and a man would get nearer to God by abiding by its precepts, than by any other book'.[5] Twice in the Doctrine and Covenants we read that the fullness of the gospel is found within the Book of Mormon: 'the Book of Mormon; which contains a record of a fallen people, and the fulness of the gospel of Jesus Christ to the Gentiles and to the Jews also';[6] 'Moroni, whom I have sent to you to reveal the Book of Mormon, containing the fulness of my everlasting gospel.'[7]

In view of the above, why does the Book of Mormon contain nothing about many key Mormon doctrines? For example:

God is an exalted man with a body of flesh and bones, the plurality of gods, the pre-existence, priesthood organisation, temple marriage, three degrees of glory. These were all added later by Joseph Smith in the Doctrine and Covenants, or elsewhere in his teachings.

Some of these teachings actually conflict with the Book of Mormon. For example:

Teachings of the Prophet Joseph Smith, compiled by Joseph Fielding Smith, 1979, p. 345: 'God himself was once as we are now, and is an exalted man.' The Book of Mormon says: 'for do we not read that God is the same yesterday, today and forever, and in him there is no variableness neither shadow of changing' (Mormon 9:9).

Teachings of the Prophet Joseph Smith, compiled by Joseph Fielding Smith, 1979, p. 346: 'you have got to learn how to be Gods yourselves, and to be kings and priests to God, the same as all Gods have done before you, namely by going from one small degree to another.' This again is denied in the Book of Mormon: 'And now, behold, this is the doctrine of Christ, and the only true doctrine of the Father, and the Son, and of the Holy Ghost, which is one God, without end, Amen' (2 Nephi 31:21).

Changes

There have been nearly 4,000 changes to the Book of Mormon, not all of them punctuation, spelling and grammar. Many of them are key doctrinal changes, and they are still going on. As recently as 1978 they changed 'white and delightsome' to 'pure and delightsome' where the Book of Mormon promises Lamanites that their curse of dark skin will be lifted if they repent. This was because modern-day Lamanites who join the church plainly do not change colour.

> Both the 1840 and the 1842 editions [of the Book of Mormon] were carefully revised by Joseph Smith. In Mosiah 21:28 and Ether 4:1 the first edition had 'Benjamin' where the name Mosiah now appears...In the 1837 edition, the Prophet Joseph Smith made this correction.[8]

In the 1830 edition of the Book of Mormon, 1 Nephi 11:18 says, 'Behold, the virgin which thou seest, is the mother of God, after the manner of the flesh.' 1 Nephi 11:21 says, 'And the angel said to me, behold the Lamb of God, yea, even the Eternal Father!' And 1 Nephi 13:40 says, 'And shall make known to all kindreds, tongues, and people, that the Lamb of God is the Eternal father and the Saviour of the world.' However, in the 1981 edition, these verses read: 'is the mother of the *Son of* God'; 'even the *Son of* the Eternal Father!' and 'that the Lamb of God is the *Son of* the Eternal Father' respectively. Didn't God really know who Jesus was?

Archaeological evidence

Mormons claim that the Book of Mormon is authenticated by archaeological evidence. No such evidence has been found:

- 1 Nephi 1:2 and Mosiah 1:4 state that the native language of the Hebrews between 600 and 130 BC was Egyptian. Archaeological discoveries show that they spoke Hebrew prior to the Babylonian captivity of 586–538 BC, and then the common language became Aramaic.

- 1 Nephi 18:24 mentions seeds which were supposed to have been brought from the land of Jerusalem to America where they were blessed in abundance. No trace of these crops is found until after the Europeans brought them much later.

- Alma 11:4–19 mentions eight different coins, not one example of which has ever been discovered.

- Ether 9:18,19 mentions a number of animals for which there is no evidence of their existence at the time. It also mentions cureloms and cumoms as animals that were especially useful for man. Nobody even knows what they are!

The Smithsonian Institute in Washington has had so many requests from people believing that there is archaeological evidence, and that the Book of Mormon has been used by the

Institute for their research, that they have issued an official disclaimer:

> The Smithsonian Institution has never used the Book of Mormon in any way as a scientific guide. Smithsonian archaeologists see no connection between the archaeology of the New World and the subject matter of the Book.[9]

The word of God?

The Book of Mormon convinces many people because it sounds like the word of God. This is because it contains large sections lifted directly from the Bible, and many biblical truths are interwoven with falsehood. It is also written in the same form of language as the King James Authorised Version of the Bible, and Mormons are instructed to use only this version. Once you realise this, its apparent spiritual charm is broken.

Notes

1. Lucy Smith, *Biographical Sketches*, p 85, quoted in Fawn M. Brodie, *No Man Knows My History*, 1966, p 35.
2. Fawn M. Brodie, same source, p 50.
3. Joseph Fielding Smith, *Doctrines of Salvation*, Vol. 3, p 209.
4. James E. Talmage, *The Articles of Faith*, p 274.
5. Joseph Smith, History of the Church 4:461.
6. Doctrine and Covenants 20:8,9.
7. Doctrine and Covenants 27:5.
8. George Horton, *Ensign* magazine, December 1983, pp 24–28, our brackets.
9. Jerald and Sandra Tanner, *Mormonism: Shadow or Reality?*, 1982, p 97.

Chapter 16
Priesthood

> Members of the priesthood belong to the greatest fraternity,
> the greatest brotherhood in all the world – the brotherhood of
> Christ – and they have the obligation to do their best each day,
> all day, and to maintain the standards of the priesthood.[1]

Thus spoke David O. McKay, ninth president of the
church, on the subject of the priesthood. The Mormon
concept of priesthood is formal and definite. It is the power
and authority to act for God, to administer gospel ordinances
and spiritual blessings. This authority presides in, and is
exclusive to, the Mormon church. All authority outside the
church is seen as presumed or usurped and totally ineffectual
in the administration of God's rule.

Joseph F. Smith, the church's sixth president, clearly
defined the nature and purpose of priesthood:

> What is the Priesthood? It is nothing more nor less than the
> power of God delegated to man by which man can act in the
> earth for the salvation of the human family...and act legiti-
> mately; not assuming that authority, nor borrowing it from gen-
> erations that are dead and gone, but authority that has been
> given in this day in which we live by ministering angels and
> spirits from above, direct from the presence of Almighty
> God...It is the same power and Priesthood that was committed
> to the disciples of Christ while he was upon the earth, that
> whatsoever they should bind on earth should be bound in
> heaven, and that whatsoever they should loose on earth should
> be loosed in heaven.[2]

John Taylor further explained that priesthood is the governing principle and power, not only on earth, but in heaven:

> What is priesthood?...it is the government of God, whether in the earth, or in the heavens, for it is by that power, agency, or principle, that all things are governed on the earth and in the heavens, and by that power that all things are upheld and sustained.[3]

The Mormon priesthood is not to be underestimated for, as we will see, it is central to every church member's life. Every activity, from a simple family event to a conference of the whole church, is presided over by one with priesthood authority. The effects of such an all-pervasive priesthood are far reaching.

Key words in the foregoing definitions are 'power', 'authority' and 'government'. In the earliest days of the church, Joseph Smith, a man described as a natural organiser, developed a unique concept of priesthood – one that would naturally draw men to him and win their loyalty. By 'democratically' sharing the power and authority to govern with his followers – under Joseph's ultimate authority – he satisfied men's natural thirst for power while keeping them submitted to his own autocratic rule. Fawn Brodie describes it well in her biography of Joseph Smith:

> Joseph's clergy was...entirely composed of laymen; moreover, of practically all the laymen in his church. The result was a pyramidal church structure resting on the broadest possible base and possessing astonishing strength. By giving each man a share in the priesthood Joseph quickened a sense of kinship and oneness in the church.
>
> What Joseph had created was essentially an evangelical socialism...Nearly every man had a New Testament title – deacon, teacher, priest, elder, 'seventy', or bishop. Each title carried a certain rank, progression from lower to higher being dependent upon a man's faith, his zeal for the church, and the good will of his superiors in the hierarchy. Each convert had not only the dignity of a title but the duties attending it. He was expected to work strenuously for the church, and he did. His

only recompense, and it was ample, was a conviction that he was furthering the work of the Lord in the last days.[4]

Today's priesthood holder enjoys the same privileges, and the initiation of a new convert into this 'fraternity' is a very solemn affair, leaving the initiate in no doubt as to his new status in 'the only true church on the face of the earth'.

Authority in the church

If the Priesthood is executive power the authority structure of the church reflects this, with the President or Prophet having complete authority. He is said to have all the 'keys' of the kingdom and delegation of authority is described as 'conferring the keys' of a particular office.

The top echelon of the church is very much a power structure and can be likened to that at the top of a large corporation. At the top you have the President, or chief executive. He is assisted by two Counsellors, or Vice Presidents. Below them is the council of the Twelve Apostles who may be looked upon as the board of directors. Further down the scale is the council of Seventy who, along with the Presiding Bishopric, might be the senior executives.

President
(Chief Executive)

Counsellor 1   Counsellor 2
(Vice Presidents)

Council of The Twelve
(Board of Directors)

Council of Seventy and Presiding Bishopric
(Senior Executives)

Given the size of the Corporation of The Church of Jesus Christ of Latter-day Saints (a legitimate title), which has an estimated daily income from tithes alone of 11 million dollars, it is clear that these men wield the kind of power found at the top of any of the leading corporations in the world today.

Cynics both in and out of the church have suggested that,
behind the ecclesiastical titles, this is really what the church is
all about.

The priesthood line of authority

The lowliest male saint is, dependent on worthiness, ordained
to the priesthood. Indeed, priesthood can only be conferred by
the laying on of hands by one already having authority. When
advanced to the Melchizedek Priesthood he is presented with
his Line of Authority tracing an unbroken genealogy back
through previous generations of ordinations to Joseph Smith
and Oliver Cowdery and through them to Peter, James and
John and ultimately Jesus Christ.

As a priesthood holder he can be called to certain responsibilities in the church by those who hold higher office than
himself – the Bishop or his Quorum President. It is every worthy Mormon's goal to serve the church and a call to service is
often seen as an advancement as, along with the call, come the
'keys' or authority.

'Uninitiated' non-Mormons are ignorant of what they are
asking of their Mormon friends when they suggest that they
leave the church. Here is an organised church in the fullest
sense of the word. More than a place to attend, it is a place to
belong. Mormons may not be fully aware of the hold such a
system has on them but it gets under one's skin. Being a
Mormon is frequently an enriching experience and holding
the priesthood, the very power that is wielded in the heaven-
lies, is seen as making one rich indeed.

Two orders of priesthood

There are two orders of priesthood in the church.

Aaronic Priesthood

The Aaronic Priesthood is named after Aaron and 'has power
in administering outward ordinances'.[5] Simply put this means
attending to baptisms, collecting tithes and offerings, administering sacraments and generally attending to 'temporal'
affairs.

Melchizedek Priesthood

The Melchizedek Priesthood is named after Melchizedek because, like Melchizedek king of Salem, it is said to be an eternal priesthood without beginning of days or end of life. (Hebrews chapter 7 is believed to refer to Jesus' priesthood not Jesus himself.) This is the presiding priesthood of the church, fully God's authority, to which the Aaronic, or lesser priesthood, is subject. This priesthood is said to

> [hold] the mysteries of the revelations of God. Wherever that priesthood exists, there also exists a knowledge of the laws of God; and wherever the gospel has existed, there has always been revelation; and where there has been no revelation, there never has been the true gospel.[6]

The Melchizedek Priesthood, then, is the key to 'revelation knowledge'.

Personal worthiness

Personal worthiness is essential to the effective operation of priesthood power. Apostle Boyd K. Packer has said, 'Your authority comes through your ordination; your power comes through obedience and worthiness.'[7] President Spencer W. Kimball stated that there 'is no limit to the power of the priesthood which you hold. The limit comes in you if you do not live in harmony with the Spirit of the Lord and limit yourselves in the power you exert'.[8]

While personal worthiness is as important to any Christian, for a Mormon all blessings are predicated upon it, a constant theme the reader will notice throughout this book. This raises the question of whether the Mormon can ever truly know God's grace, or undeserved love, in his life.

The priesthood holder and the Bible

Mormons are taught, and believe, that the priesthood of their church is typical of that found in the Bible. They also believe that the organisations of the Christian churches are disordered to the point of chaos for lack of proper priesthood authority, and that they bear no resemblance to the biblical model.

In speaking of priesthood and the Bible, the average Mormon's first point of reference will be Hebrews chapter 5, verse 4. Applying this reference to the Mormon priesthood they will insist that authority to act for God must be conferred. Priesthood holders must be called of God, 'just as Aaron was'. Aaron, they will point out, was called by a living prophet, Moses, and by the laying on of hands. They will then direct you to Exodus chapter 28. As their church is, indeed, led by a 'living prophet' it follows that it is in that church that the authority of God will be found today.

Hebrews chapters 5–10

It is true that 'Every high priest is selected from among men and is appointed to represent them in matters related to God, to offer gifts and sacrifices for sins' (Heb 5:1). It is also true that 'No-one takes this honour upon himself; he must be called by God, just as Aaron was' (Heb 5:4). The next three words give us the true intent of the writer: 'So Christ also.' It is the calling of Jesus that is being compared with the calling of Aaron. It is the high priesthood of Jesus that is being compared with the high priesthood of the Old Testament: 'Just as Aaron...So Christ also.'

Mormons will argue that if Jesus himself could not take the honour upon himself then neither can we. A good point, but irrelevant in this context. The writer is making a clear comparison as already shown. The natural question is 'How does Jesus' priesthood compare with the priesthood of the Old Testament?' It is in answering that question that true biblical priesthood is understood.

The Old Testament priest, the writer tells us in Hebrews chapter 5 verses 1–3:

- Was called of God as was Aaron
- Represented people in matters related to God
- Offered gifts and sacrifices for sins
- Identified with the weaknesses of the people so as to deal gently with those who are ignorant and are going astray.

We find all the above qualities in Christ who:

- Was called of God as was Aaron – 'But God said to him, "You are my Son; today I have become your Father." And he says in another place, "You are a priest forever, in the order of Melchizedek"' (Heb 5:5–6).

- Represented people in matters related to God – 'Therefore he is able to save completely those who come to God through him, because he always lives to intercede for them' (Heb 7:25).

- Offered gifts and sacrifices for sins – 'He offered up prayers and petitions with loud cries and tears to the one who could save him from death, and he was heard because of his reverent submission. Although he was a son he learned obedience from what he suffered and, once made perfect, he became the source of salvation for all who obey him' (Heb 5:7–10).

- Identified with the people: 'For we do not have a high priest who is unable to sympathise with our weaknesses, but we have one who has been tempted in every way, just as we are – yet was without sin' (Heb 4:15).

The same but different

The writer goes on to tell us about significant differences between Old Testament priests and Christ. These differences explain the role of Jesus as our mediator with God. To miss this is to miss the point of the gospel story.

Hebrews 10:1–3 tells how inadequate the law was to bring freedom from guilt and sin. Therefore, when Christ came into the world, he said: "Sacrifice and offering you did not desire, but a body you prepared for me; with burnt offerings and sin offerings you were not pleased."...Then he said, "Here I am, I have come to do your will"' (Heb 10:5–6). The sacrifices of the high priests were not pleasing to God because they were temporal and temporary. They had to be repeated as a reminder of sins but were unable to take away sins (Heb 10:1–3). So Jesus, as a high priest called of God, offered a sacrifice that was sufficient. Having offered himself, *'He sets aside the first to establish the second'* (Heb 10:9).

What is the first he sets aside? The priesthood of Aaron. It is made redundant at the cross because

> Day after day every high priest *stands* and performs his religious duties; *again and again* he offers the same sacrifices, which can never take away sins. But when this priest had offered for all time *one sacrifice* for sins, he *sat down* at the right hand of God...by one sacrifice he has made perfect for ever those who are being made holy. (Hebrews 10:11–14.)

What is the second for which the first is set aside? The priesthood of Jesus who is 'a priest forever in the order of Melchizedek' (Heb 5:6). That word 'forever' is very significant.

The nature of the Aaronic Priesthood is temporary. While the whole tribe of Levites had responsibilities in the tabernacle, one family was set apart for special service – the family of Aaron. They were the priests. While a whole family were priests, only one man served as high priest. There was only ever one high priest at a time. Sacrifices had to be offered 'again and again' by high priests who died and had to be replaced.

The nature of the Melchizedek Priesthood is eternal. It is named after Melchizedek for this reason. Unlike the priests of Israel, Melchizedek has no recorded genealogy, making him 'timeless' and a 'type' of Jesus. Like Melchizedek, Jesus remains a priest for ever (Heb 7:3). His priesthood was not passed on.

> Now there have been many of those priests, since death prevented them from continuing in office; but because Jesus lives forever, he has a permanent priesthood. Therefore he is able to save completely those who come to God through him because he always lives to intercede for them. (Hebrews 7:23–24.)

The function of priesthood was to intercede for men before God. Jesus' sacrifice was once for all time, his priesthood is eternal, his intercession continuous.

Christian priesthood

In Exodus chapter 19, verse 6, Israel is called 'a kingdom of priests and a holy nation'. This idea is developed in the New Testament in relation to the church. Peter speaks of believers as being 'like living stones being built into a spiritual house to be a royal priesthood offering a spiritual sacrifice acceptable to God through Jesus Christ' (1 Pet 2:4–5). He goes on to say, 'You are a chosen people, a royal priesthood, a holy nation, a people belonging to God that you may declare the praises of him who called you out of darkness into his wonderful light' (1 Pet 2:9).

The Concise Dictionary of Christian Tradition points out that the New Testament uses 'priest' only in the plural to describe Christians, further pointing out that a Christian is not a priest individually but only in so far as he is a member of the people of God.

> The whole church is a priesthood...Believers offer sacrifices of praise to God and also intercede for human needs. The church in service of God in the world offers further spiritual sacrifice of obedience to God's will in the love of the neighbour.[9]

The church is the body of Christ and so it is only as a body that we are priests.

As a kingdom of priests we are:

- Called by God as was Aaron 'that you may declare the praises of him who called you out of darkness into his wonderful light' (1 Pet 2:9).

- To reflect the holiness of God and of our high priest: 'Let your light so shine before men, that they may see your good deeds and praise your Father in heaven' (Mt 5:16).

• To offer spiritual sacrifices acceptable to God: 'You...are...a holy priesthood, offering spiritual sacrifices acceptable to God' (1 Pet 2:5).

• To intercede for man before God: 'Pray in the Spirit on all occasions with all kinds of prayers and requests. With this in mind, be alert and always keep on praying for all the saints' (Eph 6:18).

• To represent God before man: 'Therefore go and make disciples of all nations, baptising them in the name of the Father and of the Son and of the Holy Spirit, and teaching them to obey everything I have commanded you' (Mt 28:19–20).

Built on a foundation

Mormons see the church as an institution, an organisation. They teach that, in seeking the true church, we should look for the same 'organisation' found in the New Testament with its attendant officers. Pointing to Paul's letter to the Ephesians they commend a church 'built on the foundation of the apostles and prophets' (Eph 2:20) and 'having some to be apostles, some to be prophets, some to be evangelists, and some to be pastors and teachers.'

However, as we have already seen, the church is not an institution but a 'spiritual house' built of 'living stones'. We are collectively 'a royal priesthood'. The ministries described in Ephesians chapter 4 are not offices but functions by which individual members of this royal priesthood build the church. These ministries embody gifts enabling us to speak prophetically, preach the gospel, shepherd and teach the saints. This, then, is the true priesthood of God, and it is operational in the Christian church today in its varied expressions.

Notes

1. David O. McKay, 'Priesthood', *Instructor*, October 1968, p 379.
2. Joseph Fielding Smith, *Gospel Doctrine*, pp 139–40.
3. John Taylor, *The Gospel Kingdom*, p 129.
4. Fawn M. Brodie, *No Man Knows My History*, 1966, pp 100–01.
5. John Taylor, same source, p 155.
6. As above, p 139.
7. Boyd K. Packer, *That All May Be Edified*, p 29.
8. *Teachings of Spencer W. Kimball*, p 498.
9. Douglas, Elwell & Toon, *The Concise Dictionary of Christian Tradition*, Marshall Pickering, 1989, p 305.

Chapter 17

Pardon Me, Elder, But Would You Care To Repeat That?

The importance of the Mormon 'testimony' cannot be over-stated. It is the Mormons' last bastion of safety in any discussion. The most common response Mormons will give to an attack on their faith by an appeal to the facts is their testimony. Of course, this does not make the facts go away but it does make Mormons feel virtuous for having a testimony in the face of the facts, and removes the problem of having to face those facts. It is almost as though they are saying, 'we don't care what is written, or what reason makes of it, we have a testimony.' Facts only interest Mormons so long as those facts serve them. When they cease to serve they are ignored in favour of feelings: 'It must be true, I have a testimony.'

A Mormon testimony is the ultimate delusion and a denial of the facts. This chapter is about those facts that Mormons so often testify away as though of no importance. However, they are important because they show the real confusion and the plethora of contradictions that is Mormonism. Italics are added in the following quotes to highlight the differences.

GOD – one or many?

The Bible

'You are my witnesses! Is there any God beside me? *No, there is no other Rock; I know not one*' (Is 44:8).

The Book of Mormon

'And Zeezrom said unto him: "Thou sayest there is a true and living God?"
And Amulek said: "Yea, there is a true and living God."
Now Zeezrom said: *"Is there more than one God?"*
And he answered, *"No"'* (Alma 11:26–29).

The Pearl of Great Price

'I am the Lord God Almighty...*There is no God beside me'*
(Moses 1:3–6).

'And *I, God* said: "Let there be light"; and there was light.
And *I, God* saw the light; and that light was good. And *I, God*
divided the light from the darkness' (Moses 2:3–4).

'And *they (the Gods)* said: "Let there be light"; and there was light.
And *they (the Gods)* comprehended the light, for it was bright;
and they divided the light from the darkness' (Abraham 4:3–4).

Doctrine and Covenants

'Then shall they be gods, because they have all power...they
have entered into their exaltation, according to the promises,
and sit upon thrones, *and are not angels but are gods'* (Section
132:20,37).

GOD – a spirit?

The Bible

'God is spirit' (Jn 4:24).

The Book of Mormon

'And the king said: "Is God that *Great Spirit* that brought our
fathers out of the land of Jerusalem?"
And Aaron said unto him: "Yea, he is that *Great Spirit"'* (Alma
22:9–10).

Doctrine and Covenants
'*The Father has a body of flesh and bones* as tangible as man's' (Section 130:22).

GOD – dwells in hearts?
The Book of Mormon
'The Lord hath said he dwelleth not in unholy temples, but *in the hearts of the righteous doth he dwell*' (Alma 34:36).

Doctrine and Covenants
The idea that the Father and the Son dwell in a man's heart *is an old sectarian notion, and is false*' (Section 130:3).

GOD – cannot lie?
The Bible
'He who is the Glory of Israel *does not lie*' (1 Sam 15:29).

The Book of Mormon
'Yea Lord, I know that...thou art a God of truth, and *canst not lie*' (Ether 3:12).
'*Woe unto the liar*, for he shall be thrust down to hell' (2 Nephi 9:34).

The Pearl of Great Price
'*The Lord said* unto me: "Behold, Sarai, thy *wife*, is a very fair woman to look upon;
Let her say unto the Egyptians, *she is thy sister*, and thy soul shall live"' (Abraham 2:22,24).

GOD – decrees unalterable?
The Bible
'He who is the Glory of Israel does not lie *or change his mind*' (1 Sam 15:29).

The Book of Mormon
'Now the decrees of God are *unalterable*' (Alma 41:8).

Doctrine and Covenants

'Wherefore I, the Lord, *command and revoke*, as it seemeth me good…Wherefore, I *revoke the commandment*…and *give a new commandment*' (Section 56:4–5).

GOD – unchangeable?

The Bible

'I the Lord *do not change*' (Malachi 3:6).

The Book of Mormon

'For I know that God is not a partial God, *neither a changeable being*; but *he is unchangeable* from all eternity to all eternity' (Moroni 8:18).

Joseph Smith

For I am going to tell you *how God came to be God. We have imagined and supposed that God was God from all eternity. I will refute that idea*, and take away the veil, so that you may see' (Teachings of the Prophet Joseph Smith, p 345).

Jesus – born of the Spirit?

The Bible

'This is how the birth of Jesus Christ came about: His mother Mary…*was found to be with child through the Holy Spirit*…
An angel of the Lord appeared to him [Joseph] in a dream and said, "Joseph son of David, do not be afraid to take Mary home as your wife because what is conceived in her is from the Holy Spirit"' (Mt 1:18,20).

The Book of Mormon

She being a virgin, a precious and chosen vessel, *who shall be overshadowed and conceive by the power of the Holy Ghost,* and bring forth a son, yea, even the Son of God' (Alma 7:10).

Brigham Young

'Now remember from this time forth, and forever, that *Jesus Christ was not begotten by the Holy Ghost*' (Journal of Discourses, Vol. 1, p 51).

Man – made of the dust?
The Bible
'The Lord God *formed the man from the dust of the ground*' (Gen 2:7).

The Book of Mormon
'The Lord God sent our first parents forth from the garden of Eden, to till *the ground, from whence they were taken*' (Alma 42:2).

Doctrine and Covenants
'We are to understand that *God...formed man out of the dust of the earth*' (Section 77:12).

The Pearl of Great Price
'And I, the Lord God, *formed man from the dust of the ground*' (Moses 3:7).

Brigham Young
'You believe Adam was made of the dust of this earth. *This I do not believe, though it is supposed that it is written in the Bible; but it is not, to my understanding...I do not believe that portion of the Bible as the Christian world do*' (Journal of Discourses, Vol. 2, p 6).

Man – natural man an enemy of God?
The Bible
'*But the natural man receiveth not the things of the Spirit of God:* for they are foolishness unto him: neither can he know them, *because they are spiritually discerned*' (1 Cor 2:14, AV).

The Book of Mormon
'For *the natural man is an enemy to God*, and has been from the fall of Adam, and will be, forever and ever, *unless he yields to the enticings of the Holy Spirit*, and putteth off the natural man and becometh a saint through the atonement of Christ the Lord' (Mosiah 3:19).

Brigham Young

'Paul says, in his Epistle to the Corinthians, "But the natural man receiveth not the things of God." But I say *it is the unnatural man that receiveth not the things of God*' (Journal of Discourses, Vol. 9, p 305).

Man – sinful by nature?

The Bible

'As for you, you were dead in your transgressions and sins, in which you used to live when you followed the ways of this world...*Like the rest, we were by nature objects of wrath*' (Eph 2:1–3).

'*Surely I was sinful at birth, sinful from the time my mother conceived me*' (Ps 51:5).

Apostle Hugh B. Brown

'Our doctrine is positive and life affirming...*We refuse to believe*, with some churches of Christendom, that the biblical account of the fall of man records *the corruption of human nature or to accept the doctrine of original sin*' (April 1964 General Conference).

Man – fate sealed by death?

The Bible

'Just as man is destined once to die, *and after that face judgment*' (Heb 9:27).

The Book of Mormon

'For behold *this life is the time for men to prepare to meet God;* yea the day of this life is the day for men to perform their labours...for after this day of life...then cometh the night of darkness wherein there can be no labour performed.

Ye cannot say when ye come to that awful crisis, that I will repent, that I will return to my God. Nay ye cannot say this.

For behold, if you have procrastinated the day of your repentance even unto death, behold, ye have become subject to the spirit of the devil, and he doth seal you his...and the devil hath all power over you; *and this is the final state of the wicked'* (Alma 34:32–35).

Doctrine and Covenants

'Behold these are they...*who received not the testimony of Jesus in the flesh, but afterwards received it'* (Section 76:72,74).

Apostle Bruce R. McConkie

'*By accepting the gospel in the spirit world,* and because the ordinances of salvation and exaltation are performed vicariously in this world, *the worthy dead can become heirs of the fulness of the Father's kingdom'* (*Mormon Doctrine*, p 673).

Polygamy – right or wrong?

The Bible

'Now the overseer must be above reproach, *the husband of but one wife'* (1 Tim 3:2).
'An Elder must be blameless, *the husband of one wife'* (Titus 1:6).
'A deacon *must be the husband of but one wife'* (1 Tim 3:12).

The Book of Mormon

'Behold David and Solomon truly had many wives and concubines, *which thing was abominable before me, saith the Lord'* (Jacob 2:24).

Doctrine and Covenants

I, the Lord, *justified* my servants Abraham, Isaac, and Jacob, as also Moses, *David and Solomon,* my servants, *as touching the principle and doctrine of their having many wives and concubines'* (Section 132:1).
'If any man espouse a virgin, and desire to espouse another, and the first give her consent, and if he espouse the second, and they are virgins, and have vowed to no other man, *then he is justified; he cannot commit adultery'* (Section 132:61).

194 MORMONISM: A GOLD PLATED RELIGION

Forgiveness – can it be bought?

The Bible

'Come all you who are thirsty, come to the waters; *and you who have no money, come buy and eat! Come, buy wine and milk without money and without cost*' (Is 55:1; Mt 10:8; Rev 21:6).

The Book of Mormon

'Yea it shall come in a day when there shall be churches built up that shall say: "Come unto me, *and for your money you shall be forgiven sins.*"
O ye wicked and perverse and stiffnecked people, why have ye built up churches unto yourselves to get gain?' (Mormon 8:32).

Doctrine and Covenants

'Behold, now it is called today until the coming of the Son of man, and verily it is a day of sacrifice, and a day for the tithing of my people; *for he that is tithed shall not be burned at his coming*' (Section 64:23).

Adam – in new world or old world?

The Bible

'A river watering the garden flowed from Eden; from there it was separated into four waterheads. The name of the first is the Pishon; it winds throughout the entire land of *Havilah* [Arabia, compare Gen 10:29; 25:18]. The name of the second river is the *Gihon; it winds through the entire land of Cush [Ethiopia]*. The name of the third river is the *Tigris*...and the fourth river is the *Euphrates*' (Gen 2:10–14).

The Pearl of Great Price

'And the name of the second river is called Gihon; *the same that compasseth the whole land of Ethiopia*' (Moses 3:13).

Doctrine and Covenants

'Three years previous to the death of Adam he called Seth, Enos, Cainan, Mahalaleel, Jared, Enoch, and Methuselah...

with the residue of his posterity…into the valley of *Adam-ondi-Ahman*' (Section 107:53).

'Spring Hill [Davies County, Missouri] *is named by the Lord Adam-ondi-Ahman*' (Section 116).

It is noteworthy that the tenth president of the Mormon church, Joseph Fielding Smith, said of Joseph Smith: 'If his claims and declarations were built on fraud and deceit, there would appear many errors and contradictions, which would be easy to detect…The world has been unable to place a finger upon anything that is inconsistent, or out of harmony in the revelations to Joseph Smith, with that which has been revealed before, or predicted by the prophets and the Lord himself' (*Doctrines of Salvation*, Vol. 1, pp 188, 189).

Chapter 18

A Cultured Pearl — The Fall of the Book of Abraham

When Franklin D. Richards became president of the British Mission in 1850 he collected together materials that he felt would provide valuable instruction but which were not readily available. They were published in Liverpool in 1851, in a pamphlet called the 'Pearl of Great Price'. The next edition was revised and expanded in Utah, and was accepted as one of the church's standard works on 10 October 1880.[1]

The *Pearl of Great Price* consists of: the Book of Moses; the Book of Abraham; Joseph Smith – Matthew; Joseph Smith – History and the Articles of Faith of the Church of Jesus Christ of Latter-day Saints.

The Book of Moses and Joseph Smith – Matthew, are Joseph's writings interpreted in his own way from the Bible. The Book of Moses is a revision of Genesis chapters 1–6 and Joseph Smith – Matthew, is a revision of Matthew chapter 23, verse 39 and chapter 24.

Joseph Smith – History and the Articles of Faith, is an original writing by Joseph Smith.

The Book of Abraham

In 1835, Michael H. Chandler arrived in Kirtland, Ohio with his travelling exhibition of Egyptian mummies and papyrus scrolls. Having heard that Joseph Smith could translate from ancient records, he came to see him. Joseph examined the papyri and declared, 'I commenced the translation of some of the characters or hieroglyphics, and much to our joy found that one of the rolls contained the writings of Abraham, another the writings of Joseph of Egypt, etc.'[2]

The church purchased the mummies and papyri, and Joseph translated the Book of Abraham. This was published in 1842 in the *Times and Seasons*, along with three drawings from the scroll. No further work was done before Joseph died.

In Joseph Smith's day there was little or no knowledge of Egyptian hieroglyphics, so his ability as a translator could not be challenged. The Rosetta Stone, the key which unlocked Egyptian writing, was only discovered in 1799 and not deciphered until 1837, and very few scholars understood anything about it. By the time that some of the printed facsimiles from the Book of Abraham were challenged, the original papyri were not available for examination. They were believed to have been destroyed in a fire in Chicago in 1871. If this record was authentic, its value would be incalculable, for it would predate the record of Genesis in the Bible. (Genesis was written after the events it records had taken place.)[3]

Papyri found

Imagine the rejoicing, then, when the papyri were found. On 27 November 1967 the *Deseret News* announced:

> NEW YORK – A collection of pa[p]yrus manuscripts, long believed to have been destroyed in the Chicago fire of 1871, was presented to The Church of Jesus Christ of Latter-day Saints here Monday by the Metropolitan Museum of Art...
>
> Included in the papyri is a manuscript identified as the original document from which Joseph Smith had copied the drawing which he called 'Facsimile No. 1' and published with the Book of Abraham.

Since the papyri were originally translated by the prophet of the church, one would have expected the current prophet to use his gifts as 'seer and revelator' to complete the job. However, the papyri were given to Dr Hugh Nibley, who is supposed to be the top Mormon authority on the Egyptian language. Although he is a linguist with some knowledge of the

Egyptian language, he is by no means an expert. He called in Professor Dee Jay Nelson, a church member who is an expert.

The result of their studies was a great embarrassment to the church. Dr Nibley's first comments were: 'The papyri scripts given to the Church do not prove the Book of Abraham is true...LDS scholars are caught flat footed by this discovery.'[4] No full translation of the papyri was published in six years of work by Dr Nibley, only articles and eventually a book attempting to explain away what they did contain. Professor Nelson did translate the papyri, but the church declined to publish his findings. Eventually he withdrew his membership from the church.

Book of breathings

Egyptologists who have studied the papyri find no mention of Abraham or his religion, only the names of many pagan gods who were worshipped by the Egyptians. The drawing known as 'Facsimile No. 1' which Joseph Smith labelled 'Abraham fastened upon an altar', is actually a picture of an Egyptian named Hor being prepared for burial. The text on the papyri is an excerpt from the 'Book of Breathings'.

> The 'Book of Breathings' is one of a number of short funeral works...it was addressed to the deceased by the chief priest conducting the funeral service...The 'Book of Breathings' represents the attempt to include all essential elements of belief in a future life in a work shorter and more simple than the Book of the Dead...To give the work an enhanced value it was declared to be the production of Thoth, the scribe of the gods.[5]

The identity of the papyrus cannot be disputed because the name 'Book of Breathings' appears clearly on the fourth line of the fragment. This has been substantiated by several respected experts, including Dr Nibley![6]

Words count

Not only is there no comparison between the real translation of the papyrus text and the Book of Abraham, but there is an enormous difference in the number of words used. The average number of words that the Egyptologists use to convey the text is eighty-seven. The Book of Abraham has a total of one hundred and thirty-six verses divided between five chapters. Most of the verses are over twenty words long, some very long. This gives an estimate of at least 3,000 words!

Dr Nibley tried to explain this away by saying that Joseph Smith treated the characters as super-cryptograms. In other words, that they had hidden meanings. However, Professor Richard Parker stated that he knew of 'no Egyptologist who would support such a claim'[7] and the suggestion has since been dropped.

The only scriptural basis for the Mormon doctrine on negroes and the priesthood prior to 1978 is found in the Book of Abraham 1:21-27. With the discrediting of the Book of Abraham, there is now no basis for such a doctrine. Perhaps this led, in part, to the decision in 1978 to abandon it.

Credibility gap

Although many church members have had their faith shaken, the church has made no attempt to play down the Book of Abraham. It still appears in the Pearl of Great Price, and is still quoted to support church doctrine. Once again, there is a gap between the way the church portrays itself, and the way it actually operates. If the church is led by a 'prophet, seer and revelator', he should have been able to translate the papyri correctly in the first place, and the present prophet should be able to explain what was actually found.

Notes

1. Introductory note, The Pearl of Great Price.
2. Joseph Smith, History of the Church, Vol. 2, p 236.
3. Dr Sidney B. Sperry, *Ancient Records Testify in Papyrus and Stone*, 1938, p 39.
4. *The Daily Universe*, 1 December 1967, Brigham Young University.
5. E.A. Wallis Budge, *The Book of the Dead: Facsimiles of the Papyri of Hunefer, Anhai, Kerasher and Netchemet*, London, 1899, p 33.
6. Dr Hugh Nibley, *The Message of Joseph Smith Papyri: An Egyptian Endowment*, Deseret Book Company, 1975, p 20.
7. Professor Parker of the Department of Egyptology, Brown University, Letter to Marvin Cowan, 9 January 1968.

Chapter 19
Temples

Very early in the history of the Mormon church, in 1831, Joseph Smith claimed to have received a revelation in which the Lord promised that faithful saints would 'be endowed with power from on high'.[1] Around 1843–44 he taught that 'God gathers together His people in the last days, to build unto the Lord a house to prepare them for the ordinances and endowments, washings and anointings, etc.'[2]

The temple was to be

> A house whereby He could reveal unto His people the ordinances of His house and the glories of His kingdom, and teach the people the way of salvation; for there are certain ordinances and principles that, when they are taught and practiced, must be done in a place or house built for that purpose.[3]

Mormon temples are not chapels but the modern-day equivalent of the temple in the Old Testament. Mormons believe that the law of Moses finished with Christ who brought the law of the gospel. The work to be done in New Testament temples could only be revealed directly by God, in the same way that he revealed the rituals and sacrifices in the beginning. Because of the apostasy following Christ's death there was no priesthood authority to receive such revelations. Thus it could not be revealed until the church was restored through Joseph Smith.

The purposes of Mormon temples are twofold:

1. That faithful members of the church should receive endowments of knowledge and authority in order to qualify for a place in the highest heaven.
2. That they should receive the same vicariously on behalf of their dead forebears.

Salvation and exaltation

In order to understand the purpose of Mormon temples, we need to have a look at the Mormon theology of salvation and exaltation. Mormons believe that 'some degree of salvation will come to all who have not forfeited their right to it'.[4] Beyond that, Mormons believe that there are 'numerous degrees of exaltation' in heaven, known as degrees of glory. Faithfulness to Mormon doctrine qualifies a person to a place – the more faithful, the higher the degree. Indeed, one of the key functions of priesthood is to prepare oneself to pass the angels, who guard the way to heaven, by having the appropriate authority and secret signs.

This doctrine of degrees of glory is based on 1 Corinthians 15:40–42:

> There are also heavenly bodies and there are earthly bodies; but the splendour of the heavenly bodies is one kind, and the splendour of the earthly bodies is another. The sun has one kind of splendour, the moon another, and the stars another; and star differs from star in splendour.
>
> So will it be with the resurrection of the dead. The body that is sown is perishable, it is raised imperishable.

The argument is that the sun, the moon and the varying splendours of the stars represent various degrees of glory or levels of heavenly reward.

However, this section of 1 Corinthians chapter 15 sets out to answer the question: 'How are the dead raised? With what kind of body will they come?' (1 Cor 15:35). In the Corinthian church some people taught that there is no resurrection. Paul refutes such teaching in chapter 15, concluding that if there is no resurrection 'our preaching is useless and so is your faith' (1 Cor 15:14). Aware that some may sceptically ask, 'How are the dead raised?', Paul answers at length and concludes in verse 42: 'The body that is sown is perishable, it is raised imperishable.' These are the only two states Paul ever refers to.

The point being made, of course, is that we must not expect our heavenly, resurrection bodies to be the same as our earthly ones. There is variety in creation. What we sow differs from what we reap (1 Cor 15:37), not all flesh is the same (1 Cor 15:39), heavenly bodies differ from earthly ones (1 Cor 15:40), and even heavenly bodies differ from each other (1 Cor 15:41). There is no reference here to degrees of glory. As in so many other cases, the reference to degrees of glory is found only in Mormon scripture:

> These are they who are just men made perfect through Jesus the mediator of the new covenant...whose bodies are celestial, whose glory is that of the sun, even the glory of God, the highest of all, whose glory the sun of the firmament is written of as being typical.
>
> And again...these are they who are of the terrestrial, whose glory differs from that of the church of the Firstborn who have received the fulness of the Father, even as that of the moon differs from the sun in the firmament.
>
> Behold, these are they who died without the law...
>
> And again, we saw the glory of the telestial, which glory is that of the lesser, even as the glory of the stars differs from that of the glory of the moon in the firmament.
>
> These are they who received not the gospel of Christ, neither the testimony of Jesus.[5]

In order to merit the celestial glory, a Mormon must have not only been obedient to the 'laws of the gospel' but also the 'ordinances'. These are baptism, priesthood ordination, washing and anointing, the endowment, and celestial marriage. Baptism and priesthood ordination are performed in ordinary Mormon chapels, but the other ordinances only take place within the temple.

MODERN TEMPLE ORDINANCES

Washing and anointing

Clothed only in a loose covering open at the sides, you are rit-
ually washed and anointed with oil, as each part of your body
is blessed and consecrated to the Lord. You are given a new
name.

The idea of the 'new name' is taken from the Book of
Revelation: 'To him who overcomes, I will give some of the
hidden manna. I will also give him a white stone with a new
name written on it, known only to him who receives it' (Rev
2:17). 'Him who overcomes I will make a pillar in the temple of
my God...and I will also write on him my new name' (Rev
3:12).

Those who receive their new name in the Mormon temple
are impressed with how sacred it is. They must never reveal it
to anyone, not even their husband or wife. This is the name by
which they will be 'called forth on the morning of the first resurrection'. They are told that it is a key word: 'And a white
stone is given to each of those who come into the celestial
kingdom, whereon is a new name written, which no man
knoweth save he that receiveth it. The new name is the key
word.'[6]

The temple rituals are full of secret signs and passwords,
which enable the faithful to gain entrance into heaven, past the
angels who guard the way. This new name is obviously one of
these secret passwords. However, a study of the context of the
new name, both in the Bible and in Mormon scriptures, shows
that this name is given to 'him who overcomes' and to 'those
who come into the celestial kingdom', not to those who attend
the temple here on earth. Whatever the significance of the
new name, it is to be a part of the reward, not part of the prepa-
ration.

It is also quite a let-down to discover that the new name is
not revealed supernaturally for each individual. Each day, one
female and one male name is chosen from the next letter of
the alphabet and used for every new attendee that day. The letter of the day when the authors attended for the first time was
J, and our names were Josephine and Jacob. These were the

names for everyone who also attended for the first time on the same day as ourselves.

Temple garments

A temple garment is given to you after you have been washed and anointed. It consists of a one-piece or two-piece garment, like a T-shirt and long-johns, to the knee. It is worn at all times next to the skin.

> It represents the garment given to Adam when he was found naked in the Garden of Eden, and is called the Garment of the Holy Priesthood. Inasmuch as you do not defile it, but are true and faithful to your covenants, it will be a shield and a protection to you against the power of the destroyer until you have finished your work on the earth.[7]

Four marks are cut and embroidered into the garment:

- On the right breast, the mark of the square. This is a reminder of the covenants made in the temple.

- On the left breast, the mark of the compass. This is to indicate that 'all truth is circumscribed into one great whole, and that desires, appetites and passions are to be kept within the bounds the Lord has established'.[8]

- The navel mark. This is a 'reminder of the constant need of nourishment to body and spirit'.[9]

- The knee mark 'indicates that every knee shall bow and every tongue confess that Jesus is the Christ'.[10]

The garment also ensures modesty, as clothes have to cover it. Originally the garment had a high neck and reached to the wrists and ankles. Church leaders roundly condemned those who sought to alter them to come into line with fashion. Yet in 1923 they eventually bowed to pressure and agreed that the garments would now reach to the knee and the elbow. Since then they have been shortened even further, with the women's garments having a lower neckline and only small cap sleeves.

The Endowment

> This course of instruction includes a recital of the most promi-
> nent events of the creative period, the condition of our first par-
> ents in the Garden of Eden, their disobedience and consequent
> expulsion from that blissful abode, their condition in the lone
> and dreary world when doomed to live by labor and sweat, the
> plan of redemption by which the great transgression may be
> atoned, the period of the great apostasy, the restoration of the
> Gospel with all its ancient powers and privileges, the absolute
> and indispensible condition of personal purity and devotion to
> the right in present life, and a strict compliance with Gospel
> requirements.[11]

Originally the sequence of events was shown in separate rooms with participants moving from room to room as the story unfolded: the creation room, the garden room, the lone and dreary world or Telestial kingdom, the Terrestrial king-dom, culminating in a ritual permitting entrance through the veil into the Celestial kingdom. In modern temples partici-pants remain in one room and the sequence is depicted on film with only the final initiation into the Celestial realm taking them into a different room.

Covenants

> ...covenant and promise to observe the law of strict virtue and
> chastity, to be charitable, benevolent, tolerant and pure; to
> devote both talent and material means to the spread of truth
> and the uplifting of the race; to maintain devotion to the cause
> of truth; and to seek in every way to contribute to the great
> preparation that the earth may be made ready to receive her
> King – the Lord Jesus Christ. With the taking of each covenant
> and the assuming of each obligation a promised blessing is pro-
> nounced, contingent upon the faithful observance of the condi-
> tions.[12]

Each covenant follows the revelation of a new piece of knowledge, which includes a sign and a name to be used to pass the angels to gain admittance to the Celestial kingdom. Until recently, each covenant also carried a penalty of a different form of death, should it ever be revealed. These blood oaths were dropped from the ceremony in 1992.

Robes

Everyone wears white clothes: dresses for women, with white tights or socks; white shirts, trousers and socks for men, with optional white tie. Male temple workers wear white suits. Robes go on over this, as the ceremony progresses.

The robe is a long narrow piece of fabric worn over the shoulder, gathered or pleated and tied at each side of the waist. It is the robe of the priesthood and is worn on the left shoulder for the Aaronic Priesthood and on the right shoulder for the Melchizedek Priesthood.

There is a green apron embroidered with leaves to symbolise the apron of fig leaves made by Adam and Eve to cover their nakedness.

The robes also include a sash around the waist, which is tied on the right side for the Aaronic priesthood and on the left for the Melchizedek priesthood, slippers, and a hat for men and a veil for women. At a certain point in the ceremony, women used to be required to veil their faces. This has now been dropped, and the veil is worn at the back of the head throughout.

Sealing in celestial marriage

> In the celestial glory there are three heavens or degrees;
> And in order to obtain the highest, a man must enter into this order of the priesthood [meaning the new and everlasting covenant of marriage];
> And if he does not, he cannot obtain it.[13]

Thus celestial marriage is necessary for exaltation. Also, a woman can only benefit from the priesthood through marriage, and without this benefit she cannot be saved.

Mormons have not derived the doctrine of marriage for time and eternity from the Bible. It was revealed, they claim, to Joseph Smith. They do appeal to the Bible to illustrate its necessity and its prevalence in New Testament times.

Civil marriage is only until death; celestial marriage is for eternity. Mormons claim the authority given by Jesus to his disciples: 'I will give you the keys of the kingdom of heaven; whatever you bind on earth will be bound in heaven' (Mt 16:19). When Jesus was challenged by the Sadducees concerning the woman who married seven brothers in turn, he said, 'The people of this age marry and are given in marriage. But those who are considered worthy of taking part in that age and in the resurrection from the dead will neither marry nor be given in marriage' (Lk 20:34–35). The Mormon interpretation of this is that, since no marrying is done in heaven, all marrying must be done on earth. It is a 'sealing' in this life to be effective in the next, and the same by proxy for those already dead.

Let us look more closely at the story in Luke:

> Some of the Sadducees, who say there is no resurrection, came to Jesus with a question. 'Teacher,' they said, 'Moses wrote for us that if a man's brother dies and leaves a wife but no children, the man must marry the widow and have children for his brother. Now there were seven brothers. The first one died childless. The second and then the third married her, and in the same way the seven died, leaving no children. Finally, the woman died too. Now then, at the resurrection whose wife will she be, since the seven were married to her?'
>
> Jesus replied, 'The people of this age marry and are given in marriage. But those who are considered worthy of taking part in that age and in the resurrection from the dead will neither marry nor be given in marriage, and they can no longer die; for they are like the angels. They are God's children, since they are children of the resurrection.' (Luke 20:27–36.)

It is astonishing how often the Mormon explanation for a Scripture answer has no bearing on the question asked, as is well illustrated here. In all passages where the speaker's exposition is prompted by a question, it is best to go back to the question and start from there. The Sadducees asked the question about whose wife the woman would be at the resurrection (Lk 20:27–33). Usually these people asked questions to challenge Jesus' teachings. The teachings they were challenging here concerned the resurrection. They did not believe in it – but Jesus taught it.

Mormons would have you believe, however, that the issue in verse 33 is marriage. But we have already established that the issue is resurrection. Why then are the Sadducees talking about marriage? The point they are making is this. If the woman and the seven brothers conducted themselves according to the law of Moses, and there is a resurrection, you have a problem. A woman with seven husbands! Look at the mess you find yourself in if you are daft enough to believe in the resurrection.

Jesus' answer is simple. The question does not arise because the marriage state is only to be found in this life. There is no marriage in heaven. If, as Mormons would have us believe, eternal marriage was a doctrine of the early church then Jesus' answer would have been different: whoever she was sealed to in the temple, or none of them because they had not entered into the new and everlasting covenant of temple marriage.

Other sealing ordinances

> Even as husband and wife though legally wedded under the secular law must be sealed by the authority of the Holy Priesthood if their union is to be valid in eternity, so must children who have been born to parents married for time only be sealed to their parents after father and mother have been sealed to each other in the order of celestial marriage.[14]

This work of 'sealing' one generation to another continues back through all the generations until the whole line is sealed in an eternal family unit. Children whose parents are already sealed for time and eternity are 'born under the covenant' and part of that eternal family.

The work that goes on in these buildings sets forth God's eternal purposes with reference to man, God's child and creation… Much of the work that goes on within temples is concerned with the family…the treasured and satisfying relationships of mortality, the most beautiful and meaningful of which are found in the family, may continue in the world to come.[15]

WORK FOR THE DEAD

Necessity of obedience to the laws and ordinances of the gospel

The Mormon Third Article of Faith states: 'We believe that through the Atonement of Christ, all mankind may be saved, by obedience to the laws and ordinances of the gospel.' They believe that faith is not enough for salvation. Not only works, but ordinances such as baptism are essential. They also declare that these 'laws and ordinances of the gospel' apply to the dead as well as the living:

> Compliance with the laws and ordinances of the gospel is an absolute and irrevocable requirement for admission into the Kingdom of God…and that this requirement is universal, applying alike to every soul that has attained to age and powers of accountability in the flesh…It follows as a necessary consequence that if any soul has failed, either through ignorance or neglect, to render obedience to these requirements, the obligation is not removed by death.[16]

Missionary work to the dead

Mormons believe that during the three days between Christ's death and resurrection, he preached the gospel to those who had not heard it in their lifetime and were therefore in prison. They argue that although Jesus told the thief on the cross 'today you will be with me in paradise' (Lk 23:43), nevertheless Christ did not ascend to God that day because three days later he said, 'I have not yet returned to the Father' (Jn 20:17). Mormons use these references and tie them in with the statement made by Peter: 'For Christ died for sins once for all, the righteous for the unrighteous, to bring you to God. He was put to death in the body but made alive by the Spirit, through whom also he went and preached to the spirits in prison' (1 Pet 3:19–20).

This was the inauguration of missionary work among the dead. Mormons ask the question, why would he preach to them if they were not able to repent? If repentance is possible after death, then the other requirements of the gospel must also apply.

But is this the true interpretation of these verses? There are three possible explanations:

1. Some hold that in his pre-incarnate state Christ went and preached through Noah to the wicked generation of that time.

2. Others argue that between his death and resurrection Christ went to the prison where fallen angels are incarcerated and there preached to the angels who are said to have left their proper state and married human women during Noah's time (Gen 6:1–4; 2 Pet 2:4; Jude 6). The 'sons of God' in Genesis 6:2,4 are said to have been angels, as they are in Job 1:6; 2:1. The message he preached to these evil angels was probably a declaration of victory.

3. Still others say that between death and the resurrection Christ went to the place of the dead and preached to the spirits of Noah's wicked contemporaries. What he proclaimed may have been the gospel, or it may have been a declaration of victory for Christ and doom for his hearers.[17]

Mormons insist on their interpretation because it fits in with the message they want to preach:

> No soul will be punished for sin beyond the time requisite to work the needed reformation and to vindicate justice, for which ends alone punishment is imposed. And no one will be eligible to enter any kingdom of glory in the abode of the blessed to which he is not entitled through obedience to law.
>
> It follows as a plain necessity that the Gospel must be proclaimed in the spirit world.[18]

Vicarious service of the living for the dead

If the dead need to be obedient in the same way as the living, they have a problem with those things which require a physical body. In the temple, all the ordinances, including baptism and priesthood ordination, are performed on their behalf.

Vicarious service (that which is performed in someone else's place) is a biblical principle. Part of the Old Testament Temple ritual was that of the scape goat.

> [Aaron] is to lay both hands on the head of the live goat and confess over it all the wickedness and rebellion of the Israelites – all their sins – and put them on the goat's head. He shall send the goat away into the desert in the care of a man appointed for the task. The goat will carry on itself all their sins to a solitary place; and the man shall release it in the desert. (Lev 16:21–22.)

This was the forerunner of Jesus' atonement, which was a vicarious sacrifice for us all. 'He himself bore our sins in his body on the tree, so that we might die to sins and live for righteousness; by his wounds you have been healed' (1 Pet 2:24).

Once again, Mormons take unrelated scriptures and put them together to support their doctrine. This time they join the above (valid) argument with two other scriptures:

> [Speaking of the heroes of the faith:] God had planned something better for us so that only together with us would they be made perfect. (Heb 11:40, our brackets.)
>
> See, I will send you the prophet Elijah before that great and dreadful day of the Lord comes. He will turn the hearts of the fathers to their children, and the hearts of the children to their fathers; or else I will come and strike the land with a curse. (Malachi 4:5–6.)

Joseph Smith gave an explanation for this scripture from Malachi:

> It is sufficient to know, in this case, that the earth will be smitten with a curse unless there is a welding link of some kind or other between the fathers and the children, upon some subject or other – and behold what is that subject? It is baptism for the dead. For we without them cannot be made perfect; neither can they without us be made perfect.[19]

Authority to labour on behalf of the dead

The command to build the Kirtland Temple was received in June 1834[20] and was dedicated in March 1836. It was to be 'a house of prayer, a house of fasting, a house of faith, a house of learning, a house of glory, a house of God'.[21]

One week after the dedication, Joseph Smith and Oliver Cowdery claimed that Elijah appeared to them in a vision in the Kirtland Temple and gave them the keys for temple work:

> Elijah the prophet, who was taken to heaven without tasting death, stood before us, and said: Behold, the time has fully come, which was spoken of by the mouth of Malachi – testifying that he (Elijah) should be sent, before the great and dreadful day of the Lord come –
> To turn the hearts of the fathers to the children, and the children to the fathers, lest the whole earth be smitten with a curse –
> Therefore, the keys of this dispensation are committed into your hands; and by this ye may know that the great and dreadful day of the Lord is near, even at the doors.[22]

Elijah and John the Baptist

Luke stated that when the angel of the Lord appeared to Elizabeth to announce the forthcoming birth of John the Baptist, he said, 'And he will go on before the Lord, in the spirit and power of Elijah, to turn the hearts of the fathers to their children and the disobedient to the wisdom of the righteous – to make ready a people prepared for the Lord' (Lk 1:17).

Jesus himself said, 'For all the Prophets and the Law prophesied until John. And if you are willing to accept it, he is the Elijah who was to come' (Mt 11:13–14). 'But I tell you, Elijah has already come, and they did not recognise him...Then the disciples understood that he was talking to them about John the Baptist' (Mt 17:12–13).

Despite this, Mormons refute that John the Baptist was Elijah, because the 'great and dreadful day of the Lord' did not come after him. The passage in Malachi explains what will happen on that day: "'Surely the day is coming; it will burn like

216 MORMONISM: A GOLD PLATED RELIGION

a furnace. All the arrogant and every evil doer will be stubble, and that day that is coming will set them on fire," says the Lord Almighty' (Mal 4:1). John the Baptist himself explained that this referred to Jesus: 'But after me will come one who is more powerful than I, whose sandals I am not fit to carry. He will baptise you with the Holy Spirit and with fire. His winnowing fork is in his hand, and he will clear his threshing-floor, gathering his wheat into the barn and burning up the chaff with unquenchable fire' (Mt 3:11–12).

In the Gospel of John, chapter 1, we see the priests and Levites questioning John as to his identity. They asked if he was Elijah and John said that he wasn't. A misunderstanding of this incident usually stems from a misunderstanding of what the people were asking John. It was known that Elijah had not died (2 Kings 2:11) and it was commonly believed that the same prophet would return to announce the end time. Against this background we can understand John's denial. He was answering a different question to the one many people think was being asked. Clarity comes in light of the angelic prophecy of Luke 1:17 and Jesus' own verdict on John in the gospels. He was *not* Elijah but he did come in the *spirit* of Elijah thus fulfilling the prophecy of Malachi.

There are, furthermore, remarkable parallels between the ministry of Elijah and that of John.
1. They were both forerunners, Elijah to Elisha and John to Jesus.
2. Elijah's name means, 'The Lord is my God', and characterised his ministry which was to call the people to repentance and back to God, especially the King of Israel. The name of Elisha, who came after him, means, 'God is salvation', in turn characterising his ministry which was to channel the covenant blessings to the faithful in Israel.

John's ministry was one of repentance and a calling of the people back to God, especially the King of Judea. Jesus' ministry was one of reconciliation in which he became the channel of God's blessings to the 'household of faith'.
3. If Elijah is compared with Moses then Elisha becomes the Joshua of his day in that, like Joshua, he was to complete the work begun by Moses and lead God's people into the

promised blessings. John the Baptist began a work that was completed by Jesus. Jesus is the Greek form of Joshua which means 'the Lord saves'.

Baptism and salvation

Baptism is referred to many times in Scripture but the reference Mormons use to validate their claim that baptism is essential to salvation is where Jesus informs Nicodemus that in order to be saved it is essential that we are 'born of water and the Spirit' (Jn 3:5). Mormons believe that the reference to being born of water is a reference to baptism. Two things should be noted here.

First, the Mormon one is not the only interpretation of this verse. Water and wind are both symbols used in Scripture when referring to the Spirit and in this particular instance it could as easily be interpreted as a reference to purification by the Spirit. Certainly, salvation comes only to those who are born of the Spirit. This birth, or rebirth, brings regeneration and purification.

Secondly, there is the question of whether baptism is a means whereby salvation is received or a sign that salvation has been received. The weight of Scripture seems to favour the latter although the Mormons are not by any means the only group to subscribe to the former. They are, however, the only group to believe that baptism can be performed by the living for the dead. One, more orthodox, way of dealing with the problem is infant baptism where baptism is done as soon as possible and becomes of effect when the infant, grown to accountability, accepts freely the baptism done in infancy.

The Scriptures do teach that 'if you confess with your mouth, "Jesus is Lord", and believe in your heart that God raised him from the dead, you will be saved' (Rom 10:9). This being the case, then once saved we are baptised as a sign and a seal on that which has already taken place. Baptism follows salvation, it does not lead to it. Nor, therefore, can it contribute to the salvation of the dead.

Baptism for the dead

Mormons reinforce this practice with another misinterpretation of scripture: 'What will those do who are baptised for the dead? If the dead are not raised at all, why are people baptised for them?' (1 Cor 15:29). This scripture does not say that *Christians* were baptising for the dead. Paul is writing to Christians and refers to *those who are baptised for the dead* and asks why people are baptised for them. He then goes on to say 'And as for us...' (1 Cor 15:30). There is a clear distinction between 'us' and 'them'. What Paul is saying is that the pagans in Corinth were baptising for the dead, which is no mandate for us to do it today.

Consequent to Mormons' belief in baptism for the dead is the practice of other physical ordinances for the dead. In Mormon theology this means washings and anointings, ordination to the priesthood, the endowment, and celestial marriage. James E. Talmage promised faithful Mormons that they would be saviours of their dead along with Christ:

> ...and as He [Christ] by effort, sacrifice, and suffering, did for men what they never could accomplish for themselves, and so became in very truth the one and only Saviour and Redeemer of the race, so may each of us by opening the way to our departed dead whereby they may be brought within the saving law of the Gospel, become in a small measure saviours unto those who would otherwise be left in darkness.[23]

Mormons lift a verse out of 1 Peter which they say indicates that the gospel is taught to the dead, who are able to be obedient in spiritual things, but need our help to be obedient 'in regard to the body': 'For this is the reason the gospel was preached even to those who are now dead, so that they might be judged according to men in regard to the body but live according to God in the spirit' (1 Pet 4:6). The word 'now' does not occur in the Greek, but is necessary to make it clear in the English that the preaching was done while the people were still alive. This is also shown from the tense: the gospel *was* preached. Earlier in the same letter, Peter says, 'Concerning this salvation, the prophets...spoke of this grace that was to come to you' (1 Pet 1:10).

No salvation after death

The writer to the Hebrews made it clear that there will be no opportunity for people to be saved after death: 'Just as man is destined to die once, and after that to face judgment' (Heb 9:27). The Book of Mormon is actually in agreement with Hebrews: 'Nevertheless there was a space granted unto man in which he might repent; therefore this life becomes a probationary state; a time to prepare to meet God.'[24] The Book of Mormon prophet Alma lays great emphasis upon the teaching that this life is the time to prepare:

> For behold, this life is the time for men to prepare to meet God; yea, behold the day of this life is the day for men to perform their labors.
>
> And now, as I said unto you before...I beseech of you that ye do not procrastinate the day of your repentance until the end; for after this day of life, which is given us to prepare for eternity, behold, if we do not improve our time while in this life, then cometh the night of darkness wherein there can be no labor performed.[25]

This passage clearly says that nothing can be done after death. It goes on to explain why repentance is not possible after death:

> Ye cannot say, when ye are brought to that awful crisis, that I will repent, that I will return to my God. Nay, ye cannot say this; for that same spirit which doth possess your bodies at the time that ye go out of this life, that same spirit will have power to possess your body in that eternal world.
>
> For behold, if ye have procrastinated the day of your repentance even until death, behold, ye have become subjected to the spirit of the devil, and he doth seal you his.[26]

The Book of Mormon does not teach that there is a spirit prison where the wicked go until they have been preached the gospel. It teaches that between death and resurrection the righteous go to paradise and the wicked to outer darkness:

> Now, concerning the state of the soul between death and resurrection – Behold, it has been made known unto me by an angel, that the spirits of all men, as soon as they are departed from this mortal body, yea, the spirits of all men, whether they be good or evil, are taken home to that God who gave them life.
>
> And then it shall come to pass, that the spirits of those who are righteous are received into a state of happiness, which is called paradise...
>
> And then it shall come to pass, that the spirits of the wicked, yea, who are evil...these shall be cast into outer darkness; there shall be weeping, and wailing, and gnashing of teeth, and this because of their own iniquity, being led captive by the will of the devil.[27]

No other provision is made in the book that is said by Mormons to contain the fullness of the gospel.

Clearly if we cannot repent after death we cannot be baptised, nor receive priesthood ordination or endowments, nor enter into eternal marriage covenants. Why then are Mormons doing vicarious work for the dead? Jesus said that all the Father had would be given to those who believe. He did not say that some would get more than others because they had learned secret signs. He also said, 'I am the way and the truth and the life. No-one comes to the Father except through me' (Jn 14:6). There are no rituals or secret knowledge which can improve on that.

Notes

Doctrine and Covenants 38:32.
2. Joseph Fielding Smith (compiler), *The Teachings of the Prophet Joseph Smith*, p 308.
3. As above.
4. James E. Talmage, *The House of the Lord*, p 80.
5. Doctrine and Covenants 76:69–72,81–82.
6. Doctrine and Covenants 130:11.
7. Jerald and Sandra Tanner, *Mormonism: Shadow or Reality?*, 1982, p 462.
8. As above, p 472.
9. As above.
10. As above.
11. James E. Talmage, same source, pp 83–84.
12. As above, p 84.
13. Doctrine and Covenants 131:1–3, our brackets.
14. James E. Talmage, same source, p 91.
15. Gordon B. Hinckley.
16. James E. Talmage, same source, p 64.
17. *The New International Version Study Bible*, Hodder & Stoughton, 1987.
18. James E. Talmage, same source, p 77.
19. Doctrine and Covenants 128:18, sentences 2–4. Letter from Joseph Smith to the church, September 1842.
20. Doctrine and Covenants 105:33.
21. Doctrine and Covenants 109:8.
22. Doctrine and Covenants 110:13–16.
23. James E. Talmage, same source, pp 66–67.
24. Alma 12:24.
25. Alma 34:32–33, our italics.
26. Alma 34:34–35.
27. Alma 40:11–12.

Chapter 20
Fraud, Bombs and Fallibility[1]

On 19 March 1981, the church's Public Communications Department released the following announcement to the media:

> A handwritten document, which appears to be a father's blessing given by Joseph Smith Jr., first President of The Church of Jesus Christ of Latter-day Saints, to his son Joseph Smith III has been acquired by the Church Historical Department.
>
> Initial examination of the document, dated January 17, 1844, indicates that it may be in the handwriting of Thomas Bullock...
>
> The document was obtained from Mark William Hofmann, a collector of historical documents and antiques relating to the Church. He said he received it from a descendant of Thomas Bullock.[2]

Understandably, the church was very excited over this acquisition, and much was made of it in the church press.

The *Ensign* magazine (October 1982) reported another important find:

> A previously unknown 1829 letter by Lucy Mack Smith to her sister-in-law in which the mother of the Prophet Joseph Smith Jr., discusses her son's work has been made available to the Church Historical Department.
>
> The letter, dated 23 January 1829, is 'the first [earliest] known dated document relating to the history of The Church of Jesus Christ of Latter-day Saints,' said Heber C. Wolsey,

managing director of the Public Communications Department
of the Church, in a news conference held Monday, August 23,
in Church Historical Department offices...

The letter was acquired by Brent F. Ashworth, a Provo, Utah,
member of the Church, from a private collector who obtained
it from another collector in the eastern United States.[3]

The private collector who obtained the letter for Brent
Ashworth was also Mark Hofmann.[4] It had been authenticated
by Dean Jessee, senior research historian of the Joseph
Fielding Smith Institute of Church History at Brigham Young
University.

The Mormon church purchased many other documents
from Mark Hofmann, including in 1983 a letter from Joseph
Smith to his brother Hyrum, written in 1838. This letter was in
its entirety a revelation from the Lord, beginning with the
words 'verily thus saith the Lord' and ending with the word
'amen'.

In 1985 Mark Hofmann claimed that he had discovered the
'McLellin collection', and offered to help the church obtain it
so that it would not fall into the hands of anti-Mormons who
would use it to embarrass the church. William E. McLellin
was one of the original members of the Quorum of the Twelve
Apostles. He was well acquainted with Joseph Smith and other
church leaders and knew a great deal about what was going on
in the early church. Later, however, he turned against the
church and accused Joseph Smith of altering the revelations
which are found in the Doctrine and Covenants.

> His faith was first shaken by the changes made in the revela-
> tions. He had been careful to keep copies of the originals, pre-
> sented proof that all the early revelations were changed three
> times, and considerably amended before they appeared in their
> present form.[5]

The Doctrine and Covenants contains an 'Explanatory
Introduction' which claims to be the 'Testimony of the Twelve
Apostles to the truth of the Book of Doctrine and Covenants'.
William McLellin claimed that this 'Testimony' was 'a base

forgery'. William McLellin was very upset that Joseph Smith
would change revelations given by God.

In 1838, Oliver Cowdery, one of the Three Witnesses to the
Book of Mormon, claimed that Joseph Smith had 'a dirty,
nasty, filthy affair' with a young woman named Fanny Alger.
William McLellin claimed to have some explosive information
on this matter. He asserted that Joseph Smith's wife, Emma,
had told him about this affair.

When Mark Hofmann approached the church in 1985 it was
eventually decided that Hugh Pinnock, a General Authority in
the church, would help him obtain a loan of $185,000 from the
First Interstate Bank so that he could go to Texas and obtain
the McLellin collection. Steven F. Christensen, a Mormon
bishop and businessman in Salt Lake City, was supposed to
authenticate the McLellin collection on 15 October 1985. That
morning he was killed by a bomb. Later that morning,
Kathleen Sheets, the wife of another bishop and associate of
Steven Christensen, was killed when she picked up a package
containing a booby-trapped shrapnel bomb. The following day,
Mark Hofmann was seriously injured when a bomb exploded
in his car.

After intensive investigation it was discovered that Mark
Hofmann was the bomber. All the documents he had obtained
for the church were forgeries, and he did not have the
McLellin collection as he claimed. He killed Steven
Christensen, and attempted to kill his associate, that morning
so that the authentication could not take place. At the time of
the last explosion Hofmann was transporting a third bomb he
had constructed. Although this bomb was prepared to kill
someone else, it accidentally went off in his own car. Hofmann
later confessed to the murders and was sent to the Utah State
Prison.

It also transpired that the Mormon leaders had been helping Mark Hofmann to obtain a collection from Texas which
they already had in their own vault. The existence of the collection was discovered by accident. The discovery was
reported by Richard Turley, managing director of the Church
Historical Department:

March 1986 brought a startling discovery. Historical Department personnel seeking information about William McLellin had contacted Dean Jessee...Jessee visited the department and explained to Glen Rowe that he had found some interesting information about McLellin in his research files. Jessee's notes referred to correspondence in the department's uncatalogued Joseph F. Smith collection. The correspondence mentioned McLellin's diaries and other belongings...Rowe and his staff searched the collection and located papers that amazed church officials.

Rowe had kept his new supervisor, Richard Turley, informed about Jessee's clue and the letters to which it led. Turley told Dean Larsen about the letters, and Larsen informed [Apostles] Packer and Oaks, who in turn contacted the First Presidency. When Gordon Hinckley [counsellor in the First Presidency] learned of the letters, he asked Francis Gibbons if the First Presidency's vault contained the items the letters mentioned. Gibbons searched the vault. Hinckley and the other church officials then learned to their astonishment, that the *church had owned McLellin's journals and manuscripts all along.*[6]

In 1908 Joseph F. Smith, he sixth prophet of the church, had ordered the church to purchase the collection to keep it 'from falling into unfriendly hands'. The collection was then hidden in the First Presidency vaults and not even listed in the catalogue.

While Mormons might expect this to happen at some bureaucratic agency, they will have a difficult time explaining how it could happen in a church which is supposed to be led by direct revelation from God. The implications are very serious indeed.

At a press conference a week after the bombings, President Gordon B. Hinckley said, 'Throughout the investigation the Church and its officers have cooperated with law enforcement officials, responding to every inquiry and request. We will continue to do so.'[7] In view of the circumstances, it would be very difficult for church leaders to come and admit they had made such a serious mistake over Mark Hofmann. On the other hand, they faced a far more serious problem if they did not reveal the existence of the McLellin collection. Church leaders would have to keep a key piece of evidence deliberately hidden from investigators who were working on the Hofmann case. Unfortunately for the Mormon church, Richard Turley makes it clear that church leaders chose to keep law enforcement officials completely in the dark concerning the existence of the McLellin collection.

> To most members of the prosecution team, it was plain that Mark Hofmann had blackmailed the church. It was equally clear that leaders of the church were terrified that Gordon B. Hinckley would be required to testify against him and would be forced to testify, under oath, about his dealings with Hofmann. From the first weeks of the investigation, lawyers for the church sought to head off this possibility.[8]

This raises a very important question: what if the suppression of the McLellin collection by church leaders made it impossible for prosecutors to get Hofmann bound over for trial? If prosecutors had failed to make a strong enough case, we would have a cold-blooded murderer walking the streets of Salt Lake City today.

While it is true that the General Authorities of the Mormon Church have preached openness, honesty and trust in God from the pulpit, when it came right down to it, some of the very highest leaders of the church were unable to live up to their lofty teachings. Apparently, they did not believe that the God they served was able to handle the embarrassing situation the church found itself in. Their behaviour with regard to this matter did not match up to their Twelfth Article of Faith: 'We believe in being subject to kings, presidents, rulers, and magistrates, in obeying, honoring, and sustaining the law.' Following Hofmann's confession, the church issued a statement which included the following:

> The Church, its early leaders, its doctrine, and its members have been abused by much of the commentary about the meaning and impact of the questioned documents which are at the center of these tragic events.
> Like other document collectors throughout the nation, the Church has relied on competent authorities in document

acquisition and with the others has been the victim of the fraudulent activities which have now been acknowledged in the courtroom.[9]

The Mormons claim to be led by revelation from God. Apostle Bruce R. McConkie made these claims regarding Mormon revelation:

> Our Lord's true Church is established and founded upon revelation. Its identity as the true Church continues as long as revelation is received to direct its affairs...without revelation there would be no legal adminstrators to perform the ordinances of salvation with binding effect on earth and in heaven...the Spirit is *giving direct and daily revelation to the presiding Brethren* in the administration of the affairs of the Church.[10]

Unfortunately for church leaders, Mark Hofmann has put the claim of revelation in the church to the acid test and found that the 'living oracles' are just as fallible as other men. At a time when revelation was really needed, they seemed to be completely in the dark as to what was going on.

The forged 1838 Joseph Smith letter was supposed to be a revelation from the Lord. The fact that Mormon leaders were not able to recognise the spurious nature of these revelations casts doubt upon their ability to discern the truthfulness of the other revelations given by Joseph Smith. The church has always claimed that it is virtually impossible for a person to write a revelation that would compare with Joseph Smith's. It now appears, however, that there *is* someone who can write revelations comparable to Joseph Smith's, and that it is even possible to get them past the scrutiny of the highest leadership of the Mormon church.

There is an interesting footnote to this story. A small item in the News of The Church section of the *Ensign* magazine for February 1993 declared 'McLellin Papers Available for Research'.

> In 1908, the Church acquired some papers written by William E. McLellin, one of the first Apostles in this dispensation. The records were stored away in the Church Historical Department

and eventually forgotten. Those papers – several journals and four small manuscript books – have now been catalogued and are available for study by qualified researchers.[11]

If the church had not been so sensitive about its past, and so secretive about its documents, the tragedy of the Mark Hofmann bombings would never have happened.

Notes

1. Material for this chapter has been used with permission from Jerald & Sandra Tanner of Utah Lighthouse Ministry.
2. *Ensign* magazine, May 1981, p 107.
3. As above, October 1982, p 70.
4. Robert Lindsey, *A Gathering of Saints*, Corgi, 1990, p 99.
5. *Salt Lake City Tribune*, 6 October 1875.
6. Richard Turley, *Victims: The Latter-day Saints Church and the Mark Hofmann Case*, pp 248–51, our italics.
7. *Ensign* magazine, December 1985, p 72.
8. Robert Lindsey, same source, p 311.
9. *Ensign* magazine, April 1987, p 77.
10. Bruce R. McConkie, *Mormon Doctrine*, 1979, pp 646,647,650, our italics and brackets.
11. *Ensign* magazine, February 1993, p 74.

Chapter 21
False Credibility

With nearly 50,000 full-time missionaries working across the globe and a motto of 'every member a missionary', Mormons are an example that many orthodox churches would do well to emulate. Of course they are not the only group whose first point of contact is the doorstep or street corner. They do surpass all others however for the variety and novelty of their approaches to the public. No one has worked harder than the Mormons to get a message across in a way that is attractive and respectable.

Public relations are a high priority for Mormons and every effort is made to appear acceptable, legitimate and substantially orthodox. The church has its own Public Affairs Department. Each of its twenty-two geographical areas has an area director of public affairs and each region and stake in turn has public affairs directors. All are either professionals or church trained in media and community relations.

An interview in *Ensign* magazine (May 1995) with the department's director of area relations, Michael R. Otterson, gives an insight into the goals of the church in its relationships with the communities within which it operates. Each area, we are told, has a five-year public affairs plan with the primary goal of helping people understand the church better. Being 'acceptable' is paramount when seeking recognition in a new area, approval for new buildings, or permission to microfilm genealogical records.

Aware of 'those who like to talk about what the Church is

not', Mr Otterson says that 'the Church stands a better chance of being accurately portrayed when it takes the initiative'. Today's Mormon church is clearly image conscious and anxious to own the correct reputation. This is in stark contrast to the attitude the church had in the first seventy years of its existence. From its inception the church has endured persecution, mob violence, even martyrdom. It responded with strong polemics against the 'gentile' nations around it and against the government of the United States in particular. Hostility towards the church was more than matched, indeed preceded, by the church's hostility toward all who would question its claim or its right to self government. Battle lines were drawn and Mormon jingoism was at its height.

In the early years of the church, Apostle Orson Hyde stated: 'What the world calls "Mormonism" will rule every nation. Joseph Smith and Brigham Young will be the head.'[1] In 1859 Heber C. Kimball of the first presidency, said, 'And so all Nations will bow down to this kingdom.'[2] In 1865 John Taylor, who became third president of the church, said, 'We do believe it, and honestly acknowledge that this is that kingdom which the Lord has commenced to establish upon the earth, and that it will not only govern all people in a religious capacity, but also in a political capacity.'[3]

Such talk inevitably provoked the enmity of their neighbours who felt threatened by the Mormons and their ambitions to govern. The Mormons responded vigorously. Brigham Young stated that they were to become free and independent of all other kingdoms, predicting:

> God Almighty will give the United States a pill that will put them to death, and that is worse than lobelia[4]. I am a prophet enough to prophecy the downfall of the government that has driven us out...Woe to the United States: I see them going to Death and destruction.[5]

Early Temple ceremonies included an oath to avenge the blood of the prophets Joseph and Hyrum Smith on the government of the United States substantially in these words:

> You and each of you covenant and promise that you will pray
> and never cease to pray Almighty God to avenge the blood of
> the prophets upon this nation, and that you will teach the same
> to your children and to your children's children unto the third
> and fourth generation.[6]

The consequences of such extreme posturing began to make themselves felt in many ways. Early Mormons were driven beyond the jurisdiction of law and government to the Rocky Mountains. Later the westward expansion of 'civilisation' brought their persecutors to them. Later in the century, in 1889, two Mormons, John Moore and W.J. Edgar, were denied citizenship of the United States because it was felt that the aforementioned oath was deemed incompatible with the oath of citizenship. By 1890 the pressure on the Mormons to renounce polygamy was no longer bearable and the famous manifesto was published announcing the cessation of the practice. Before the end of the century a concerted effort was made to break the political control church leaders had on the people of Utah.

The 1800s ended with much of the church leadership either in jail or in hiding from the authorities. By this time the spirit of defiance amongst Mormons had been broken and only through compromise, even capitulation, on the part of the church was any vestige of Mormon identity preserved.

Shortly after the turn of the century Mormon Apostle Reed Smoot was elected to the United States' senate. Claims that an oath against the US government constituted part of the temple oaths he would have taken as a Mormon, along with rumours that Mormons were still practising polygamy, led to an investigation. Despite strident objections by opponents of the church the outcome of the investigation saw Reed Smoot take his seat in the senate and go on to serve Utah for thirty years.

It has been observed that:

> The Church entered the twentieth century in anxious pursuit
> of respectability. The Mormons had long been accused of
> being immoral and un-American...At last the Saints could be
> 'respectable'...they became not only loyal Americans but patri-
> ots, determined to prove their Americanism to any doubter.

> Soon after the turn of the century the new Boy Scouts of
> America program was adopted by the church with great
> enthusiasm. Thousands of Mormon boys could now pledge to
> do their duty to God and country, with none of the old
> schizophrenia.[7]

While this change has not gone unremarked, its significance and impact on subsequent church growth and prosperity has been lost to many. While other cults have gone to great
lengths to keep their distinctive identity in the modern world,
Mormons have jumped into the twentieth century with both
feet. In a remarkable reversal of policy and thinking they have
embraced the system they once vowed to destroy. While other
groups have stood apart believing that friendship with the
world is enmity with God, Mormons have successfully made
companions of both. The result is that Mormonism enjoys, in
this century, a wider scope of influence and a greater degree
of respectability than any of the other traditional Christian
cults. No legitimate area of activity is barred to the Mormon
by his faith.

Education

The Mormon church has from earliest days encouraged its
members to be educated and informed in the things of the
world. The result is a group of people who can, and do, com-
pete with the world on the world's terms and in pursuit of the
same achievements.

In the nineteenth century the church tried to establish an
exclusively Mormon system of education. Nowhere is this better illustrated than in the story of the 'Deseret alphabet'. One
account states:

> At a meeting of the board of regents, held in October 1853,
> Parley P. Pratt, Heber C. Kimball, and George D. Watt were
> appointed a committee to prepare a small school-book in char-
> acters founded on some new system of orthography, whereby
> the spelling and pronunciation of the English language might
> be made uniform and easily acquired. A further object was
> exclusiveness, a separate people wishing to have a separate lan-
> guage, and perhaps in time an independent literature.[8]

In the twentieth century church education is very much on the pattern of the world, with Church Educational System schools and colleges seeking full accreditation and association with other institutions across the world. Over 26,000 students enrolled in Church Educational Programmes at Brigham Young University in 1985. Another 18,664 enrolled in other church schools including elementary schools and colleges in the Pacific, Latin America and New Zealand. Many young people from Britain have attended Brigham Young University, but this flow is beginning to reverse with American students now attending the newly opened Centre for Mormon Studies at Nottingham University, England.

The *Ensign* (September 1995) reported on the commencement exercises attended by 5,342 graduates of Brigham Young University in April of that year. Young men and women being sent out into the world with a firm Mormon education and the words of President Gordon B. Hinckley ringing in their ears: 'Drink deeply from this ever springing well of wisdom and human experience'. With such encouragement they will go out to ensure that no worthy enterprise is left without the benefit of their education or the influence of their convictions.

Government

In the nineteenth century, church and state were one to the Mormon voter. John Taylor, who became third president of the Mormon church, stated: 'Was the kingdom that the Prophets talked about, that should be set up in the latter times, going to be a Church? Yes. And a State? Yes. It was going to be both Church and State. To rule both temporarily [sic] and spiritually.'[9]

In 1838 Thomas B. Marsh, president of the Council of the Twelve Apostles, left the church stating in an affidavit: 'The plan of said Smith, the Prophet, is to take this state, and he professes to his people to intend taking the United States and ultimately the world.'[10] Such ambitions are reflected in the crowning of Joseph Smith as king shortly before his death in 1844. In 1844 Joseph ran for presidency of the United States with Sidney Rigdon as running mate. Although he had no chance of election, his candidature further illustrated his own ambitions and those of the church.

In their book, *Mormonism: Shadow or Reality*, Jerald and Sandra Tanner point out that 'in early Utah the Mormon people were taught to vote one way'. They quote Joseph F. Smith who became sixth president of the church: 'We move as a man, almost; we hearken to the voice of our leader; we are united in our faith and in our works, whether politically or religiously.'[11]

The influence of church leaders in political matters was exercised through the People's Party, the official party of the church. It was effectively the only party in Utah. In 1891, in a remarkable turn around, church leaders announced the disbanding of the People's Party and encouraged members to divide on national party lines, voting either Democrat or Republican. This was an important contributory factor in the granting of statehood to Utah, by then a major Mormon ambition.

The twentieth century saw democratic elections become the norm in Utah with Reed Smoot elected to the senate in 1903. The church's Political Manifesto, published in 1896, now emphasised the separation of church and state and the withdrawal of overt church influence in the political arena. Since then Mormons have thrown themselves fully into the democratic process, making it difficult to imagine that it could ever have been any other way.

Today the church boasts of its representatives in state and national government. Notable among these was Ezra Taft Benson, thirteenth president of the church, who was Secretary of State for Agriculture in President Eisenhower's administration. Throughout the church members are encouraged to see office in government as a noble ambition and a positive help to the church.

Ecumenism

The attitude of the Mormon church toward other churches was very clear in the nineteenth century. The message of the First Vision contained the injunction to Joseph to 'join none of them for they were all wrong; and the Personage who addressed me said that all their creeds were an abomination in his sight; that those professors were all corrupt.'[12] Even in the twentieth century intolerance has been evident. The Mormon apostle and apologist Bruce R. McConkie wrote of other churches:

> Speaking of harlots in the figurative sense, he (Nephi) designated the Catholic Church as 'the mother of harlots' (1 Nephi 13:34; 14:15–17), a title which means that the protestant churches, the harlot daughters which broke off from the great and abominable church, would themselves be apostate churches.[13]

Until recently the Mormon temple endowment ceremony included a portrayal on film of the typical clergyman, presumably one of the corrupt professors referred to above. This man is in the pay of Satan and receives his instructions from him. He preaches for material gain, bartering with Satan for his wages. His message – 'orthodox religion' – is ridiculous and incomprehensible, 'the philosophies of men mingled with scripture'. He denies the power of God and is saved in the end only through leaving his ministry and joining the Mormons. This drama is no longer part of the endowment ceremony, which is not surprising considering the church's efforts in the area of ecumenism.

When the first Parliament of World Religions was convened in Chicago in 1893, the Mormon church still held to the view expressed by John Taylor, their third President:

> We talk about Christianity, but it is a perfect pack of nonsense...Myself and hundreds of the Elders around me have seen its pomp, parade, and glory; and what is it? It is a sounding brass and a tinkling symbol [sic]; it is as corrupt as hell; and the Devil could not invent a better engine to spread his work than the Christianity of the nineteenth century.[14]

In 1993 the centenary of that first parliament was marked by a second convention. Among Hindus, Jews, Muslims, Pagans, Witches, Sikhs, Taoists, Catholics, Protestants and New Agers sat Elder Russell M. Nelson of the Quorum of the Twelve

Apostles of the Mormon church. In a fifty-minute address he spoke of the need for tolerance and understanding and the need to be rid of interfaith contention, maligning, and intolerance. He ended by wishing all delegates 'success in all your worthy endeavours'.[15]

Such conciliatory overtures are reflected across the world with church members in Denver, Colorado, helping in the accommodating of the Pope's visit to that community in 1993; Mormons in England sitting on parish councils, and church participation in interfaith activities across the world. The acting chair of the Interfaith Forum in Gateshead, England, at the time of writing, is a Mormon, and the church played a major role in the 'One World Festival' sponsored by the Interfaith Fellowship in Huddersfield, England, in 1993.

When Michael J. Barrett, a returned Mormon missionary, was censured and then excommunicated in 1994 it was because he insisted on writing to newspapers telling the truth about Mormon history. The reason for his excommunication was disobedience because the 'public has no business knowing about church history and doctrine' (Mr Barrett's Stake President, T. Lamar Sleight in conversation with Mr Barrett). Reporting a visit he received from church leaders, Mr Barrett said, 'F. Burton and F. Enzio Busche [both members of the first quorum of seventy] came out on separate occasions and told me we have an obligation to conceal our doctrines; *we are trying to be a mainstream christian church.*'[16]

So keen is the Mormon church's eye for the main chance that in 1995 a major British documentary maker was allowed to film a fifty-minute programme following the training and work of Mormon missionaries. This is the first documentary of its kind in this country. In America the church features regularly in every media form. Its clean cut, family image is a familiar feature in every home with satellite TV or a copy of the *Reader's Digest* on the bedside table.

With such exposure it is perfectly possible that a Mormon Stake will one day be as familiar to British people as a diocese, and a ward as a parish. The Elder or local Mormon Bishop will be as much a part of the community as the Priest or the Vicar, and women will go to Relief Society as readily as they now go to Mothers' Union. Such are the ambitions of today's ecumenical Mormonism.

All this and heaven too

Fawn Brodie said that 'the Paradise of Joseph Smith had much of the earth in it', and that 'Mormon theology was never burdened with otherworldliness'.[17] The whole church still identifies prosperity with the goodness of God. The Mormon church is the wealthiest church of its size in the world, in Mormon thinking a reflection of God's favour.

Like the prosperity teachers of today, Mormons have always taught that heaven is merely a continuation of what is best on earth. Their teaching that 'families are forever' reflects this rather well. Brigham Young said, 'If we will work unitedly, we can work ourselves into wealth, health, prosperity and power; and this is required of us. It is the duty of a saint of God to gain all the influence he can on this earth.'[18]

Taking care of business

The Mormon church has, this century, amassed enormous wealth and has used that wealth to gain power and influence in every area where money talks. Many of the characteristics of the nineteenth-century church are still in evidence: enthusiasm for education; the thrift and industry of the members; the pioneer spirit; even the hold the leaders have over members' lives. The isolationism has gone. It nearly destroyed the church towards the end of the century with the passing of the Edmunds Tucker Act which dissolved the church, disenfranchised Mormons, and confiscated all church property over 50 thousand dollars. Attempts by the church to build a kingdom apart from the world had failed. From such inauspicious beginnings the twentieth-century church had its start. A church that has successfully built a kingdom in the world.

The authority structure of the church today resembles a corporate rather than an ecclesiastical organisation. We have already seen that the general authorities of the church form an effective executive power base. It is noteworthy that generations of these men have already been fabulously successful in business before entering into full-time church service. Who better to run the Corporation of The Church of Jesus Christ of Latter-day Saints?

What better explanation for the fabulous wealth of this church? In the preface we saw how church holdings were estimated in 1976 to be valued at over 2 billion dollars, placing them among the top fifty corporations in America. Income in contributions and sales was estimated at that time to be in excess of 3 million dollars a day. More recent estimates put their income in tithing alone at over 15 million dollars a day. Their worldwide holdings are conservatively estimated to be almost 12 billion dollars, and their income from business enterprise and investments is over 6 billion dollars annually.

With such wealth, and with a theology developed to lend respectability to its accumulation, the appropriate image can be manufactured: an image designed to attract our neighbours, our friends and our families. Mormon enthusiasm for the world and all it has to offer affords them more opportunities for witnessing than any other cult.

The peculiar emphasis on genealogical work has come into its own in recent years as genealogy has become a major leisure pastime. The church's well-funded genealogical programme is the best in the world and people seeking to trace their ancestors are more than welcome at the genealogical libraries that now comprise part of every main unit of the church.

The influence of Mormonism is so strong in some parts of the world, quite apart from Salt Lake City, that tourists cannot visit without being offered a well-packaged invitation to 'investigate the church'. A notable example is Hawaii where there is an impressive Mormon temple and a strong Mormon presence in business and education.

Scouting is an area where Mormons have a long and 'honourable' history. Whole troops are made up of Mormon youth and in some areas parents who wish to involve their children in the scouting programme find that the only local troops are Mormon. They also often have the best facilities money can buy.

The large Marriott hotel chain which has recently entered Britain is privately owned by a Mormon family, the Marriotts.

Most hotel rooms have, along with the Gideon Bible, a copy of the Book of Mormon.

The welfare programme of the church, while teaching the admirable principle of looking after your own, affords even more opportunities to attract people to the Mormon church. The knowledge that one will be looked after is, for some people, one of the main pulling factors to the church. A single mother on a low income, for example, can be helped financially, or by someone coming round to dig the garden or paint a room.

A further advantage of this programme is the facility for acquiring land in the name of charity. We have seen this recently in the purchases the church has made of large tracts of land in East Anglia for an estimated 12 million pounds. This makes them the second biggest landowners in the area after the Queen.

Outstripping all other cults, Mormonism is arguably the wealthiest new religion in the world and has been said to be the first major religion to emerge on the world scene since Islam. This is a comforting thought for the Latter-day Saints. It should be a voice of warning to Christians who are frankly too complacent and often too indifferent to their responsibilities to take the truth to their neighbours, friends and families before the errors of Mormonism overtake them and claim them for their own.

Notes

1. *Journal of Discourses*, Vol. 7, p 53.
2. As above, p 170.
3. As above, Vol. 11, p 53.
4. Lobelia is a herbaceous plant. The context in which Brigham Young used this is not known.
5. *Quest for Empire*, pp 116–17.
6. Jerald and Sandra Tanner, *Mormonism: Shadow or Reality?*, 1982, p 475.
7. Davis Bitton, *Dialogue: A Journal of Mormon Thought*, Autumn 1966, p 126.
8. Bancroft, *History of Utah*, p 712.
9. *Journal of Discourses*, Vol. 6, p 24.
10. Jerald and Sandra Tanner, same source, p 414.
11. *Journal of Discourses*, Vol. 12, p 328.
12. Joseph Smith, History of the Church 1:19.
13. Bruce R. McConkie, *Mormon Doctrine*, 1958, pp 314–15.
14. John Taylor, *Journal of Discourses*, Vol. 6, p 167.
15. *Ensign* magazine, November 1993, pp 102–08.
16. *Reachout Trust Newsletter*, Winter 1994, p 10, our italics and brackets.
17. Fawn M. Brodie, *No Man Knows My History*, 1966, p 187.
18. *Journal of Discourses*, Vol. 12, p 376.

Part Four

OUTREACH

Chapter 22
Sharing the Gospel

The list of points below is an excellent outline of how to share the gospel effectively with Mormon friends. They are reproduced here with permission from Sandra Tanner, Utah Lighthouse Ministry.

1. You are already witnessing to your Latter-day Saint friends – one way or another.

2. Start with a positive witness for Christ.

3. If they say they believe like you, ask them to define their terms. Also ask for a reference from the Bible.

4. Be aware of Latter-day Saints' teaching and pet arguments so you won't get caught off guard. [Not to argue but to better understand and be prepared.]

5. Make a list of scriptures that refute their claims [memorise even] and keep it in your Bible.

6. Stress Christ and the need of committing life to him. The gospel is the good news of Christ's atoning work, not a church system.

7. Don't get sidetracked defending your denomination – their first need is Christ.

8. If they say the Bible has been changed to the point it no longer is reliable for doctrine, kindly ask them for documentation. Such claims should be challenged. [A good book on this is F. F. Bruce, *The New Testament Documents: Are They Reliable?* Inter-Varsity Press.]

9. Challenge them to study the Bible. If Mormonism is a 'restoration' of Christ's church, it will agree with the Bible. [Acts 17:11–12.]

10. Pray for God's love and patience. You are to plant and water but God gives the increase. [1 Cor 3:6.] Winning a Mormon takes TIME.

11. Challenge them to think for themselves – truth can stand up to examination. [2 Tim 2:15.]

12. Sharing is not arguing! Don't raise your voice or argue [2 Tim 2:23–26; Titus 3:2–9.] Is your love showing?

13. Share with them how you saw yourself as a sinner, separated from God and your repentance and turning to Christ for salvation.

14. Keep grace and works in proper order. Explain how works are a result of grace, not a way to earn it. [Gal 5:22–23; Eph 2.]

15. Mormons limit the result of the fall [Latter-day Saints say it brought mortality but not a sinful nature, as man is supposed to be a god in embryo], thus they limit the need of atonement [they say Christ brought resurrection to all, but our place in heaven is based on our good works]. A Mormon doesn't usually understand he is a lost sinner in need of salvation. Salvation only means something to you when you are lost. [Luke 7:35–47.] They believe they commit sin but don't understand man's basic sin-nature.

16. A Mormon quickly senses if you are talking from genuine concern and conviction or if you are just out to put down Mormons. Check your motives and attitude. You hinder the work of God if your motive is less than to share Christ's love. 'Always be full of joy in the Lord; I say it again, rejoice! Let everyone see that you are unselfish and considerate in all you do' [Phil 4:4–5, *Living Bible*].

Reachout Trust have another way of reaching out to Mormons with the gospel by the use of the following letter.

Dear Mormon

Will you take a moment in your busy day and consider anew the message of your faith? A message of hope. Do you personally enjoy that hope? The Bible describes it as a sure hope (Heb 11:1. See the footnote in your Bible which speaks of assurance). Is that the kind of hope you bring?

Can you confidently promise people eternal life? Are you able to guarantee people who believe your message that they will not be condemned? Can you assure them safe passage from death to life right now? That is the sure hope Jesus brought (Jn 5:24; 3:14–18).

Can you say to your converts, as John was able to say to his, 'You have eternal life' (1 Jn 5:13)? When hands are laid on them in order that they may receive the Holy Spirit, can you, with Paul, assure them that it 'is the earnest of our inheritance' (Eph 1:14; 2 Cor 1:22; 5:5)? 'Earnest' in these verses literally means 'guarantee' or 'pledge'.

What inheritance are you guaranteeing your listeners? What hope are you offering them? Are you faithfully conveying the same sure hope of Jesus, John, Paul and other New Testament writers? Compare the passages quoted above with your third Article of Faith: 'We believe that through the Atonement of Christ, all mankind *may be* saved *by obedience* to the laws and ordinances of the Gospel.' How were they able to offer a guaranteed inheritance, a sure hope, while you can only offer a 'may-be' gospel?

We testify to you that there is only one God. Not just one

God 'pertaining to us'. There are no other gods anywhere. If there were, God would be a liar: 'Is there a God beside me? Yea there is no God; *I know not any*' (Is 44:8, our italics). Can you imagine there being other gods besides the God of the Bible and God not knowing about it?

We testify to you that obedience to laws cannot get us into his presence no matter how noble the code or how earnest the intentions of those who follow it: 'for if there had been a law given which could have given life, verily righteousness should have been by the law' (Gal 3:21).

Law does, however, serve a very good purpose: 'Therefore by the deeds of the law there shall no flesh be justified in his sight: for by the law is the knowledge of sin' (Rom 3:20). Law does not justify us but it does make us conscious of sin and of our need for a redeemer. Paul speaks of the law as being a 'schoolmaster to bring us unto Christ' (Gal 3:24). For what purpose? To teach us obedience that we may be justified? No! – 'That we might be justified by faith' (Gal 3:24).

The way to God, then, is without any written code: 'But now the righteousness of God *without the law* is manifested...which is by faith of Jesus Christ' (Rom 3:21,22, our italics).

You see, 'The wages of sin is death; but the *gift* of God is eternal life through Jesus Christ our Lord' (Rom 6:23). Paul reasoned this out in Romans chapter 4: 'Now to him that worketh is the reward not reckoned of grace [it's not a gift if you work for it], but of debt [if you have worked for your salvation God owes it to you as wages]. But to him that worketh not, but believeth on him that justifieth the ungodly, his faith is counted for righteousness' (Rom 4:4–5, our brackets).

We know that you are convincing yourself that we have misinterpreted the Scriptures. That, if they do say what we claim, they must have been translated incorrectly. That the Bible is wrong. Stop for a moment to consider the gravity of that thought. It has become so much a part of your life. After all, hasn't the Mormon church come to shed light where the Bible has been interfered with? It is second nature to you to regard the rest of us as lost and deceived. But to find fault with God's inspired word is a serious business. Can you back up such a charge? We're sure you can't.

You are very sincere, and the idea that all you have come to believe is wrong is unthinkable. We know how you must feel.

God knows too and has such a gift of love for you; a gift that can truly affect your eternity now. It has been said that the Mormon faith stands or falls on the Book of Mormon. This is not true. It stands or falls on the Bible – a Bible your church regards as faulty. Once the myth of a faulty Bible is removed, Mormonism falls. For not one claim of the Mormon church can be substantiated from the Bible. Can we back up such a claim? Yes, we can.

When the Bible speaks in John 3:16 it speaks to you. When Romans 5:6–8 was written it was written for you. Galatians 3:1–14 is especially for you, as it was for us. Will you take the trouble in your time of prayer and Bible study to find out for yourself if what we are saying is true? Don't just read the verses we have given you, read around them. Get the context. Read the cross references and get the broader picture.

Then, if you can rise to the challenge, contact us for more information. We are not pushy and we do understand how difficult such a move would be for you. But we are talking here about eternal life. Not something to be faint-hearted about. God bless and keep you as you search the deeper things of God.

You are in our prayers.

Mike and Ann Thomas
Reachout Trust Swansea
PO Box 75
Swansea
SA1 6YX

Chapter 23

Helping People To Freedom

When the person with whom you are sharing the gospel finally sees the deception in the Mormon church, they may not run from the false Jesus to the real one. Some people are so hurt by the realisation that they have been deceived, and so damaged by their experience in a cult, that they find it impossible to trust another religion. This is very sad, but we must be patient and show the true gospel in the loving support we give them rather than in preaching at them. They need space to recover from the past before they can consider the future. Actions speak louder than words.

To bring full healing and wholeness, only the saving power of Jesus Christ and the enabling of the Holy Spirit will do. But much of what follows is still relevant in helping ex-Mormons to become totally free from the influence of the Mormon church, even if they do not become a Christian.

Clear the house

At some point there must be a clean break with the past. If they have been a Mormon for many years, the house will be full of Mormon things: scriptures, manuals, books, pictures, certificates, etc. All these are reminders of the Mormon faith, and ties to the past. In addition, there is a need for the person to demonstrate that they really do want to leave the church. We have found an incredible reluctance to part with things, even though they have verbally rejected them.

Maybe the thought of destroying valuable books and items

which have been precious in the past is too much. Offer to remove them all and keep them safe. At some time in the future they can have their property returned to them, or ask you to dispose of it. This is often more reassuring. One couple we worked with were horrified at the thought of destroying everything, but agreed to store it all in our loft. Three months later we reminded them that it was still there, and without a moment's hesitation they said, 'Burn it!'

Remember that the decision to clear the house must be theirs. While you should be firm in explaining the necessity of it, forcibly taking away their possessions will achieve nothing, and may cause bad feelings between you. You must be sensitive to the right moment to introduce the subject, and be willing to recognise that they are not yet ready. Make it clear that it will be necessary, but allow them space to get used to the idea. The object of the exercise is for *them* to reject Mormonism and everything to do with it.

Renounce

It is one thing to talk to friends in the privacy of your own home and agree that the faith you have been following is false. It is similar to a private decision to commit your life to Christ. If they have been a faithful Mormon there will be little fruit in changed lifestyle because Mormons work very hard to keep the commandments. This is why it is necessary to make a public declaration of faith in Christ, before baptism for example. In the same way, it is often beneficial for an ex-Mormon Christian to publicly renounce any hold that the church may have on their life.

We all have a need to burn bridges, make commitments and take a stand. Having got rid of all the physical things that attach us to the Mormon church, there is a need to get rid of the mental, emotional and spiritual things too. This does not have to be a big, formal affair. Some people are shy of large crowds anyway. At a home group, a prayer meeting or with a small group of their new Christian friends, they can come out and say it for all to hear: that they reject any hold that the Mormon church may have had in their lives, they no longer recognise its authority, and they want no more to do with it.

Once again, the key thing is not that it is said, but that it is meant. Nothing forced is valid. It must come from the heart, and then it can be sealed with prayer.

Deliverance

Following any way that is not of the true Jesus is fraught with dangers. There are subtle occult influences in the Mormon church, but the strongest influence is in the rituals of the Temple. Among other things, sacred oaths are taken: promises of chastity, loyalty, obedience, and the consecration of all your time, talents and money to the building up of the Mormon church. Even though the signs of grisly death which used to accompany these oaths have now been removed from the ceremony, they are no less serious.

It is not true in every case, but there may be some people who are unable to become totally free from the influence of the Mormon church in their lives without deliverance ministry. The temple oaths may need to be broken and ties cut in the name of Jesus, to set them free. It should go without saying that this is a very sensitive issue. Be certain that it is not only required, but appropriate, before attempting this. Only a small percentage of Mormons have attended the temple. Many people are freed by the sovereign power of God in their lives and do not need deliverance ministry.

Ask to have names removed from records

The Mormon church counts its membership by the number of names on the records, not by the regular attendance at church. Those who fall away still remain on the records. Periodically there will be a drive to reactivate lost members, and lists will be given out to teams who go visiting. If the person you are helping does not ask to have their name removed from the church records, they may be visited at various times in the future.

Some people do not feel this is a bad thing. Their new-found faith in the real Jesus is such that they welcome the opportunity that they might have in the future to witness to visitors from the Mormon church. Others are happy that they are strong enough to tell visitors that they are not welcome, and close the door.

There are two ways of looking at the question of Mormon membership. Some people feel that, once the church has been renounced, it has no power or authority over that person, and the request to remove the name from the records is recognition of an authority that no longer exists. Others feel that the membership record is a tie which should be broken. We have found that it is best to explain this to the ex-Mormon, and give them the choice.

Should they feel that they want to have their name removed, the procedure is simple, but may be upsetting. There is no honourable way out of the Mormon church. When they request to have their name removed from the records, the church will excommunicate them. Reassure them that this means nothing, as they have no authority and no power to affect their salvation.

The first step is for them to write to their Bishop with a formal request:

> Dear Bishop
> I want you to remove my name from the records of the Church of Jesus Christ of Latter-day Saints. I want no further contact from the Church except to inform me that my request has been dealt with.
> Yours sincerely.

This will also prevent persistent callers from the church attempting to persuade them to change their mind. If there is no reply (and some bishops are very stubborn), try again, and then the person to contact is his superior, the Stake President. Simply state that the request has been made to the Bishop and nothing has been done. In rare cases, you can simply work your way up the hierarchy until somebody moves.

The Mormon church is totally legalistic. There will be a Bishop's court for women and for men who do not hold the priesthood. Priesthood holders have a Stake court for excommunication. One can see the reasoning behind it if the court is called for disciplinary action, but it is pointless in this case.

The Bishop's court consists of the Bishop and his two coun-sellors, with the Ward Clerk to take minutes. This Stake court consists of the Stake President and his counsellors, and the entire Stake High Council (twelve men).

There is, however, absolutely no need for the person to be present. There are set procedures that the church officers have to take to ensure that the person is not in the building (!), and then they will excommunicate them in their absence. We went to our courts because we wanted to take the opportunity to bear witness to the truth, but it is not recommended.

They will then be informed in writing of the court's deci-sion. If they do not receive this letter, they cannot be certain it has been done, so help them to nag the Bishop until they get it.

Reachout Trust

Reachout Trust is a Christian ministry concerned with people involved in the cults, occult and New Age movement. Its primary aim is reaching out to the people involved in these groups. It also offers training, resources, counselling and advice to Christians seeking to minister in this area. Address: 24 Ormond Road, Richmond, Surrey, TW10 6TH. Tel: 0181 332 7785. Fax: 0181 332 0286. E-mail: Reachout@ dircon.co.uk

Chapter 24
Aftercare

Mormons are polytheistic (they believe in many gods) and indeed expect, through faithfulness, to become gods themselves. Thus they believe they can earn their way to heaven. This is one of the most dangerous aspects of any cult. Instead of trusting in the all-sufficient Saviour of the Bible, the followers end up doing anything their leaders tell them in order to come up to the mark. It can be a life of incredible doubt and insecurity and has led to tragedies of all types, including the break-up of relationships and even suicides.

Special needs

Latayne Scott, in her book *Mormon Mirage*, states:

> People who leave Mormonism have two acute needs: solid Bible teaching and warm (even sacrificial) fellowship and friendship. These are both essentials, non negotiable and irreplaceable. Without the first the new ex-Mormon Christian will go from one system of error to another; without the second they will wither and die no matter how biblical the teaching they receive.

Here is part of a letter we received:

> Presently I am feeling that before I came out of the church, Christians bent over backwards to witness to me. However, now that I am out of the church they are totally disinterested in my personhood. It's as if I was some sort of a prize catch, like

getting me out of Mormonism would gain them some smartie
points; however, once I was out the novelty wore off. If only
they could realise that there is still a lot of Mormonism in me.
I may have come to know Jesus as my personal Saviour, however there are still so many things within me that are rooted in
Mormonism. There are still so many things that I am unsure
of.

Leaving the Mormon church often means losing all your
friends, and it is not always easy to make new ones. Many people may not be aware that the Mormon church caters for
every area of an individual's life: social, spiritual, educational
and physical. Most Mormons do not have any activities outside the church, except their jobs. As we have seen, there are
social functions, dances, drama, sports, arts and crafts, music,
camping, scouts, as well as meetings for youth, children, men
and women. Life outside can be suddenly very empty.

Legalism
Obedience
It is impossible to over-emphasise the emotional and psycho-
logical damage that cults do to their members. The Third
Article of Faith of the Mormon church states: 'We believe that
through the atonement of Christ, all mankind may be saved, *by
obedience to the laws and ordinances of the Gospel*' (our italics).
Those who join the Mormon church are not set free in Christ
but introduced to a whole set of laws and ordinances through
which they may prove their faith and earn their salvation. The
impossibility of keeping all the commandments, especially in
their own strength, imposes an increasing burden of guilt,
unworthiness and condemnation.

This doctrine of obedience to ordinances is supported by
reference to James chapter 2, verse 17: 'faith without works is
dead'. This scripture is interpreted to mean that works are
necessary in order to prove that you have the faith. A closer
study of the context will show that works are the fruit of faith,
not the cause of it (see chapter 14). This may be obvious to a
Christian, but will be a recurring problem for ex-Mormons

who will be continually seeking Christian 'rules to live by' to replace the Mormon ones.

Answers for everything

Cults also have an answer for everything and a rule for everything. This is very comforting, and encourages members to cease to think for themselves. Christianity is not so clear-cut, and ex-cult members have to cope with feelings of insecurity and doubt as they struggle with difficult questions and the need to think things out for themselves. How can a faith be true and yet not have all the answers? How can there be 'one Lord, one faith, one baptism' when different denominations and even different people in the same church disagree?

We have found people believing that the Christian church they now belong to is 'the only true church' and they are intolerant of other churches.

Personal problems

Everyone in the world has problems of one kind or another, and some cope better than others. But when you add to them the harsh rule of law, unworthiness and condemnation, you make things much worse.

Leaders are chosen from within the congregation by those in authority over them. They often have no special gifting and are totally untrained in any form of counselling. When those in their care bring their problems to them they have to rely on their own ideas, plus the rules and regulations laid down by the church. It would not occur to them to seek other help because that would be a failure on their part to uphold their calling. So, problems which may have been readily solved in the beginning become compounded until it may be only the legalism which holds them together. Take that away and they fall apart.

When you show people freedom from the law, you may then spend long traumatic hours trying to piece them back together again before they can begin to enjoy the fruits of the true gospel.

Practical tips

Doctrine

Many new Christians have few, if any, preconceived ideas and are like a blank page on which to write the truths of the gospel. Ex-Mormons have a whole package of wrong beliefs, many of which are close to the truth or a subtle twisting of it, and gospel teaching can cause great confusion. You must be prepared to refute error and teach the truth. Some doctrines will be discarded easily, others will take in-depth teaching and repetition before the truth is grasped.

Feelings

The Mormon testimony is gained by means of a feeling (see chapter 8). This feeling is very easily found, and along with the encouragement to accept blindly, creates a testimony that holds fast even in the face of clearly proven error. New Christians will find it very difficult to let go of this idea, and will look for feelings along the way. This is reinforced by the fact that the act of commitment to the Saviour is often accompanied by a good feeling. The early days of adjustment and confusion can lead to doubt and panic when the feelings disappear. Constant reassurance and reinforcement of their status before God is essential.

Social life

As mentioned above, leaving the Mormon church creates a great gulf in their social life. Most Mormon friends will desert them, and those who don't will often put on a lot of pressure to return. Meetings, activities and social events are all lost. Like most new converts, they may be attending a church where they don't know anyone. They may have held responsible positions in the Mormon church. In the Christian church it will be some time before they are equipped to serve. This gulf needs to be filled, and much love and support is needed for some time until they feel at home and a part of the Christian community. Introducing them to a nurture group, house-group, or just assigning one or two people to spend time visiting them is essential.

Oaths and covenants

Those people who have been through the Mormon temple ceremonies have made very serious oaths and covenants, similar to those in Freemasonry. Sometimes freedom in Christ breaks these chains completely without further need, but you should be aware that these oaths and covenants may need to be specifically broken in a person's life. In any case, it is good to bring the person to a point where they formally renounce and cast off everything to do with Mormonism (see previous chapter). It may be good to do this in public before baptism.

Chapter 25
Our Testimony

Ann

Before I was taught by the Mormons in my teens, I only knew what I had learned at Sunday school as a small child and in RE lessons in school. Like many people, I thought that a Christian was someone who tried hard to do good things, read the Bible and prayed to God. I learned from my Mormon friends that Jesus had paid for the fall of Adam, so that we are all born sinless and are held accountable only for the sins we ourselves commit. Because Jesus died for my sins, I could work to be acceptable to God and hope one day to be judged worthy of heaven. It certainly sounded right, and I looked no further.

I was introduced to the Mormon church via a card through the door offering a free copy of the Book of Mormon. I had been asking a lot of questions about God and the purpose of life, so I sent it off. The book was delivered by two Mormon missionaries when I was out, so my mother made an appointment for them to come back and speak to me. Through their teaching, and visits to the church, my whole family were eventually baptised in March 1968.

Mike

I was eighteen years old when I first encountered the Mormon church. I have always maintained that the first thing that got my attention was the fact that they paid attention to me and valued my opinion. I knew nothing about religion although I had felt for some time that there must be more to life than the little I was experiencing then. This feeling had been increasingly distracting for me and so by the time the Mormons came along I imagine I was ripe and ready for picking.

I took the missionary discussions, all the time feeling quite embarrassed about my ignorance of spiritual matters. I had had no religious upbringing except the usual Sunday school, and certainly my family were not churchgoers. This was an adventure and the missionaries presented answers to questions I had never considered. Everything was new and everything seemed right. So I joined on 29 September 1972.

I mostly enjoyed being a Mormon. I had experienced the 'burning in the bosom' promised to all true seekers and, as a shy boy with nothing outstanding to boast of in my life, I felt special for having the inside track on truth. I was ordained an elder in the church on 25 February 1973 after over a year of study and faithful application, and had more reason to feel good as I was assured that I now had more authority than any of the so-called spiritual leaders in the world.

It was through the church that I met Ann and we both had many happy times as Mormons. Our family started there and we found the church most helpful and supportive as we struggled with the usual difficulties encountered by young parents. Together we had gone to the temple and had been 'sealed for time and eternity' and together we continued to enjoy the 'blessings' of temple worship.

There were, of course, down times. However the church was always there for us. Looking back I feel perhaps we needed them more than most but they did not let us down and we have much to thank them for. Indeed it seems natural to ask, if it was so good why did you leave?

Ann

I didn't know that what I had found was not the truth but a counterfeit, a deception. It took me eighteen years before I finally had the courage to admit that my faith wasn't working, and that all my efforts to please God only left me feeling inadequate.

Mike

For all the church had going for it there was one area in which it singularly failed me. I was looking for something when I joined and, with hindsight, I can see that it was the one thing the church was incapable of delivering: peace with God. When Ann and I became dissatisfied we really did not understand why. We just knew – I knew – that something fundamental was missing from our spiritual experience. It was only as we began seeking with a determination we had never known before that we saw how radical the change in our lives would have to be if we were to go on with God. We were genuinely surprised to be faced with the choice of God or Mormonism.

Ann

A Christian friend asked us to read the book of Romans in the Bible, in a modern English version, and with no Mormon commentary. There we discovered the grace of God. I realised that the one thing I had never done in my life was to submit in obedience to Christ and ask him to be my Saviour. I had believed in him for eighteen years, but I had been taught that the way to salvation was by obedience to the Mormon church. They had effectively put themselves between me and God.

When I set out to read the book of Romans I was looking for a solution to the problems of my faith in the Mormon church. I wanted to get right with God so that I could be a better Mormon. I certainly got more than I bargained for! Now I was faced with a dilemma. Could I give up some things that had been very precious to me, had been my whole life for eighteen years, and leave all my Mormon friends? Or could I compromise and stay when I knew their teaching was false? Jesus promised us abundant life, but he never promised it would be easy.

So many people think obedience is about the ten commandments and that sort of thing. Really it is about attitude. What really is the most important thing in your life? When I thought about it like that, there was no other choice I could make. I chose Jesus and the true gospel, and left the Mormon church. I can honestly say that I have never regretted it. My life since really coming to know Jesus bears no comparison to all those previous years when I only *thought* I knew him.

Mike

We made the right choice, I believe, and discovered a God who truly proves his faithfulness. So many Scripture promises came true for us when we sought him and discovered that 'If you seek him, he will be found by you' (1 Chron 28:9). Coming from a system that saw obedience to law as the way to God we rejoiced in the fact that 'a righteousness from God, apart from law, has been made known, to which the Law and the Prophets testify' (Rom 3:21). The assurances of God's word were, and are, a blessing to us beyond anything we could hope for or ask for. We know that through faith in Jesus we have eternal life as a present possession and a guaranteed inheritance (Jn 5:24).

I suppose the biggest surprise was that Christianity, far from being the hopelessly confused and frighteningly confusing religion painted by the Mormons, actually makes sense. In all its expressions and in every aspect it is a beautifully harmonious faith. If it is seen by the power of the Spirit, seen for what it really is, it is irresistible, and for honest seekers a love affair is inevitable.

OUTLINE CHRONOLOGY – HISTORY

1805	23 Dec. Joseph Smith born in Sharon, Vermont.
1820	Spring. Joseph Smith receives the First Vision (aged 14).
1823	Moroni visits Joseph four times (aged 17).
1827	22 Sept. Joseph receives the Book of Mormon plates (aged 21).
1828	116 Book of Mormon manuscript pages lost.
1830	March. The Book of Mormon published.
	6 April. Joseph Smith organises the Church of Jesus Christ of Latter-day Saints, with 6 official members.
	June – Dec. The Book of Moses is revealed.
1833	May – July. The Book of Commandments published.
1835	Feb. Joseph Smith publishes the Doctrine and Covenants, begins work on the Book of Abraham.
1837	Several leading brethren apostatize.
1838–39	Joseph Smith and others imprisoned in Liberty Jail on false charges of treason and murder.
1839	City of Nauvoo founded.
1844	Joseph Smith becomes a candidate for United States president.
	27 June. Smith dies at Carthage Jail, Illinois (aged 38).
	24 Sept. Seventy presidents are called to preside over all seventies.
1846–47	Brigham Young leads the exodus from Nauvoo to Salt Lake City and returns to Winter Quarters.
1847	23 July. The advance group enters the Salt Lake valley and camps. Orson Pratt dedicates the land to the Lord and the men begin ploughing and planting.
1849	The Perpetual Emigration Fund is organised.
1853	6 April. Brigham Young lays the cornerstone for the Salt Lake Temple.
1866	The Parent Sunday School Union is organised.
1867	The Relief Society is organised.
1868	Zion's Cooperative Mercantile Institution (ZCMI), the first department store west of the Mississippi River, is organised.

1869	The young men's and young women's mutual improvement associations organised.
1876–79	The Saints establish more than one hundred settlements in Utah, Wyoming, Nevada, and Arizona.
1878	11 Aug. Primary Association organised.
1880	The Pearl of Great Price is accepted as one of the standard works at general conference.
1882	22 March. The Edmunds-Tucker Act, making 'unlawful cohabitation' a crime, is signed into law.
1885	1 Feb. John Taylor delivers his last public sermon and goes into 'retirement' [hiding].
1888	Stake boards of education are established.
1890	The 'Manifesto' announces discontinuation of the practice of plural marriage.
	25 Oct. Weekday religion classes are instituted.
1896	Utah achieves statehood.
1936	The Church welfare plan is established.
1938	12 Aug. Deseret Industries is inaugurated.
1939	Missionaries are withdrawn from Europe as World War II begins.
1941	Assistants to the Quorum of the Twelve are called.
1958	Dedications of the New Zealand Temple, the Church College of New Zealand, and the Church College of Hawaii.
1964	Oct. The ward priesthood executive committee and ward councils are created.
1967	The unified Church magazine begins publishing in nine languages: Danish, Dutch, Finnish, French, German, Norwegian, Portuguese, Spanish, Swedish.
1968	1 Jan. The first Regional Representatives are called, to aid the Twelve in their responsibilities around the world.
1971	Jan. New correlated Church magazines begin publication: the Ensign, the New Era, and the Friend.
1972	Nov. New programme announced for the single adults of the Church.
1973	Jan. A Welfare Services Department is created.

Feb. First Church agricultural missionaries go out, to the Guatemala-El Salvador Mission.

1975   3 May. Six General Authorities are assigned to serve as Area Supervisors and to reside in their areas away from Church headquarters.

1976   A missionary training complex is opened in Provo, Utah.

Oct. First Quorum of Seventy organised as a General Authority Quorum.

1978   Genealogical name extraction program introduced.

28–30 June. Nauvoo Monument to Women dedicated.

16 Sept. First annual women's meeting held.

30 Sept. Emeritus Status created for certain members of the General Authorities from time to time.

1979   New Latter-day Saint edition of the King James Version of the Bible published.

1980   Consolidated meeting schedule instituted following several months of pilot studies. Sacrament, Sunday School, Melchizedek and Aaronic Priesthood, Relief Society, Young Women, and Primary meetings are grouped into a three-hour time block on Sunday.

March. Church takes a stand opposing the Equal Rights Amendment.

1981   New edition of the 'triple combination' – three books of Mormon scripture in one volume, is published.

A satellite network is established to carry church programs.

1982   2 April. Single young men to serve only 18 months on a mission, instead of two years, for economic reasons.

1985   1 Jan. Two year missions return for single elders. Single females under 40 continue to serve 18 months, over 40 12 months. Married couples can choose either 12 or 18 months.

Mar. Missionary Training Centre established in England.

15 Oct. Two bombs kill two members, with a third seriously injuring a document dealer the next day.

The dealer, Mark Hofmann, later confesses to the bombings, which were to cover up his sale of fake historical documents to the church. Church hides information to save face.

1986   Mar. Church announces Book of Mormon now in 70 languages.

10 Oct. Stake Seventies Quorums discontinued.

Nov. Church announces availability of computerised guide to the scriptures. Word searches on all 4 standard works of the church.

1987   1 Jan. Relief Society organisation changed.

1992   Church publishes 4-volume Encyclopaedia of Mormonism.

1993   April. First Presidency announces that 4,855,167 copies of the Book of Mormon were sold during 1992, but re-emphasises that they 'have not authorized efforts to express the doctrinal content of the Book of Mormon in familiar or modern English.' (Ensign, April 93, p 74).

1994   Jan. First Presidency responds to extensive media coverage of six recent church disciplinary councils in Utah, where prominent members were excommunicated. (Ensign, Jan 94, p 75).

Feb. Sunday School opening exercises eliminated to provide more time for study.

OUTLINE CHRONOLOGY – DOCTRINE

When Joseph Smith began writing the Book of Mormon, his theology was basically orthodox, but his ideas developed along with the book. Later, as the challenges of creating a church arose, the doctrine grew to meet them, and in some cases to meet Joseph's growing ego.

Other early church leaders also had input into the new theology, the most prominent of which was Brigham Young. Some of his pronouncements were so extreme that the church today does its best to have them ignored.

Apart from this, there is virtually no deviation from the original doctrine that grew with the beginnings of the church. Where there have been major deviations, these have been announced as fresh revelations from God, so there is no embarrassment in acknowledging the differences before and after. The church's commitment to education, with gospel classes for all ages every week, has ensured the purity of the faith.

1829	May – June. The priesthood is restored.
1830	Joseph Smith begins work on the 'new translation' of the Bible.
1831	9 Feb. Joseph Smith receives Doctrine and Covenants section 42 and introduces the law of consecration and stewardship.
1832	16 Feb. Joseph Smith receives Doctrine and Covenants section 76, the revelation on the three degrees of glory.
1833	27 Feb. Joseph Smith receives Doctrine and Covenants section 89, a revelation on the Word of Wisdom.
1840	Lorenzo Snow receives a revelation on the nature of God and man.
1843	12 July. Smith writes a revelation on marriage, Doctrine and Covenants section 132.
1846	Brigham Young receives section 136 of the Doctrine and Covenants. Sees Joseph Smith in vision and is given valuable instruction.

1853   Brigham Young discourses on the redemption of
        fallen beings.

1877   Church leaders define duties of the priesthood and
        restructure stakes.

1890   The 'Manifesto' announces discontinuation of the
        practice of plural marriage.

1898   Lorenzo Snow sees the Saviour in the Salt Lake
        Temple, of which he was President.

1909   First Presidency issues a statement on the doctrine
        of the origin of man.

1915   The First Presidency stresses holding a home
        evening.

1916   First Presidency issues a 'doctrinal exposition' on the
        Father and the Son.

1918   3 Oct. Joseph F. Smith has a vision of the redemption
        of the dead.

1921   David O. McKay beholds a vision of the celestial city
        during world tour.

1962   Oct. The First Presidency unveils the priesthood
        home teaching programme.

1965   Oct. The First Presidency re-emphasises a family
        home evening programme.

1976   3 Apr. In general conference, Joseph Smith's vision
        of the celestial kingdom and Joseph F. Smith's vision
        of the redemption of the dead accepted as part of the
        standard works of the Church. They become
        sections 137 and 138 in the Doctrine & Covenants.

1978   8 June. The First Presidency announces priesthood
        blessings are extended to all worthy male members.
        30 Sept. Announcement accepted as 'the word and
        will of the Lord' and added to the Doctrine &
        Covenants as Official Declaration – 2 (announcement
        discontinuing plural marriage to be renamed Official
        Declaration – 1).

1982   2 April. Members warned not to involve the church
        in politics.

1993   Jan. First Presidency issues statement on
        observance of the Sabbath day. Church members are

urged to refrain from worldly activities on the
Sabbath.

1994   Nov. First Presidency emphasises temple worthiness
and family home evening.

OUTLINE CHRONOLOGY –
PRESIDENTS OF THE MORMON CHURCH

Presidency dates	Name	Age on becoming President
1830–1844	Joseph Smith	24
1847–1877	Brigham Young	46
1880–1887	John Taylor	71
1889–1898	Wilford Woodruff	82
1898–1901	Lorenzo Snow	84
1901–1918	Joseph F. Smith	63
1918–1945	Heber J. Grant	62
1945–1951	George Albert Smith	74
1951–1970	David O. McKay	78
1970–1972	Joseph Fielding Smith	93
1972–1973	Harold B. Lee	73
1973–1985	Spencer W. Kimball	78
1985–1994	Ezra Taft Benson	86
1994–1995	Howard W. Hunter	86
1995–	Gordon B. Hinckley	84

Joseph Smith designated himself President when he organised the Church of Jesus Christ of Latter-day Saints, on 6 April 1830. The succession in the Presidency was by no means clear, when he died on 27 June 1844 at Carthage Jail, Illinois.

There were several contenders, but two main ones at the time, and one later. Sidney Rigdon was first counsellor in the First Presidency, and claimed that he should be caretaker of the church until God called the next Prophet. He called a special conference on 8 August to decide the matter.

Brigham Young's claim was that the keys of the kingdom resided with the Quorum of the Twelve Apostles, and he was the President of the Quorum. His claim was strengthened, and Sidney Rigdon's defeated, by a remarkable event in the special conference meeting. Many who were present testified that as Brigham Young rose to address the meeting, his face was transfigured, and appeared to be Joseph Smith. A week later the Twelve sent an epistle to all the Saints, stressing that they were the proper successors to Joseph Smith because they held the keys. Brigham Young led the Church as President of the Quorum of the Twelve.

It was not until 5 December 1847 that the Quorum of the Twelve sustained Brigham Young as President of the Church. This was ratified on 27 December when the Saints, assembled in general conference at Kanesville (Council Bluffs), Iowa, voted to sustain Brigham Young as President of the Church.

Later, another faction arose. Joseph's family and many others believed that the Presidency should be hereditary, and the Presidency should fall on his son, Joseph Smith III. The split was so strong that when his claim was refused, his followers left and began what is now the Reorganised Church of Jesus Christ of Latter-day Saints. Their Presidents have all claimed direct descent from Joseph Smith.

When Brigham Young died in 1877, the Quorum of the Twelve once again led the Church. John Taylor was President of the Quorum, but he was not sustained as President of the Church until 1880. It was from this time onwards that the President of the Quorum of the Twelve automatically became the new President on the death of the previous one.

In 1965 there was another temporary change, when two additional counsellors to the First Presidency were chosen, to assist President David O. McKay. On his death, the number of counsellors returned to two.

For a comprehensive description of the structure of the First Presidency, see chapter 2.

OUTLINE CHRONOLOGY –
THE CHURCH IN BRITAIN

1837	4 Jun. Heber C. Kimball called on a mission to England.
	20 July. Elders Kimball and Hyde arrive in Liverpool.
	30 July. First baptisms in the British Isles – in Preston.
	6 Aug. First Branch organised in England – in Preston.
1839	8 Aug. John Taylor serves a mission to the British Isles.
	20 Dec. First missionaries arrive in Scotland.
1839–41	Brigham Young and Wilford Woodruff serve a mission to Great Britain.
1840–43	Lorenzo Snow serves a mission to Great Britain, presents a copy of the Book of Mormon to Queen Victoria.
1840	17 April. First British patriarch ordained – P. Melling.
	8 May. First Scottish branch organised – in Paisley.
	27 May. Millennial Star magazine first published.
	6 June. First church-approved emigration from England.
	31 July. First baptism in Ireland.
	Sept. First Branch in Ireland – in Hillsborough.
	6 Oct. First missionary arrives in Wales.
1841	21 Jan. The Book of Mormon published in Liverpool.
1844–46	Wilford Woodruff presides over the European Mission.
1845	3 Jan. Wilford Woodruff and other missionaries arrive in Liverpool, England.
	Dec. Dan Jones appointed to preside in Wales.
1846–47	John Taylor serves a second mission to Great Britain.
1849	26 Feb. First Welsh Saints leave for the United States.
	Sept. Perpetual Emigration Fund Company organised.

	Oct. Tabernacle Choir organised around a core of Welsh singers.
1850	More members in Britain than in North America.
1851	Pearl of Great Price published in England.
1853	1 Nov. Journal of Discourses first published.
1860–63	Joseph F. Smith, the son of Joseph's brother Hyrum, serves a mission to Great Britain.
1894	June. Emigration to America discouraged.
1897	David O. McKay, later to become 9th President of the Church, serves a mission in Great Britain.
1899	Joseph Fielding Smith, later to become 10th President of the Church, serves a mission to England.
1904–6	Heber J. Grant, later to become 7th President of the Church, presides over the British and European Missions.
1906	26 Aug. First Prophet visits Britain – Joseph F. Smith.
1919–21	George Albert Smith, later to become 8th President of the Church, serves as president of the European Mission.
1922–24	David O. McKay, later to become 9th President of the Church, serves as president of the European Mission.
1934–37	Meetinghouse acquisition programme.
1948	8 Mar. First church property in Ireland dedicated.
1952	June. First chapels in Scotland dedicated. 10 Aug. London Temple site dedicated.
1958	7 Sept. London Temple dedicated.
1960	17 Jun. First English stake organised – in Manchester.
1962	26 Aug. First stake created in Scotland – in Glasgow. 17 Nov. First chapel dedicated in Ireland – in Belfast.
1970	First Institute of Religion in Britain.
1971	Aug. Joseph Fielding Smith presides over the first area general conference of the Church, in Manchester, England, where Harold B. Lee also speaks.
1973	11 Feb. 600th stake – Southampton, England.

1974	9 Jun. First Irish stake organised – Belfast.
1980	7 Jul. First Bishop's store house in England – Birmingham.
	16 Oct. First multi-regional conference – London.
1985	Mar. Missionary Training Centre established in England.
1986	7 Sept. First Regional Conference for Ireland, in Belfast.
1987	25–26 Jul. Commemoration of 150th anniversary of the church in the British Isles.
1994	12 June. Ground breaking for second British Temple in Chorley outside Preston.
1995	First Stake created in the Republic of Ireland, in Dublin.

BIBLIOGRAPHY

Mormon Sources

Answers to Gospel Questions

Bancroft, *History of Utah*

William E. Berrett, *The Restored Church*, 1969.

The Book of Mormon, 1959 and 1982 editions

Brigham Young Studies, Spring 1969

The Daily Universe, Brigham Young University, 1 December 1967

Deseret News

Dialogue: A Journal of Modern Thought

Discourses of Brigham Young

Doctrine and Covenants, including 1835 edition

Encyclopaedia of Mormonism

Ensign magazine

Gospel Essentials Manual, 1979

Gospel Principles Manual, 1981

Hymns, 1985

Milton R. Hunter of the First Quorum of the Seventy, *Gospel Through the Ages*, 1945

Improvement Era

Instructor

Journal of Discourses

John L. Lund, *The Church and the Negro*, 1967

Bruce R. McConkie, *Mormon Doctrine*

Bruce R. McConkie, *The Mortal Messiah*

My Kingdom Shall Roll Forth: Readings in Church History, manual, 1979

Dr Hugh Nibley, *The Message of the Joseph Smith Papyri: An Egyptian Endowment*, Deseret Book Company, 1975

Preston Nibley, *Joseph Smith the Prophet*, 1944

Boyd K. Packer, *That All May Be Edified*

The Pearl of Great Price

Arch S. Reynolds, *How Did Joseph Smith Translate?*, Springville, Utah, 1952

Legrand Richards, *A Marvelous Work and a Wonder*, 1979

The Seer

Joseph Smith, *Diary*, original in Latter-day Saints' Historical Department

Joseph Smith, History of the Church

Joseph Fielding Smith, *Doctrines of Salvation*, 1954

Joseph Fielding Smith, *Gospel Doctrine*

Joseph Fielding Smith, Letter to Morris L. Reynolds, 9 May 1966

Joseph Fielding Smith, *The Way to Perfection*, 1935

Dr Sidney B. Sperry, *Ancient Records Testify in Papyrus and Stone*, 1938

James E. Talmage, *The Articles of Faith*

James E. Talmage, *The House of the Lord*, 1969

James E. Talmage, *Jesus the Christ*, 1976

John Taylor, *The Gospel Kingdom*

John Taylor, *Mediation and Atonement*

Teachings of the Prophet Joseph Smith, 1976

Truth Will Prevail: A History of the Church in Britain, 1987

Richard Turley, *Victims: The Latter-day Saints and the Mark Hoffman Case*

280 MORMONISM: A GOLD PLATED RELIGION

Non-Mormon Sources

Gleason Archer Jr, *A Survey of the Old Testament*, Chicago: Moody Press, 1964, 1974

Fawn M. Brodie, *No Man Knows My History*, 1966

The Christian Baptist

The Concise Dictionary of Christian Tradition, 1989

Larry S. Jonas, *Mormon Claims Examined*

The Life, Conversion, Preaching, Travels and Sufferings of Elias Smith, Portsmouth, NH, 1816

Robert Lindsey, *A Gathering of Saints*, Corgi, 1990

Josh MacDowell and Don Stewart, *Answers to Tough Questions*, Campus Crusade for Christ, 1980

Floyd C. McElveen, *The Mormon Illusion*, 1979

Floyd C. McElveen, *Mormon Revelations of Convenience*, Bethany Fellowship Inc., 1978

The New International Version Study Bible

Reachout Trust Newsletter, Winter 1994

The Salt Lake City Messenger

Salt Lake Tribune

Jerald and Sandra Tanner (eds), *The Changing World of Mormonism*, 1981

Jerald and Sandra Tanner, Latter-day Saints Apostle Confesses Brigham Young Taught Adam-God Doctrine

Jerald and Sandra Tanner, *Mormonism: Shadow or Reality?*, 1982

E. A. Wallis Budge, *The Book of the Dead: Fascimiles of the Papyri of Hunefer, Anhai, Kerasher and Netchemet*, London, 1899

Wesley P. Walters, *New Light on Mormon Origins from the Palmyra (New York) Revival*, Utah Christian Tract Society, 1967

The Wayne Sentinel, 22 October 1823

INDEX